Praise for *The Sea*

'Part elegy, part manifesto, a
travelogue with a chaser of hist
without sentiment the great E
political thought and bar snacks'

'A wholehearted celebration of the old-fashioned pub and all it
represents'   *Time Out*, Book of the Week

'Part road trip, part pub guide and part lament, Paul Moody and
Robin Turner's book takes its lead from George Orwell's fantasy pub
. . . the enthusiasm for fine beers and charming independent pubs
makes reading it very thirsty work'   *Financial Times*

'Makes an excellent case for using and encouraging our pubs'
                              Independent on Sunday, Books of the Year

'A book so persuasive you'll resolve to visit at least one pub every day
for the rest of your life'   Paul De Noyer, *WORD* magazine

'A timely and heartfelt reminder of how pubs are far more than
simple boozing dens (although there's nothing wrong with a simple
boozing den) and why we need them now more than ever'
                              Pete Brown, Beer Writer of the Year 2012

'A serious investigation of the decline of pub culture'
                              Giles Foden, *Conde Nast Traveller*

'Written with a personality and intelligence that gives the book the
feel of an informed, passionate chat down the pub'   *The Quietus*

'A rattling good yarn, the fruit of a three-year journey measuring –
surprisingly favourably – today's pubs with a template set 65 years
ago by George Orwell'   *Scotland on Sunday*

'The enthusiasm shines through. The authors put themselves in
the firing line without any worries for their own health or, at
times, sanity'   *London Drinker*

Paul Moody is a writer, journalist and musician from north London. His work has appeared in publications ranging from the *NME* and *Guardian* to the *Bangkok Post*. He now resides south of the river and can regularly be seen in The Asylum, SE15.

Robin Turner, along with Paul, is the co-author of *The Rough Pub Guide*. He was introduced to Wales's greatest pub gardens by his dad at an early age. He is one of the people behind the acclaimed nature website *Caught by the River* and is the creator of the mobile library art project, Roam.

By the same authors:

The Rough Pub Guide

THE SEARCH FOR THE
PERFECT PUB

LOOKING FOR THE MOON UNDER WATER

Paul Moody and
Robin Turner

An Orion paperback

First published in Great Britain in 2011
by Orion
This paperback edition published in 2013
by Orion Books Ltd,
Orion House, 5 Upper St Martin's Lane,
London WC2H 9EA

An Hachette UK company

1 3 5 7 9 10 8 6 4 2

A CIP catalogue record for this book is available
from the British Library.

ISBN 978-1-4091-3928-7

Printed and bound in Great Britain by
CPI Group (UK) Ltd, Croydon, CR0 4YY

The Orion Publishing Group's policy is to use papers that
are natural, renewable and recyclable products and
made from wood grown in sustainable forests. The logging
and manufacturing processes are expected to conform to
the environmental regulations of the country of origin.

www.orionbooks.co.uk

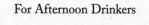

For Afternoon Drinkers

THE MOON UNDER WATER

by George Orwell

Evening Standard, 9th February 1946

My favourite public-house, the Moon Under Water, is only two minutes from a bus stop, but it is on a side-street, and drunks and rowdies never seem to find their way there, even on Saturday nights. Its clientele, though fairly large, consists mostly of 'regulars' who occupy the same chair every evening and go there for conversation as much as for the beer.

If you are asked why you favour a particular public-house, it would seem natural to put the beer first, but the thing that most appeals to me about the Moon Under Water is what people call its 'atmosphere'.

To begin with, its whole architecture and fittings are uncompromisingly Victorian. It has no glass-topped tables or other modern miseries, and, on the other hand, no sham roof-beams, ingle-nooks or plastic panels masquerading as oak. The grained woodwork, the ornamental mirrors behind the bar, the cast-iron fireplaces, the florid ceiling stained dark yellow by tobacco-smoke, the stuffed bull's head over the mantelpiece – everything has the solid, comfortable ugliness of the nineteenth century.

In winter there is generally a good fire burning in at least two of the bars, and the Victorian lay-out of the place gives one plenty of elbow-room. There is a public bar, a saloon bar, a ladies' bar, a bottle-and-jug for those who are too bashful to buy their supper beer publicly, and, upstairs, a dining-room.

Games are only played in the public, so that in the other bars you can walk about without constantly ducking to avoid flying darts.

In the Moon Under Water it is always quiet enough to talk. The house possesses neither a radio nor a piano, and even on Christmas Eve and such occasions the singing that happens is of a decorous kind.

The barmaids know most of their customers by name, and take a personal interest in everyone. They are all middle-aged women – two of them have their hair dyed in quite surprising shades – and they call everyone 'dear', irrespective of age or sex. ('Dear,' not 'Ducky': pubs where the barmaid calls you 'ducky' always have a disagreeable raffish atmosphere.)

Unlike most pubs, the Moon Under Water sells tobacco as well as cigarettes, and it also sells aspirins and stamps, and is obliging about letting you use the telephone.

You cannot get dinner at the Moon Under Water, but there is always the snack counter where you can get liver-sausage sandwiches, mussels (a speciality of the house), cheese, pickles and those large biscuits with caraway seeds in them which only seem to exist in public-houses.

Upstairs, six days a week, you can get a good, solid lunch – for example, a cut off the joint, two vegetables and boiled jam roll – for about three shillings.

The special pleasure of this lunch is that you can have draught stout with it. I doubt whether as many as 10 per cent of London pubs serve draught stout, but the Moon Under Water is one of them. It is a soft, creamy sort of stout, and it goes better in a pewter pot.

They are particular about their drinking vessels at the Moon Under Water, and never, for example, make the mistake of serving a pint of beer in a handleless glass. Apart from glass and pewter mugs, they have some of those pleasant strawberry-pink china ones which are now seldom seen in London. China mugs went out about 30 years ago, because most people like their drink to be transparent, but in my opinion beer tastes better out of china.

The great surprise of the Moon Under Water is its garden. You go through a narrow passage leading out of the saloon, and find yourself in a fairly large garden with plane trees, under which there are little green tables with iron chairs round them. Up at one end of the garden there are swings and a chute for the children.

On summer evenings there are family parties, and you sit under the plane trees having beer or draught cider to the tune of delighted squeals from children going down the chute. The prams with the younger children are parked near the gate.

Many are the virtues of the Moon Under Water, I think that the garden is its best feature, because it allows whole families to go there instead of Mum having to stay at home and mind the baby while Dad goes out alone.

And though, strictly speaking, they are only allowed in the garden, the children tend to seep into the pub and even to fetch drinks for their parents. This, I believe, is against the law, but it is a law that deserves to be broken, for it is the puritanical nonsense of excluding children – and therefore, to some extent, women – from pubs that has turned these places into mere boozing-shops instead of the family gathering-places that they ought to be.

The Moon Under Water is my ideal of what a pub should be – at any rate, in the London area. (The qualities one expects of a country pub are slightly different.)

But now is the time to reveal something which the discerning and disillusioned reader will probably have guessed already. There is no such place as the Moon Under Water.

That is to say, there may well be a pub of that name, but I don't know of it, nor do I know any pub with just that combination of qualities.

I know pubs where the beer is good but you can't get meals, others where you can get meals but which are noisy and crowded, and others which are quiet but where the beer is generally sour. As for gardens, offhand I can only think of three London pubs that possess them.

But, to be fair, I do know of a few pubs that almost come up to the Moon Under Water. I have mentioned above ten qualities that the perfect pub should have and I know one pub that has eight of them. Even there, however, there is no draught stout, and no china mugs.

And if anyone knows of a pub that has draught stout, open fires, cheap meals, a garden, motherly barmaids and no radio, I should be glad to hear of it, even though its name were something as prosaic as the Red Lion or the Railway Arms.

CONTENTS

PROLOGUE

Robin Turner & Paul Moody

A Thursday lunchtime in late April 2009 and Leicester Square is half demented, furious with heavy weather and direction-less tourists. A hailstorm, unseasonably late – well, late if you still believe the British seasons mean anything any more – has just passed through. Vicious and intense, it's all but bleached the dirt from the streets. A Hollywood premiere is being set up outside the Odeon. Security barriers branch out like creepers, penning in crowds braving the weather in the hope of catching a glimpse of someone they saw in *Heat* a few weeks ago. Befuddled, soaked and losing my bearings, I veer off into the pub next to the cinema.

Long and slipper-thin, the bar edges its way awkwardly away from the Square. It's standing room only. The cast of characters is reliably one-dimensional. Solo drinkers, men of a certain age, cradle glasses and mentally count out pennies and pounds into pint-sized denominations. The looks on their faces are all the same. Every one of them contemplating what to do between now and last orders, that moment of cruel and unusual punishment heralded with the words: 'Time, gentlemen, please!'

There is no music, nothing here to distract you from the slow throb of stolen time. In fact, there isn't anything to raise the blood pressure other than the reflective tick and tock of steady daytime drinking. Nothing, that is, except for Sky News flickering away silently from big-screen televisions, a constant high-def tickertape of bad vibes, just in case you'd forgotten what it was like out there in the real world.

On the upside, there are lots of options at the bar, not just the usual cooking lagers. I get change from £2.50 for a pint of Brains SA Gold, which is pretty amazing for a pub in the beating heart of central London.

Why, then, am I sat here just five minutes later, stunned numb and staring at the foam-flecked sides of a half-empty pint glass? This pub should be the perfect respite from the craziness outside, but it's just not clicking. There's nothing glaringly wrong here other than a lack of personality, the kind which should come swelling out of the hand pumps. The problem is that you could be in a flat-pack boozer anywhere in the UK. This isn't a place where you could make friends from strangers. To me, it feels like the booze equivalent of a burger joint – quick, cheap, cheerless, soulless. Would you like fries with that, sir? Next!

It's called The Moon Under Water, named after George Orwell's essay from 1946 about the perfect pub, yet it doesn't provide the warming glow of a proper local – the kind of place that feels like a hug from a loved one, that sends the blood rushing to your cheeks like a roaring log fire.

There used to be another Moon Under Water not 500 yards from the pub I'm sat in, a pub so vast it ran from street to street, tunnelling under an entire block of central London. You could enter on Greek Street in sunshine and exit onto Charing Cross Road in snow.

That Moon was formerly the Marquee Club. When refitted, the rock 'n' roll ghosts were exorcised from the venue, leaving something that resembled a vast Bavarian beer hall designed by the Temperance Movement as a harsh lesson to discourage social drinking. Although epic in scale, you would never hear the din of chinking tankards and bawdy songs, of shared jokes and declarations of love between friends both lifelong and fair-weathered.

The West End isn't the only place where you could chance upon Moon Under Water pubs. From Balham to Boston (Lincs), Cheltenham to Cradley Heath, there are pints being pulled in licensed establishments inspired by Orwell's wistful paean to the perfect pub. Perhaps the most notable tribute was the one opened in 1995 in a converted cinema space in Manchester. *The Guinness Book of Records* states that the Deansgate pub-cum-stadium is the largest boozer in Britain, regularly packing in up to 1,700 drinkers on busy weekends. In his bestselling treatise on nationhood, *The English*, Jeremy Paxman states: 'There are sixty-five staff and an effigy of the *Coronation Street* character Ena Sharples, brooding over the place like some fertility goddess. It is noisy, in your face and on a Saturday evening packed with hundreds of young men and women getting aggressively drunk on frothy, imported American beer.'

Each of these Moons is part of the J.D. Wetherspoon chain, the 815-strong, fiercely independent pub company set up by the maverick Irishman Tim Martin. Although admirable in looking to the Orwell piece for inspiration, it would be hard to argue that many of the defining traits remain recognisable. Today's versions are more like distortions; as stretched and warped as reflections in a fairground hall of mirrors.

So, what to do about it other than sit around complaining about how things aren't what they used to be?

After a decade and a half working in music (i.e., sat in lounge bars the world over with this year's model) in 2008 Paul and I started work on *The Rough Pub Guide*, a tribute to some of the country's more eccentric watering holes. However, as we combed our high streets and side streets, looking for the quirky and the quixotic, we found fewer and fewer pubs you'd want to idle away your time in. Instead, we discovered a silent army of identikit establishments offering a soulless, homogenised experience, with any chink of individuality ironed out.

In the years since, frustration has turned into bewilderment and, at times, despair. How could one of our most loved institutions have become so unloved and undervalued? And why does it feel as if the pub's central role in our culture is fast turning into one as a walk-on extra?

To find out, we set out to discover if George Orwell's vision of the perfect pub was actually out there, a beacon of individuality, wit and wisdom in the gloom. Did it still exist, down a winding country lane or a quiet backstreet? Or had it already been destroyed by the wrecking ball or gastro-ised, its darts teams washed away on a tide of sea bass?

Our journey took on the form of a meandering pub conversation: from the House of Commons to the Pembury Estate in Hackney; from glorious Burgh Island in Devon to apocalyptic Blackpool Pleasure Beach; from city bars full of blazing neon to the oldest pub in Edinburgh. Along the way we talked and listened to hundreds of people, from publicans and politicians, brewers and barflies, pop stars and poets, [pub] revolutionaries and raging soaks. And all along the way, we met representatives from CAMRA (Campaign for Real Ale), the pressure group fighting for drinkers' rights – after all, if you're going to tour the country pub by pub, it seems sensible to talk to the people who know where the best beer is served. In the end, pretty much the only person we didn't speak to was Orwell himself (although, as we hope you'll discover, we got pretty close).

While the results are, of course, hopelessly subjective, we'd like to think they shine a light on those pubs which still fly the flag for independence in the face of corporate domination and the onset of a homogenised 'clone town' Britain: the ones which feed the community yet give back in double measures, at happy hour prices.

More than that, we hope this book will strike a chord with anyone who has ever found themselves lost in reverie, daydreaming about their perfect pub on a long afternoon at work, at home or at the match. One where the welcome is warm, the beer is cold and you get a flash of what Charles Bukowski meant by riding 'life straight to perfect laughter'. Congratulations. You're in The Moon Under Water.

PART ONE

SHOOT FOR THE MOON

Paul Moody

've always thought that pubs are like songs; there's one to suit every mood, and the great ones stay with you for ever. You can lift the spirits in a buzzing city bar or chase away the blues in a cosy country inn. Soothe the soul in a glittering gin palace or rant and rave the night away in a grungy backstreet boozer.

With booze as the muse you'll always come out more in tune with the universe than when you went in. In a society seemingly hell-bent on making us anxious, depressed, nervous or stressed-out, pubs are mini-republics of hope; independent states of mind where we feel at our most relaxed, charming and witty (usually before stumbling home via the kebab shop). Finally free from the whir of the CCTV cameras and the clutches of advertisers, we're no longer consumers or competitors, but citizens; equals united by the three magic words: 'fancy a pint?'

'The plain fact is alcohol makes other people, and indeed life itself, a good deal less boring,' wrote Christopher Hitchens.

But the pub offers more than just a liquid escape route from the daily grind. In a fast-changing world, it marks both time *and* place, mapping the co-ordinates of our lives: from first dates to break-ups; weddings to wakes; teenage idealism to middle-years pragmatism.

As we make the breathless leaps from school to college to work in search of our future, it's in the pub that we find out how the world really operates; discover its hinges, trapdoors and zips, and get to see through the cracks in life. It's a dream depository, too; where hopes and ideas, long discarded or forgotten, can flare back to life, even if just for an evening.

Scorn for such views is rife these days. The killjoys are on the rise, and mentioning one's selfless research in the field of pubology is as likely to prompt a roll of the eyes or a pointed reminder to update your LinkedIn profile than gracious thanks.

But knowing what constitutes a good pub seems as much a part of our aesthetic appreciation of life as any book, record or film.

It seems strange, then, that most books on pubs are either dry academic studies or gonzo travelogues. If the pub means so much to us, isn't it worth taking a closer look at it?

According to the latest figures from the British Beer and Pub Association, there are currently 52,000 pubs in England, Wales, Scotland and Northern Ireland. Like Radiohead albums, some of these are more accessible than others.

A visit to the Tan Hill Inn in the North Yorkshire Dales requires climbing to a remote stretch of moorland 1,732 feet above sea level where, in midwinter, patrons are often snowed in for up to a week. A trip to The Castlebay Inn in the Outer Hebrides, meanwhile, involves a flight in a twin-prop plane and a tricky beach landing on the Isle of Barra (known to the locals, incidentally, as 'Barradise'). Anyone who fancies a pint at The Marisco Tavern on Lundy Island will need to take a two-hour trip across the Bristol

Channel, where, should you miss the klaxon signalling the departure of the last boat, you'll be left with only puffins for company for three days.

So where else leaps out from this imaginary list of pubs, as rousingly British as 'Rule, Brittania'?[1] There's the oldest ones, obviously (a toss-up between Nottingham's Ye Olde Trip to Jerusalem and The Fighting Cocks in St Albans); the smallest (The Nutshell in Bury St Edmunds, Suffolk, just 15ft x 7ft); and the one boasting the longest name (deep breath: The Old Thirteenth Cheshire Astley Volunteer Rifleman Corps Inn, in Stalybridge, Manchester).

Then there's the ones who've scratched their names into our cultural history while no one was looking. Without the Bat & Ball Inn, home of the Hambeldon Cricket Club, would the game have developed, as David Gower puts it in the foreword to John Goldsmith's *Hambledon*, 'from a sport to an art'? Would the razor-wit of *Punch* magazine, launched in 1841, have been the same without a few sharpeners at The Punch Tavern in Fleet Street, where it was conceived? Would musicians in Cornish inns, Yorkshire snugs and Hebridean back rooms still sing long into the night without knowledge of the communal singsong, traceable to the 'wassails' of Anglo-Saxon ale houses? And, while we're on the subject, where would pop music be, had The Beatles not plotted their teenage masterplan at The White Star, close to The Cavern?

Other cultures have benefited, too. Both Marx and Lenin are said to have refreshed their intellects at The Pindar of Wakefield, in London's Gray's Inn Road, while Thomas Paine called the English pub 'the cradle of American Independence', having written *The Rights of Man* at, variously, The Old Red Lion, Clerkenwell, and The White Hart in Lewes.

Other pubs catch the eye for different reasons. The Marsden Grotto in South Shields, built into the cliff face by a retired quarry man called 'Jack the Blaster', comes complete with an exterior

---

1. Based on a poem by James Thomson, written at the Dove, Hammersmith, in 1730.

zigzag staircase, while The Pack of Cards in Combe Martin, Devon, comes in the exact shape of a pack of playing cards, complete with 52 windows, 13 doors and 4 floors; all the work of a gambling squire named George Ley in 1690 to commemorate a hefty win. All very odd, then, but trumped comprehensively by The Fleece Inn in Worcestershire (where chalk 'witch circles' prevent the arrival of any stray phantoms down the chimney) and The Barley Mow in Bonsall, Derbyshire, where landlord David Wragg races chickens and conducts UFO tours of the area, known locally as the 'Matlock Triangle', following the sighting of strange lights in the sky in 2000.

But then pubs and mysteries go together like gin and tonic. A Mass Observation study conducted at the end of the 1930s and published in 1943 even concluded, in answer to the question 'what is a pub?' that no typical pub existed.

As Paul Jennings writes in *The Local: A History of the English Pub*: 'It is an institution which has always been evolving. Moreover, it has done so in response to changes in the wider society, and its development cannot be understood without reference to them.'

Perhaps the problem is that the pub sometimes feels like a long-term lover, faithful for decades: you can never quite describe it without feeling a sharp tug on the heart strings. 'To write of the English Pub is almost to write of England itself,' wrote Thomas Burke in *The English Inn* in 1927, declaring it is 'as familiar in the national consciousness as the oak and the ash and the village green and the church spire'.

Dr Johnson, an enthusiastic patron of the 18th-century tavern, famously declared: 'As I enter the door of a tavern, I experience an oblivion of care, and a freedom from solicitude… there is nothing which has yet been contrived by man by which so much happiness is produced by a good tavern or inn.' Which is all very well, but it doesn't tell us what a pub actually *is*.

Personally, I prefer the description published in the *London Mercury* in May 1928. A Mr McLaren wrote that the warmth of a pub's welcome, the solidity of its architecture and the contentment of its customers made it: 'the true temple of the English genius – the poetic spirit so essentially a part of the English character'.

Does that sound fanciful? It's not meant to. It's just that pubs tend to do that, too. They're a magical halfway house between home and work where we shrug off the straitjacket of conformity and finally say what we really think. Or, as the celebrated beer writer Michael Jackson puts it: 'proper pubs are havens in which one can anchor the soul, and hope'.

To logistics, then. To visit every pub in the UK, at a steady rate of, say, five a day, would take 28½ years. Even between two of us, that still works out at just over 14 years each. Which seems a little excessive when you consider that Christopher Columbus's first voyage to the New World took just under six months, Roald Amundsen's mission to the South Pole took less than three years and *Apollo 11* travelled to the moon and back in just over eight days.

Other intrepid travellers have passed this way before, of course. *The Good Beer Guide*, compiled by the Campaign for Real Ale (CAMRA), has been listing pubs which offer a reliable service since 1974. Impressively, ten pubs have made it into every edition, thanks to their 'unwavering dedication to real ale'.[2] CAMRA's regional associations, meanwhile, provide annual garlands for best district pubs as well as one overall winner. In 2010–11 it was The Harp in London's Covent Garden.

On a normal day the Harp shimmers like a tiny emerald amidst the West End beer-o-dromes. However, when we visited on a damp Thursday lunchtime, the beer tasted good and the whiff of homemade sausages could have sent Pavlov's dog into a seizure, but squashed between some bankers and stockbrokers, the Harp's subtleties were lost.

---

2. For the record, these are The Star Tavern and Buckingham Arms in London, The Sow and Pigs in Toddington, The Queen's Head in Newton, The Blue Anchor in Helston, The Square and Compass in Worth Maltravers, The Roscoe Head in Liverpool, The Star Inn in Netherton, The Cherry Tree in Tintern and The New Inn in Kilmington.

Which brings us neatly to the point. Any search for the perfect pub is, of course, entirely subjective without some kind of agreed ideal in mind. A treasure map, if you like, universally recognised as providing the co-ordinates for pub nirvana. The good news, then, is that we've got one.

It wasn't, you may be disappointed to learn, found among Oliver Reed's possessions following his untimely death at The Pub in Valetta, Malta, having downed eight pints of lager, rum and whisky and victoriously arm-wrestled a group of sailors. Nor was it discovered underneath a bar stool at Soho's Coach and Horses, DNA verified as the work of Jeffrey Bernard. It was, in fact, written by a 42-year-old called Eric, more commonly known as George. He rarely got drunk, seldom kept alcohol in the house and only drank lager on sufferance. And to obtain it, we must travel back 65 years.

I'm sitting in booth 108 of the Microfilm Reading Room of the British Library's National Archive in Colindale, when a bored-looking girl walks over and wordlessly places a small cardboard box in front of me. Inside, there's a single oily black reel of microfilm marked 'London Evening Standard January/February 1946'.

I attach it to the spool, flick on the light box and hit the red fast-forward button. Suddenly the pages flare into life and I'm whizzing through the days like Rod Taylor in H.G. Wells's *Time Machine*; reliving news that's long forgotten but still eerily familiar: Revolt In Cairo. 276 Dead In Earthquake. Tories: Who Will Lead The Opposition? Fuel Shortage Worsens. Spy Arrested. Manhunt for child's kidnap slayer. Ten Men Fulham Take Cup Lead. Spurs Seek New Players.

It's an odd sensation, reeling in the days and months at the touch of a button. Instinctively, I pull a small black lever, the pages slowly blur into focus and suddenly I'm back where I need to be: Saturday 9 February 1946.

On the front page, block capitals proclaim: 'FLOODS CUT

LMS MAIN LINE: Travellers are warned "Do not use Euston!"'
On page three, beneath the headline: 'Why Don't They Tidy
Up Islington?' there is an angry complaint about the number of
bombsites still left uncleared after the end of the war. 'Rubble, the
remnants of Anderson shelters and barbed wire entanglements lie
abandoned in the streets' fumes the editorial, along with 'even the
wrecked remains of motor vehicles'. The adverts, meanwhile, act as
reminders of the strange dualities of post-war Britain.

In one, a sketch of a feisty female worker with rolled-up sleeves
and a polka-dot headscarf proclaims: 'Biscuits keep you going!
They are an important food – not a luxury.' Opposite it, another
advertises Maldano Cocktails, Damson Cream: 'Late Night Final,
White Heart Cherry, Limetail, Creamy Egg Flip, Whoopee! Back
on sale at 14/6d.'

On page four, a human interest story seems to capture the sense
of storm clouds slowly lifting: 'Mr Harry Driver, 74, cycled nine
miles in heavy rain to fetch a four-year-old girl's ration of bananas,
which were on sale for the first time at Alton.'

It's the weekend essay tucked away on page six that I'm looking for, however. Written by a regular columnist by the name of
George Orwell, it extols the virtues of the author's favourite pub.
'My favourite public-house, The Moon Under Water, is only two
minutes from a bus stop, but it is on a side-street and drunks and
rowdies never seem to find their way there, even on Saturday
nights,' it begins. 'Its clientele, though fairly large, consists mostly
of "regulars" who occupy the same chair every evening and go there
for the conversation as much as the beer.

'If you are asked why you favour a particular public-house it
would seem natural to put the beer first, but the thing that most
appeals to me about The Moon Under Water is what people call
its 'atmosphere".'

Orwell reports that the interior is 'uncompromisingly Victorian',
including 'grained woodwork, cast-iron fireplaces and ornamental mirrors above the bar', with the florid ceiling 'stained dark
yellow by tobacco-smoke', providing it with the 'solid comfortable

ugliness of the nineteenth century'.

The pub possesses 'neither a radio nor a piano', ensuring that it is always 'quiet enough to talk' and in winter 'there is generally a good fire burning in at least two of the bars, and the Victorian lay-out of the place gives one plenty of elbow-room'.

Service in the three adjoining bars (public, saloon and ladies) is provided by attentive barmaids who know 'most of their customers by name, and take a personal interest in everyone. They are all middle-aged women – two of them have their hair dyed in quite surprising shades – and they call everyone "dear", irrespective of age or sex.' Games, meanwhile, are restricted to the public bar 'so that in the other bars you can walk about without constantly duck-ing to avoid flying darts'.

Upstairs, a 'good solid lunch – for example, a cut off the joint, two vegetables and boiled jam roll' is available six days a week, and the pub also sells tobacco, cigarettes, aspirins and stamps, and is 'obliging about letting you use the telephone'. While you can't get dinner there is 'always the snack counter where you can get liver-sausage sandwiches, mussels (a speciality of the house), cheese, pickles and those large biscuits with caraway seeds in them which only seem to exist in public-houses.'

The pub, unlike most, also serves a 'creamy sort of stout' which 'goes better in a pewter pot' and the barmaids never make 'the mistake of serving a pint of beer in a handleless glass.'

Occasionally, beer is served in strawberry-pink china mugs, the kind rarely seen 'because most people like their drink to be transparent' but which accord with Orwell's belief that 'beer tastes better out of china'.

The pub's 'great surprise', he explains, is a garden reached via a narrow passage from the saloon bar. Here, patrons can sip beer or draught cider beneath the plane trees on 'little green tables with iron chairs around them' while children play on swings or a chute, occasionally nipping into the public bar to 'fetch their parents more refreshment'. He concludes that the garden is the pub's best feature, because 'it allows whole families to go there instead of

Mum having to stay at home and mind the baby while Dad goes out alone'.

However, just as you can smell the hops, hear the saloon bar chatter and see the dust particles glittering in the sunlight, Orwell delivers the punchline which, he suggests, the 'discerning and disillusioned reader' will 'probably have guessed already': The Moon Under Water exists only in his imagination. 'That is to say, there may well be a pub of that name, but I don't know of it, nor do I know any pub with just that combination of qualities. I know pubs where the beer is good but you can't get meals, others where you can get meals which are noisy and crowded, and others which are quiet but where the beer is generally sour. As for gardens, offhand I can only think of three London pubs that possess them. And if anyone knows of a pub that has draught stout, open fires, cheap meals, a garden, motherly barmaids and no radio, I should be glad to hear of it, even though its name were something as prosaic as The Red Lion or The Railway Arms.'

A rainy day in Soho. It's spring and I'm sitting in a pub called The Fitzroy Tavern waiting for Alan Avenall, a member of the Save the Pub Society and Orwell enthusiast.

Looking out onto the hustle and bustle of Charlotte Street, it strikes me that the capital must look very different to how it did back in 1946. Shops struggling with post-war privations have been replaced by swish pavement cafés; crop shortages replaced with obesity scares, and judging by the frantic tapping sounds from nearby tables, ration books with Facebook.

On the surface, Orwell's vision seems a long, long way away. It's doubtful there's a single pub in Britain still serving liver-sausage sandwiches, let alone beers in china mugs.

However, much like his fiction, Orwell's vision of the perfect pub continues to haunt us down the years. Entering the words: 'Moon Under Water, Orwell' into Google reveals 837,000 references to this boozy paradise, while even a casual trawl of the internet reveals bloggers of all ages, colours and creeds letting their imagination run riot on the theme.

We've agreed to meet at The Fitzroy, because, all things considered, it seemed the obvious place. Perched insouciantly on the corner of Charlotte Street and Windmill Street in the heart of London's West End, the pub once attracted Orwell and literary contemporaries such as Dylan Thomas, Cyril Connolly and Harold Acton through its doors, part of a regular clientele including Quentin Crisp, 'wickedest man in the world' Aleister Crowley and Nina Hammett, Queen of Bohemia, who would trade tales of her adventures with Picasso for the price of a gin.

I'm a little early, and I start thinking about how, seen through the prism of history, 1940s Soho[3] seems like an idyllic sort of place, a louche republic operating on its own set of rules not unlike the Republic of Burgundy in *Passport to Pimlico*.

Fitzrovia had attracted artists since the late 19th century when John Constable, Dante Gabriel Rossetti and James McNeill Whistler all lived and worked in the area, but it wasn't until the influx of writers such as Roy Campbell, Anthony Powell and Jack Lindsay into the area in the twenties that The Fitzroy Tavern's reputation began to grow as a rough 'n' ready alternative to the salons of Bloomsbury. Patrick Hamilton soon joined them, his love-hate affair with the demi-monde captured in his trilogy of novels set in the fictitious Fitzrovia pub The Midnight Bell.

'It was perhaps the only area in London where the rules didn't apply,' said the musician and writer George Melly of the square mile just north and south of Oxford Street. 'It was a bohemian no-go area, tolerance its password, where bad behaviour was cherished.'

In The French House on Dean Street, Dylan Thomas, Francis Bacon and Daniel Farson would prop up the bar, engaged in eloquent slanging matches, egged on by fellow barflies who were 'deathly pale, wore shades and looked like artistic gangsters.'[4]

---

3. In 1946, the area north of Oxford Street was known as Fitzrovia.
4 . *London Calling: A Countercultural History of London Since 1945* by Barry Miles.

Around the corner at The Wheatsheaf on Rathbone Place, Julian Maclaren-Ross would hold court in the back bar while down the road at the George on Great Portland Street, the 'BBC Bohemia' of Hugh MacDiarmid, W.H. Auden, Robert Graves, Lawrence Durrell and Muriel Spark would congregate, all before tumbling down the stairs of drinking dens such as The Mandrake, The Gargoyle and The Colony.

These days, all that remains of The Fitzroy's outrageous clientele are the photographs lining the walls of the downstairs Writers & Artists Bar, looking balefully down on a group of thrusting young advertising execs talking loudly about the need for 'guerrilla strategies'. Much like the rest of Soho, it feels as airbrushed as the glossy magazines in the newsagent opposite, more like a theme park or a film set than an artistic playground.

Alan Avenall explains that he first visited The Fitzroy in 1985. The area has changed dramatically since, but, like most things, there are good and bad sides. 'This is a Sam Smith's pub now, which brings in a lot of advertising people who don't want to spend much money,' he says wryly. 'As you can imagine, that's not the healthiest mix. On the positive side, The Newman Arms down the road is still a terrific little pub, and I don't think it was ever half as bad as Orwell makes out in *Aspidistra*.'[5]

Dressed in a tweed suit and sporting a battered leather suitcase, Avenall doesn't have the look of the typical pub aficionado. Thin as a cocktail stick, his every statement is a precise bulletin of good sense, delivered with a deadpan understatement. 'The search for the perfect pub, eh?' he says, almost under his breath. 'It's out there. You've just got to find it.'

I had the agreeable impression that, like Orwell before him, he saw society at a crossroads, and that along the way something precious had been lost. 'It's very interesting that you've dug this article up,' he says, clearly intrigued that anyone should still be

5. *Keep the Aspidistra Flying*, 1936 novel.

interested in some yellowing newsprint first published 65 years ago. 'Because, like most of Orwell's writing, "The Moon Under Water" is more relevant today than it ever was. Think about it. When Orwell wrote *The Road to Wigan Pier* the country was in the middle of a terrible recession, the government had just embarked on the most radical reduction of public spending in generations and there was an old Etonian as prime minister. Does any of that sound familiar?'

While Avenall is at the bar, I go through a mental check of Orwell's life. Apart from the typical, school-age enthusiasms for *Animal Farm* and *Nineteen Eighty-Four*, and a voracious reading of his fiction at college (I'd been spellbound by *Keep the Aspidistra Flying*, and devoured the rest) what did I really know about the author of two of our most famous novels, and greatest modern essayist?

Born Eric Arthur Blair and educated at Eton, he rejected a life of privilege following an unhappy stint in the Indian Imperial Police in Burma. While early books *Down and Out in Paris and London* and *The Road to Wigan Pier* detailed life on the peeling edges of society, his literary progress was halted by a fascist sniper's bullet while fighting in the International Brigades during the Spanish Civil War. Subsequently dogged by ill health, his journalistic output was then dwarfed by the international acclaim for *Animal Farm* and, in 1949, *Nineteen Eighty-Four*. It feels like a pretty flimsy resumé, and I'm relieved when Avenall's return finds him plunging straight in with his own interpretation of Orwell's status as the acceptable (if slightly gaunt) face of radicalism.

'It's funny, people talk about him as some paragon of principled Englishness, but he offers us far more than that. He was more of a dissenter than anything, but his strike rate in terms of predicting the way society operates is uncanny. Obviously, the buzzwords from his fiction like Big Brother, Room 101 and Newspeak are now embedded in the language, but his ideas have seeped into the way we think. Thought crime crops up everywhere from Hollywood movies like *Inception* to the current mania for hounding celebrities who have texted someone they shouldn't. As for *Nineteen Eighty-Four*'s mantra that we are in a perpetual state of war, well, that feels truer than ever. In the course of our own lifetime our supposed enemies have shape-shifted from the Russians to the IRA to Colonel Gaddafi to Al-Qaeda and now back to Gaddafi again, give or take the odd incursion into Iraq and Afghanistan. What's the difference between that and Oceania's constant war with Eastasia and Eurasia? We're being fed a seamless flow of paranoia, it's just that most people don't choose to listen.'

I'm put slightly off balance by this outburst, and clumsily attempt to steer him in a different direction. In fact, I find myself saying, 'So where does The Moon Under Water come into this?'

Alan takes a deep draught of beer. 'Well, he could, of course, just be talking about an amalgamation of his favourite pubs, which could have been any number in Islington or the West End, including this one. But Orwell cared passionately about pubs. You could interpret it as his way of saying that we should cherish our pubs or we might lose them.'

In a review of the Mass Observation's study of 'Worktown' (Bolton, Lancashire), published in 1943 as *The Pub and the People*, Orwell extolled the pub as 'one of the basic institutions of English life' and enthused about the need for it to continue 'despite the harassing tactics of non-conformist local authorities'. The pub, he wrote, with its 'elaborate social ritual, its animated conversations... its songs and weekend comedians' provided a healthy contrast with 'the passive, drug-like pleasures of the cinema and radio'.

But the smile playing around Alan's lips tells me he knows this already. 'The other key thing about The Moon Under Water is that Orwell makes it clear that it's completely free from any connotations of drunkenness. It's a place for reflection and calm, an escape from daily life. These days it seems like everyone is plugged into some form of electronic device or other. You don't need to be a genius to see the parallels between the telescreens of *Nineteen Eighty-Four* and our modern obsessions with technology, be it the internet, mobile phones or social networking sites. Most of which, let's face it, is constant chatter without any real value or importance to society. So in that sense you could argue that in "The Moon Under Water" he's celebrating the quiet things in life, aware that technology would one day have us in its grip.'

I'd never thought of the pub like that: as a defence mechanism against the modern world, but Avenall is clearly on a roll, and it seems daft to stop him.

'What I'm trying to say is, he saw the pub as a place where people are allowed to shine. In a poem about an Italian militiaman he met during the Spanish Civil War, Orwell refers to the 'crystal spirit'. I think that's also something he saw within the population, and was conscious of how the powers-that-be try to extinguish it. When Orwell talks about the "atmosphere" in The Moon Under Water, I think that's what he's talking about. It's a place where anyone can feel at home. David Cameron might go on about The Big Society but the pub has been fulfilling that role for hundreds of years.'

There's one more question I have to ask, but before I can get there he beats me to it.

'Of course, as a search, it's hopelessly subjective,' Alan says, pulling on his pint. 'The perfect pub is different for everybody, that's the beauty of it. But if you're going to look for the real Moon Under Water, it really depends on what your criteria are. If it's all about a literal search for a pub with a Victorian interior, you've narrowed down the odds instantly. Of the 50,000 pubs or so that are left, only about 250 or so are on CAMRA's National Inventory of Historic Pub Interiors. But I get the impression you're looking for something other than that. Something a little less tangible.'

As he's leaving, Alan Avenall offers one last thought. I can tell he sees the whole idea of a search faintly absurd, but wants to register his approval anyway.

'There's one other thing that's quite interesting. In *Nineteen Eighty-Four* the central character Winston Smith dreams of somewhere he can escape the non-stop supervision of The Party. He calls it "the golden country". For me The Moon Under Water feels a bit like that. It's a piece of the jigsaw puzzle that's been lost, and the picture's not quite right without it. If you can find it, you might just discover what it means to be British.'

He puts down his glass and affords himself a final chuckle. 'Funny how you can get carried away after a couple of pints, isn't it? Either way, like they say, shoot for the moon.'

It's mid-afternoon in the British Library by the time I pack away my things and hand back the microfilm to the bored girl behind the counter. As I collect my coat downstairs at reception, I remark to the security guard on the art deco beauty of the building, opened in 1932 and housing periodicals dating back to the 1500s.

'Oh yes, it's beautiful,' he says with a rueful smile. 'But it won't be here for much longer. They've sold it to developers. By this time next year it will be torn down and turned into flats.'

He makes a rubbing gesture between his thumb and forefinger. 'The old ways are going my friend. It's all about the money now.'

Outside, it's a cold but bright January afternoon, the sun sitting low in the sky, and I'm strangely optimistic. If The Moon Under Water can still exist so vividly in the imagination after all these years, then surely there's a chance that it may really exist, on a quiet side street or down a rambling country lane?

It's 4 p.m., about time for a pint, but no luck: the pub across the road has closed down. Looking through the windows I can still see empty pint glasses, dust on the bar, spirits still to be poured. As I head to the station, I have a vision of smiling faces, Nina Hammett laughing, and fifty-two thousand clues leading to a single alcoholic Arcadia. A tingling sensation shoots up my spine. Alan Avenall was right. The perfect pub was out there. We just had to find it.

Interlude:
On the Road Again

Robin Turner

It is bitingly cold and black as Hell out there on the road to nowhere and the driver is rapidly losing his patience. We're trying to find the 54th pub on the list we've drawn up and it's very clear that we're lost. From the back seat of a well-worn Saab – air toxic and sliceable with Marlboro (Red) smoke – I am trying to guide us to a tiny hamlet in the West Midlands. Although I'm certain it exists, the scribbled-down directions I'm trying to read by the dim light of a mobile phone aren't filling anyone with any confidence. From the front, regular strangled screams emanate. 'I can't do this any more!' There is a very real chance that someone will actually, physically explode before too long if we don't find our destination, like an outtake from *Scanners*. We are in search of The Yew Tree – a Victorian theme pub that doesn't seem to have made it onto any 21st-century map. We have absolutely no fucking idea where we are.

With hindsight, maybe our initial plan was too ambitious. Sat in a central London boozer in December 2007, we decided to search the country for the perfect pub. Armed with some crumpled print-outs from Google Maps and a seemingly never-ending flow of vandal-strength lager, we drew up a list that zigzagged from coast to coast and back again. Four pints in and the idea of covering Middle England in two days made total sense.

We set out from London early having blagged a lift northwards. Styrofoam cups of instant coffee that had seemingly been heated by nuclear fission were clasped in frostbitten hands, unread copies of the *Guardian* lodged frozen under armpits. It was the kind of January midweek morning where the air seemed to hang opaquely just around eye level – not quite clear, not quite fog. Without much of a plan other than to see what the lay of the land was, we hit the A1 north.

Speeding through county after county, we stop for a pint or two at various key points on the way. The soundtrack is an ear-splitting mix of shit-kicker country, doomy crunking hip hop and the kind of heavy metal that leaves the speakers like a thinly veiled threat – pretty much the usual nerve-rattling Friday night blokes-only/ after-the-pub selection.

There are ludicrously high expectations for the first stop-off point. Ye Olde Trip To Jerusalem in Nottingham claims to be the oldest pub in the country. Signage inside dates it back to 1189 although the bit you drink in is only a few hundred years old. As with those establishments purporting to be the smallest pub in Britain, there are many claimants to the title of oldest pub. And, as with the smallest pubs, more often than not the title just acts as a way of ensnaring tourists and disguising what would otherwise be a pretty boring old boozer. Ye Olde Trip is… okay. Average really. Their own beer is drinkable but nothing I'd cross town for, let alone county boundaries. Maybe the excitement of a road trip – a stags-only working alco-holiday away from London – meant that Ye Olde Trip was only ever going to be a disappointment. Glasses emptied, we are back heading north.

The early warning signs that something is wrong probably come somewhere around Derby. While Paul and I can imbibe lunchtime pints, our designated driver has to survive on nothing more stimulating that energy drinks, soup-like coffee and high tar cigarettes. While we feel the glorious rosy afterburn of alcohol, he simply starts to twitch.

Hindsight is a fantastic thing, but looking back, SatNav would have really helped. It is dark outside and foggy inside, the air less a soup and more a lumpy stew. None of us have any idea where Cauldon Waterhouses – the hamlet The Yew Tree sits in – is. From our pub perch back in London, it looked so simple. Now we might as well have been trying to navigate our way to Mars. The driving seat is screaming, Paul and I are screaming back. It feels like we've come a long, long way from the relative sanity of that central London bar. It feels like we'll be found by farmers in a ditch a week or so later, frozen and asphyxiated, the sounds of Slayer and the RZA weakly parping out of busted speakers. Just as things reach insanity pitch, the point where everyone is screaming, angry, confused and scared – just that tipping point at which hindsight tells you must be the very peak of madness – something looms out of the pitch-black freezing fog. A pub. An old pub. A pub called The Yew Tree.

The welcome inside isn't exactly what you'd call warm, but to us it feels like the enveloping embrace of a long-lost relative. The pub is magical – Santa's grotto, if Santa was dead set on making sure that all kids, naughty or nice, were going to receive Victorian ephemera for Christmas whether they liked it or not, for the rest of eternity. The bar is adorned with the classic Carling ice-cube tap covers, dismissed to landfill by pubs the country over in the mid-eighties. By that point the nation's favourite noxious tipple might as well have been Brewer's Gold served in a gold tankard topped with flecks of gold leaf. We'd made it – literally tap water would have blown our minds wide apart at that point.

Behind the bar, there are loose packets of cigarettes on sale. A player piano in the corner has everything from Coronation anthems to 'Bohemian Rhapsody' (who knew that Queen were big in the world of Victoriana?). Food is strictly of the Smith's crisps variety. One of Queen Victoria's stockings takes pride of place in a glass cabinet. The Yew Tree is a memorial to a time gone by – that time being BBC1 in the seventies, with *The Good Old Days* being broadcast on an unbreakable loop. All that is missing is Leonard Sachs and a thigh-slapping version of 'Down at the Old Bull and Bush'. It is bloody brilliant.

Landlord – and curator – Alan pours us pints of foaming nut-brown Bass from perfectly preserved antique fonts with a bemused look on his face. He's seen it all before, the press cuttings in his scrapbooks showed us that. After decompressing, Paul and I mingle with a group of bemused locals – each disappointingly displaying the trappings of the 21st century. Dave, the group's designated driver from nearby Winkhill, tells us of how local resident Roy Wood once played the hits of Wizzard on the in-house serpent (The Yew Tree doesn't double as the local reptile house – it was a bass wind instrument). 'I'm more of a Verdi man myself, but hearing "I Wish It Could Be Christmas Everyday" played on that thing after six pints of bitter really takes some beating!'

Back at the bar, when asked to pose for photos, Alan promptly leaves his place behind the taps and dons a dicky bow for the pictures. It is symbolic of his brilliant eccentricity – the whole place is built around his unique vision, his unwaning enthusiasm in the face of the kind of market forces that exist to put people like him out of business. He has stood behind that same bar for 46 years, adding to his permanent collection piece by piece. Anywhere else, this may well have felt forced. Here in Cauldon Waterhouses – roughly two miles past the turn-off for the back of beyond – it somehow makes a kind of berserk sense. Alan's obsession has morphed a backwater pub into a museum display you could get pissed in. I am sure that somewhere out of view are the pewter tankards and liver-sausage sandwiches. Orwell's words echo from the bricks and mortar. The pub is 'uncompromisingly Victorian... everything has the solid, comfortable ugliness of the nineteenth century' and it certainly provides 'what people call its "atmosphere"' in spades.

In fact, there is just one problem. Emptying pint pots and asking for the next set of directions, we are told we are 20 or so miles away from our B&B in Newcastle-under-Lyme. The only way out is the way we came in.

Enter the Saab. Cue *Reign In Blood*.

THE GOLDEN COUNTRY

Paul Moody

Every morning at precisely 7 a.m. Stan Pownall wakes to a sharp, scratching sound. This slowly builds into a steady, percussive rhythm accompanied by low moans rising to a cacophony of ear-piercing shrieks. It's been going on for 40 years and he knows who's responsible: 'the black-eyed bugger'. Or as he's more commonly known, Snowy, The Montague Arms' pet cockatoo.

Snowy's mood swings are legendary. Once, his incessant squawking continued for two days solid, and to this day anyone foolish enough to ruffle his feathers risks losing a digit.

Not that there's usually anyone to disturb in the mornings, unless you count the strange house guests who live downstairs: the (real) skeleton perched on the bar, procured from a man called

Dr Death who slept in a coffin; the mounted stags heads (one with chewing gum glass eye), and a zebra in a crimson stage coach dating to 1780.

Sitting at a table in the pub's kitchen, Stan laughs at this strange daily ritual. He's 85, and along with wife Betty and brother-in-law Peter Hoyle, he's been running The Montague since 1967. 'We haven't changed things much over the years,' he says, blue eyes still as bright as Hockney swimming pools. 'It's nothing fancy, but the welcome's always warm. And you always know you'll see a familiar face behind the bar.'

Located next to a traffic island close to London's New Cross Gyratory, The Montague isn't the sort of pub you'll find splashed across the pages of the Sunday supplements. Outside, broken-down wire-mesh fencing and peeling black paint give it a castaway feel, while the interior is filled with clutter seemingly washed up from a Victorian shipwreck. Pressure gauges, diving helmets and boots, lifebelts and a ship's wheel fill every available inch of space, a hint of *Twin Peaks* provided by blankets of electric blue fairy lights.

When Stan took the pub over it was, as he puts it, full of 'South London gangsters' rolling in the aisles to local comedians including Mike Reid. One time, two rival crime families met in the bar for clear-the-air talks. One pulled out a hand grenade and lobbed it over the bar, with only Stan's quick wits preventing a volatile situation turning explosive.

These days the sheepskin coats, flat caps and gold jewellery are strictly ironic, worn by students at nearby Goldsmiths College of Art, lured in by quirky events such as the Unwrong Quiz (where contestants have to supply incorrect answers to win) and live music ranging from ethereal freak-folk to ear-bleed death metal. Some things remain unchanged, however.

Every Saturday night, Peter Hoyle and blind organist Peter London still entertain drinkers with idiosyncratic two-man renditions of everything from 'The Lambeth Walk' to Oasis' 'Don't Look Back In Anger'. On special occasions, they'll even attempt David

Bowie's 'Star Man'. It's all part of an entertainment policy dating back to Stan's days running The King and Queen in Mottingham, south London.

'That was a huge place. The second biggest in Europe at the time,' he says. 'We'd have two rooms packed with three hundred people in each and another twelve hundred in the disco.' Part of the attraction, Stan admits, might have been the décor. With the walls covered floor to ceiling in bamboo, and animal heads lining the walls, it was their very own urban jungle. On fine days, Stan would even ride a penny farthing he'd picked up at an antiques fair around the car park, waving to regulars. These days, the bike is lashed to a pillar at The Montague, but the quirky spirit remains undimmed.

Tonight, The Montague is hosting 'Witch Night', which will climax with a performance of 'The Umbanda', an Afro-Brazilian cult ritual creating a crossroads between the living and the dead. For promoter Frog Morris, it's all part of The Montague's unique appeal. 'It doesn't look much from the outside, but once you see the interior you realise it's the nearest experience you'll ever get to walking into a TARDIS. The first time I went there I was confronted by a horde of punks with piercings and tattoos politely waiting to be poured pints of beer by a little elderly couple, as if there was nothing unusual about the situation. It's a magical place.'

Across the country, a generation of pub landlords and landladies are doing the same thing, local heroes serving their community in their own unique way.

Ninety miles away at The Lamb and Fountain in Frome, 89-year-old Freda Searle affords herself a grin. She's been pulling pints here since 1966 and is known to everyone in the area simply as 'Mother'; local minicab drivers are regularly instructed: 'Take me to Mother's.'

Freda still remembers the week she took the pub over with late husband Harry. The pub had one sole customer, convincing the couple they'd made a terrible mistake. Yet back in the pub's mid-seventies glory days they had so much custom Freda and Harry could hardly cope, people coming from far and wide attracted by a warm welcome, hearty fare (faggots and peas, sausage 'n 'mash) and the pub's intriguing past: a stone-floored inn dating to the 15th century, its cellars include a mysterious maze of underground tunnels as well as an Elizabethan ice house.

Widowed in 1975, Freda remains a regular presence during the week, still pickling the eggs available in a big glass jar on the bar, and chatting with regulars content with entertainment consisting of darts, shove ha'penny and bar skittles.

After 45 years in the trade, like Stan, she's seen all human life come and go. There was nearly a birth in the pub once, she explains, while another time a funeral wake in one bar was disturbed by the arrival of a wedding party in the other, all singing at the top of their voices. In the end, they all cried together.

Over at The Adam and Eve in Cheltenham they've seen all of creation too. Aged 78, Dot Gasson has been running the pub in Townsend Street with her husband for 33 years. She describes it as 'a traditional local' where no one ever gets any hassle, regardless of colour or creed. 'It's just a happy pub. We've got a CD player and a very tiny television, but we don't put the sport on. People put on any music they like, if they've got a CD we'll play it.'

At The Adam and Eve, the local distinctiveness extends to the beer: the pub is supplied solely by Arkell's, a small family brewery in Swindon. 'We've been in *The Good Beer Guide* nineteen years and we've won Gloucestershire pub of the year twice,' she says with understandable pride. 'It's funny, but people seem to be going back to real ale. There's lots of students in Cheltenham now, and I've noticed that a lot of the young ladies have started drinking real ale. I'm not sure why. It feels like a new generation are coming through who don't want the lagers. They appreciate the fact that it's local.'

Like at The Montague Arms, nothing much has changed at The

Adam and Eve since 1978, the year the grapevine was planted, now so sprawling you can pick fresh grapes in a back garden which doubles as a vegetable patch. On a warm summer's day, the only thing you can hear apart from the bees buzzing around the honey-suckle is the low rumble of applewood balls in the skittle alley, aimed at 'fat Annie'-fronted pin diamonds.

Skittles is serious business in this part of the world: the pub has both a men's and a women's team, part of a thriving local league involving ten men's and six women's divisions (with fourteen teams in each). She shows me the walls of the alley, covered with pictures of the teams decked out in fancy dress on various jaunts and I'm inexplicably drawn to one decked out as The Milky Bar Kid. It's all in a good cause: Dot explains that the pub's charity do's have already raised hundreds for Help for Heroes.

I'm wondering how pillars of the community like Dot, Freda and Stan aren't acknowledged for their efforts in some way when she suddenly says: 'I haven't had a holiday for seventeen years.' The people who used to look after the pub while I was away have passed on, and I don't want to risk leaving it in the hands of strangers.'

How long will this tiny piece of paradise be here? Dot affords herself a chuckle; she's already had a couple of house calls from a man in a hooded cloak, scythe in hand. 'I had a heart attack last year and I'm getting over a stroke now. But I'm here every day, we open during the day on Saturday and Sunday too. To be honest, it's not me to be sitting around doing nothing. I like to have some company and everyone talks to each other here. Chatting to people all day keeps my spirits up.'

As for the future of the pub in general, Dot isn't optimistic.

'Unfortunately I think that pubs these days are going out fast. It's going to be very very sad when there aren't any pubs left. I hope it's not in my time. I think people will think afterwards, oh no, the pubs have gone. It will be like the post offices. Suddenly they've vanished and people don't realise what they've lost until it's too late. Those little moments when you say "hello" to someone in the morning mean a lot. It's going to be very sad in terms of the community because pubs have always been the meeting place.'

Sometimes this idea of the pub pulling the drawstrings of society together feels fanciful; a politician's soundbite rather than actual fact. But sometimes the case is unarguable.

'The pub originally opened in 1848. It was basically a converted terrace house. Last year a lady came here all the way from New Zealand who said her grandmother had been born in the pub. She came and looked around and she was so thrilled it was still here. When we go, they will knock it down and no one will ever know it was here.'

I tell Dot she'll still be serving at a hundred but she laughs it off good-naturedly. 'You must be joking. I'll be long gone by then. But I'd love to celebrate my eightieth birthday here, that's my ambition.'

If you set the SatNav from Cheltenham for Callington in south-east Cornwall, then eventually, through a maze of winding country lanes, you'll find yourself at The Bull's Head. It was in this 15th-century pub that Vera Ghey, Britain's oldest landlady, served her last pint at the age of 100 in 2008 before retiring. In charge for 60 years since the day she took over with husband Sydney in 1949, Vera estimated she pulled around 50 pints a day over six decades, meaning she had served over a million beers. She also poured around 150,000 glasses of wine and 200,000 shots of whisky before handing over the reins to Gerry Foster, her loyal helper for 27 years.

'Vera always looked after the regulars,' says Gerry, pulling me a pint of Tribute on a crisp Saturday afternoon in March. 'It's a locals pub but Vera was always accommodating. If there was a new face she would go out of her way to make them feel comfortable.'

Now 74 himself, Gerry explains that the paintings of racehorses on the walls are a monument to his days as a National Hunt jockey. He once rode winners at Liverpool and Chepstow but his crowning glory was triumphing at the Gloucester Hurdle in 1957. He says he can still remember it like yesterday; the crowd on their feet, the smell of the turf, the elation as he passed the winning post.

'If there was a secret to the pub's success while Vera was here, then it was Vera herself,' he says. 'But nothing has changed here for centuries, and I've kept things exactly as they were. There's no entertainment here of any sort, it's a drinking pub, and that's the way the regulars like it. We try to keep the prices down, too, and maybe that's what keeps people loyal. Apart from that I couldn't tell you. If Vera was here she would tell you it's just a pub doing what a pub does best, which is serve good beer in a friendly atmosphere.'

He gestures to the window, which looks out onto the local village church. 'We're next to the church and so we get a regular trade from weddings and funerals. On Fridays and Saturdays we're completely packed out. And that's the way it's always been here.'

He tells me he'd love to chat but it's time to crack on, and as I gaze out of the window it's impossible not to think of Thomas Gray's 'Elegy Written in a Country Church-Yard': 'Beneath those rugged elms, that yew-tree's shade/ Where heaves the turf in many a mouldering heap/Each in his narrow cell for ever laid/The rude Forefathers of the hamlet sleep.'

'There go the church bells,' says Gerry as tumbling chimes start up. 'That means the bell ringers will be coming in soon, and they're a thirsty bunch!'

Back in 1978, Whitstable landlady Bessie Beed wrote her splendidly titled memoirs *Seventy Years Behind Bars*, but other great servants of the community have either retired or gone to the lounge bar in the sky with shamefully little fanfare or recognition. Flossie Lane pulled pints for 74 years at The Sun Inn in Leintwardine, Herefordshire, before her death, aged 94. Daisy Holland, fiercely independent former landlord of The Queens Hotel in Pelsall, Walsall, passed away age 106 in January 2010, causing her grandson Kevin, himself a publican, to pay the tribute: 'She was quite strict in the way she ran the pub; she had a very strong notion of what was right and wrong, and was very dignified with it.' And then there's Mabel Mudge. Landlady of The Drewe, in Drewsteignton, Devon, she ran the pub with her husband for 75 years from 1919 until 1994, eventually retiring aged 99.

I can't help but think of Freda Searle's last words to me. 'There won't be any pubs left in this country in ten years' time. A lot of managers don't even talk to their customers. They just want their money. When I started out pubs were the hub of the community and that's how I've tried to keep mine. I have no intention of retiring, but I can't go on for ever . . .'

Crystal chandeliers, dimmed to a seductive glow, combine with flickering candlelight and decorative feather boas to cast sexy shadows on black and silver wallpaper. Above a blood-red Regency sofa, a chalkboard suggests drink options (Cremant De Limoux – £22, Champagne Descombes – £32) as patrons peruse a menu offering: 'Plump Scottish miso salmon fillet with udon noodles tossed in low sodium soy sauce and bok choy' and 'Emma Ringshaw's chicken, liver prune and port pate'. Through the speakers, Billie Holliday suggestively whispers: 'It just had to be you.'

Kate Burt rolls her eyes and takes a swig from a pint of Beck's Vier. 'I can remember when this was a proper pub. It had a pool table, lock-ins and you'd meet local people who you'd recognise but had never spoken to and start chatting away. Some of my mates used to come in here and they loved it, but they never come in here now.'

We are sitting in The Cambria in Camberwell, south London and it's fair to say Kate preferred it as it was. As the driving force behind the 'Save the Boozer' website (tag-line: 'Say No To Gastro!') she sees it as proof that the 'gastro-revolution' of recent years hasn't just seen thousands of pubs undergo drastic face lifts, it's changed their personality, too.

'The problem is, this isn't a traditional pub any more. It's geared towards a specific market who want to eat out. It's an easier game. The trouble is, it's exclusive in the worst sense. You wouldn't come here with your nan, or your grandchildren or your dog.'

The way Kate sees it, it's just another example of the way the whole world appears to have 'gone middle class'. She gives an example of a pub down the road from where she lives in Brixton. Once, it was full of old Jamaican guys sitting at the bar slowly drinking their pints of Guinness. Now, the comfortable seats which made the regulars feel at home have been ripped out, leaving them perched on shiny chrome stools under fluorescent lighting; relics from a bygone age, being edged towards the door. 'There seems to be this insatiable desire to destroy the past which links in with the whole wave of gentrification. Family pubs which were all about being down to earth are being replaced by these aspirational bars where everyone wants to feel a bit chi-chi.'

Growing up in Wandsworth, Kate's pub baptism came via a Saturday job working in the kitchen at a hostelry called The Crane. Chi-chi, it was not. 'My parents weren't particularly outgoing and so it was a real eye-opener. There were so many characters there. The landlord and landlady were like Angie and Den from *EastEnders*. Big hair, big glasses, very charismatic, calling people "darling" all the time. It was a classic example of the pub being a melting pot of ages, races, genders, backgrounds, class and levels of mental health, all with a huge dose of eccentricity thrown in. The rich fabric of British society, in other words.'

At university in Norwich, Kate's friends petitioned her to go to trendy DJ bars. Instead, she wiled away the nights with 'an alcoholic boyfriend' in a scruffy local pub called The Ironmongers on Red Lion Street. 'It was great. My boyfriend was working behind the bar, so it became a familiar and comforting place. There were beer mats stuck everywhere, you'd meet all sorts of random people.'

On returning to London in the mid-nineties she found her hometown in the throes of a drastic reinvention. 'I remember seeing Brixton change. There was a mini riot in the mid-nineties, and allegedly the cause of it was the opening of The Dog Star, which used to be a really old proper boozer called The Atlantic. The Dog Star is great in its own way, but it made me feel sad to see so many other local pubs closing down. They're important socially and historically. There was an amazing one called The Wickwood

Tavern. They had lock-ins every night, you'd play pool with complete strangers, get pissed and tell each other your life stories. There was another one called The Hamilton Arms on Railton Road. The road got gentrified and they did up all the flats. As soon as the flats were occupied the neighbours complained about the noise and got the pub closed down. It's like, the pub was here before you were, you bastards!'

To channel her frustrations, Kate started 'Save the Boozer' and was amazed at the response. 'I got so much positive input from people, it really seemed to touch a nerve. I think it taps into what makes Britain great, and yet what other nations often scorn us for: our nostalgia. We didn't like the idea of the euro because we liked the idea of pounds and pence and we cling desperately to national institutions such as pie and mash, and Routemaster buses. The classic British boozer fits into that pattern. Yet the weird thing is, we don't seem to cherish them enough to preserve them. Which is a shame because, when we lose one, a little piece of our national identity shrivels up and dies.'

Her inbox wasn't just filled with the teary-eyed reminiscences of men of a certain age, though. 'I've had a strong reaction from lots of women who feel the same way. I could not be less interested in real ale, but I think loads of women appreciate a good dive. Which is what maddens me about gastropubs. The argument is that they somehow make it more comfortable for a woman to sit on her own. But where is any woman going to feel comfortable on her own having a drink in the evening? That's just life, sadly.'

New Year 2010, determined not to fall into the traps laid by cash hungry club promoters, Kate went to a bash at her local pub, The Canterbury Arms. 'It's a bit skanky, a proper Irish pub. The landlord closes it to anyone who's not local. It was free to get in, there was a buffet and a party room. It was lovely. I think what made it so great, and all the other pubs like it so great, is that they don't rest on their laurels. They work hard to keep the pub's heart beating. At somewhere like The Montague Arms, say, it's very inclusive. The bar staff are reassuringly old too.'

And the perfect pub? Unsurprisingly, it's along the same lines. 'The perfect pub is like that wedding reception you'll never forget because everybody – dads, babes in arms, walking-sticked grannies, the vicar, awkward teenage bridesmaids, that harmless oddball no one seems to know, the bigoted aunt charmed into enlightenment by the bride's black, gay best friend – all get down to the Nolan Sisters together. British reserve disappears. I think there's something beautiful about a proper neighbourhood boozer which makes us leave that national trait at the door. And it's not just the alcohol inside (though of course it helps). In an unpretentious pub, secure under the watchful eye and comforting hospitality of a stern but warm-hearted landlord or lady, the complex hierarchies of the outside world don't matter; we can relax and be ourselves.'

Through the speakers, Craig David segues into Kajagoogoo and Kate Nash. It's enough to make the eyes water.

It's almost time to go, but Kate smiles; one more point: 'At heart, I think we're a nation of gleeful non-conformists. We don't worship at the altar of classic chic like the French: we put Vivienne Westwood on a pedestal. We don't cherish order like the Germans – we're comforted by a bit of chaos, that's why we loved Oasis and think Tracey Emin is a legend. We love a bit of family entertainment – Bruce Forsyth, *Britain's Got Talent*. You'll find all those things in the pub. A brilliant boozer is like a microcosm of British society at its best. It's where we do what – as a nation – we're famous for: accepting others just as they are, and making them feel welcome.'

Back at The Montague Arms a man dressed in the black stovepipe hat and Puritan tunic of Witchfinder General Matthew Hopkins takes a thoughtful sip from a pint of lager. His gaze is fixed on the stage where a girl in a tight black catsuit is marking out a pentagram on a starched bedsheet using wax from a flickering altar candle. It's the artist Grace Morgan Pardo, and 'The Umbanda' is in progress. When the diabolic image is complete, she sets it alight, spindly lines of fire crackling into jagged shards of light. As it illuminates her in a wash of blue-yellow flames, the crossroads is forged.

Life and death: it's hard to miss the symbolism. Because despite the best efforts of Stan, Freda, Dot, Vera and a generation of other landlords and landladies, the pub is in a desperate battle for survival. One against an enemy who is stealthy as the Grim Reaper but no less deadly, who comes armed with spreadsheets, hard hats and cold-eyed talk of 'progress'. And it's one that's intertwined with the very spirit and soul of the nation.

THE LAST OF ENGLAND

Paul Moody

'When you have lost your inns drown your empty selves,
for you will have lost the last of England.'
Hilaire Belloc, 1907

June 2037. In the sleepy country village of Amblewick, a scrum of news teams from around the world are jostling for position outside the front door of The Rose and Crown, a traditional inn dating to 1543.

As the local church bells ring a mournful lament, 95-year-old landlady Mabel Summers leans over the counter and bellows 'Time, Gentlemen please!', a cue for regulars including a loved-up couple, a retired army colonel, some ladies-who-lunch and a group of boisterous lads to reluctantly drain their glasses. Because the pub, the last in England, is closing its doors for the final time.

On a special edition of *Newsnight*, hand-wringing politicians point the finger at each other while a social historian explains that in multi-media, multi-faith Britain, there really is no longer a need for pubs anyway. It ends with Chas & Dave performing a version of 'The Sideboard Song' and a freeze-frame of *Coronation Street*'s Bet Lynch which causes younger viewers to scratch their heads in bewilderment. After which everyone shrugs their shoulders, logs back on to their personal computer profiles, and promptly forgets all about it.

A paranoid delusion? Not according to an article in *The Times* in March 2009, when closures were at a whopping 39 every week, which calculated that the country would be pub-free within our own lifetime. Subsequent years have seen pub numbers continue to fall dramatically with over 2,700 closing in 2010 (an average of one every three hours). Beer sales, meanwhile, have fallen to their lowest levels since the Great Depression of the 1930s, with 14 million less pints a week being served than at their peak 30 years ago.

For the pub trade it's as though a combination of contributory factors – including the smoking ban, the availability of cheap beer and wine in supermarkets and regular tax hikes have combined forces in an all-out war on pubs. The effects on our towns and cities are clear to see: a once proud army of Duke of Wellingtons, Earl of Lonsdales and Red Lions standing defeated by the road-side, with The Kings Head taken as a trophy.

In the country, the effects have been even more brutal: more than half the villages of England are now 'dry' for the first time since the Norman Conquest. These closures are bringing with them a bizarre process of cultural self-immolation, as if, after centuries of loyal service, the pub is being slowly unstitched from the Bayeux Tapestry of British life, leaving a gaping hole in our own history.

The Crown and Cushion in Manchester, a classic red-brick corner pub dating to 1741, called last orders in January 2011 to make way for an 'urban redevelopment' of shops and offices. The Fleur De Lys in Cranborne, a 17th-century pub mentioned in *Tess of the D'Urbervilles* and praised by the poet Rupert Brooke for its 'fine hoppy ale and red firelight' closed its doors for the final time in 2010, as did The Crispin and Crispianus in Strood, frequented by Charles Dickens and featured in the essay 'The Uncommercial Traveller'.

Pubs familiar from pop, film and TV have fallen like dominoes, too. In March 2011 The Tavistock Arms in Westbourne Grove, better known as The Mother Black Cap in *Withnail and I* was razed to the ground to make way for flats. While The Duke of Albany, better known as The Winchester in *Shaun of the Dead*, was boarded up in 2009, and set to be converted into designer flats: a different class of zombiefication.

On a more personal note, a few months ago I found myself walking past The Archway Tavern pub in north London. The Kinks shot the cover for their *Muswell Hillbillies* album here in September 1971, and it's always been a rough 'n' ready place to enjoy live music. As I crossed the road I noticed that the original pub sign (it is now trading as 'The Archway') had been left abandoned on the roadside, and was about to be pulverised by the metal jaws of a dust cart. For any Kinks fan, it was almost as heartbreaking as seeing someone bulldoze the village green. (I later told Ray Davies about it in an interview, and he expressed a typically opaque sadness. But that's another story.)

So why does any of this matter? Isn't an emotional attachment to places you've sometimes never even been, at best, irrational? Perhaps. But as each pub goes, it feels like a tiny, often subversive insight into our history, customs, attitudes and sense of humour goes with it.

Paul Heaton, former singer and lyricist with The Beautiful South, is sitting on a silver chair outside The Star in Bentworth, Hampshire. For the last twenty-five years he has been writing beer-soaked vignettes about the disillusioned and romantically muddled. Despite the warming afternoon sun, he is wearing a bright red cagoule zipped to the collar and a pair of thigh-hugging Lycra shorts. The expression on his face is somewhere between that of healthy exhaustion (he's cycled 50 miles today) and the irritation which comes with seeing the country he loves being systematically dismantled.

'I do a lot of cycling around Macclesfield, and I'd see a lot of pubs boarded up. It was really depressing. There's this particular road which leads towards a pub called The Cat and Fiddle which closed down. It led me to thinking about what the pub was like and wonder where the people who used to go there, go to now. The damage it's causing to local communities is enormous. I've got to the stage now where I even stop and photograph each empty pub when I see a new one.'

To highlight the impact of rural closures and raise funds for struggling locals he had the idea for a fundraising tour around his local pubs in Cheshire. This inevitably mushroomed into his 'Pumps and Pedals' tour of the UK, a two-week 720 mile trek around the country, stopping off at 16 rural pubs armed with nothing more than his voice and a healthy thirst.

'I put an ad in the *Publican* (pub trade newspaper) and got nine hundred replies,' he says with a grin. 'It was really life-affirming. Most of them didn't know what the hell they were going to get, really. Ninety-five per cent had never put on any pub event before. Obviously they had to fit the bill in terms of what we needed, so they had to have a live room for music and somewhere to stay. To make it worth their while we gave them fifty tickets to sell themselves so they could get fifty locals in. I think people appreciate the fact that I turn up on my bicycle and don't bring a load of attitude.'

While Paul sees the closures as the result of a number of contributory factors, he's convinced, as many within the industry are, that the causes are man-made. 'The people who take these pubs over are quite clever. What they do is buy the property, then leave it for a year so that local people think it will reopen as a pub. Then a year later it's a Tesco, or turned into a block of flats. So they sap the life out of the community first, which takes the sting out of any opposition. Nobody actually says "we're gonna take the pub over and turn it into a supermarket", but it happens all the time. I'm the sort of person who looks at every sign on the street, and very rarely do you get any proper consultation about a new supermarket being built, especially if it's something like a Tesco Express.'

The way Paul sees it, it's not just the tour which will prove the survival of the fittest. 'I've heard a variety of reasons why pubs are closing down in such numbers. I think the smoking ban has gone now as an issue, although it's obviously had a big effect. A lot of people in the pub trade have realised that if they're going to make sure they're not the next pub to go down they have to use a bit of suss. The keenest ones are really pushing their pubs out there to be a part of the community. This pub (The Star) is really working hard, they have a blues festival, movie nights, all sorts of things. They're the ones that will survive, and the quiet ones are just going to vanish.'

On his travels, he's been showered with gifts from grateful landlords. At the Three Horsehoes in Ratledge he was presented with a cake in the shape of a bicycle. At The Plough in Dorking, he was even poured a pint of 'Beautiful South' beer.

'That's a fantastic little pub. It's one of these amazing places in the middle of nowhere. I like to think I've been to a lot of pubs, but there are so many of these places just tucked away where you'd never find them. Hidden gems.'

'I think the trouble is, a lot of us feel the same way about these pubs but we don't know what to do about it. We feel powerless, yet something we love and believe in is being taken away from us. Pubs are what we all grew up with, and now they're disappearing, and nothing seems to be being done.'

So is there any light at the bottom of the beer glass? On the way home, I start reading Paul Jennings' book *The Local*. A history of pubs and how they've changed down the centuries, it's a fascinating reminder that that the pub has constantly changed shape to fit the social environment. If we're to understand the current climate, it seems important for us to examine it in the light of the past.

According to the Greek commentator Dioscorides, Britons have been drinking communally since the first century BC. It took the Romans to get us organised, their roadside tavernae being simplicity itself: a single room where ale, wine and food could be enjoyed over a game of chequers, at locations marked by hanging vine leaves.

The first attempts to curb binge drinking came as early as the seventh century, King Edgar's edict that drinking horns in Saxon ale houses should be marked with pegs to measure each draught quickly resulting in medieval drinking games (hence the phrase 'to take down a peg or two').

We boozed our way through the growth of Christianity, too, and by the Middle Ages the inns, mostly run by monks, acted as handy pit stops for pilgrimages to shrines at Glastonbury, Winchester, and, after the assassination of Archbishop Thomas Beckett in 1170, Canterbury. It was only with the dissolution of the monasteries by Henry VIII that inn-keeping moved from the control of monks to the lay gentry, ushering in a new age of revelry.

In these flashy Tudor taverns, given heraldic names like The Red Lion and The White Horse, strolling players would entertain drinkers with songs from a central courtyard, and by the late 17th century, these various inns, taverns and ale houses even had a collective name: the 'public house'.

The arrival of William of Orange on the throne provided the pub with a fresh enemy: the dram shop. By 1740 there were 9,000 in London alone, public concern at this epidemic of drunkenness summed up by Hogarth's 1751 engraving *Gin Lane*, a picture of moral degeneracy in sharp contrast to sister drawing *Beer Street*, where prosperous businessmen go about their bawdy business.

It took the Duke of Wellington's 1830 Beer Act, however, to fully reinstate beer as the nation's drink of choice. Effectively allowing any householder to start up a pub in their own home for the price of two guineas, it sparked nothing short of beer mania. 'If Satan himself had had a seat in the counsels of the nation, the Beer Act was the very kind of measure which the great enemy of mankind would have suggested,' wrote a horrified Reverend Thomas Page of Virginia Water Parsonage in 1846, and the effects of the act were certainly dramatic. Within a little over three months, more than 26,000 new licences had been granted, prompting free trade advocate Sydney Smith to comment in 1831:

'Everybody is drunk. Those who are not singing are sprawling.'

To cope with demand, grand, purpose-built locals were erected in city centres, designed to attract a more professional clientele, their sumptuous fittings, decorative flourishes and glittering mirrors cropping up on street corners like boozy Xanadus. This Victorian golden age couldn't last.

The Licensing Acts of 1869 and 1872 ushered in a new era of regulation and red tape for the nation's publicans, while the 1908 Licensing Bill even banned women from working behind the bar. Suitably encouraged, the wartime Liberal government of Lloyd George curtailed opening hours drastically, with state-owned pubs set up in their place offering weak beer and distractions including newspapers, billiards and bowling greens. Scant consolation, you'd imagine, for battle-scarred veterans of Loos, Verdun and the Somme, hoping for a stiff drink on their return from the front line.

Much as now, the Depression of the 1930s saw a slump in beer sales and the pub's declining place in the nation's affections was summed up by J.B. Priestley in his brilliantly waspish 1934 travelogue *English Journey*.

While faring slightly better than Birmingham (written off with the words 'I saw nothing, not one single tiny thing, that could possibly raise a man's spirits'), the pub is pointedly left off the guest list for Metroland, where 'factory girls looking like actresses' enjoy a world of cocktail bars and 'giant cinemas and dancehalls'. Instead, the pub (or at least 'public houses with red blinds') are described as an unwanted reminder of drab, 19th-century England, a cultural relic as unattractive as 'cindery waste ground, mill chimneys, slums and sooty dismal little towns.'.

Throughout, the pub, much like Doctor Who, has battled all manner of reoccurring enemies. A shape-shifting cabal known variously as the Puritans, the Temperance Society and Health and Safety take on the Daleks role, but the dreaded coffee shop has caused its fair share of problems, too. 'When you come into them, they are but ale-houses, only they think that the name of coffee-house gives them a better air,' wrote a disgruntled Daniel Defoe on a visit to what was presumably called Ye Olde Starbucks in Shrewsbury in 1714.

In recent years, however, it's another sci-fi analogy which seems to fit: *Invasion of the Bodysnatchers*. The rise of the pub companies (known within the trade as pubcos) over the last 15 years has seen a massive growth in identical chain pubs as O'Neill's, All Bar One and the Slug and Lettuce. This 'McDonaldisation' of pubs has left us with thousands of strange, characterless premises, robbed of once vibrant personalities. Using techniques developed in pizza and sandwich chains, these companies have succeeded in 'growing revenues' by filling our high streets with bars known within the trade as 'high volume vertical drinking establishments'. Designed specifically to encourage patrons to do one thing, and one thing only: drink.

Where once most pubs stocked local ales, lovingly cared for by a landlord who knew his beers and the regulars by name, these identikit pubs stock only a handful of major brand lagers, as well as heavily marketed bottled beers, ciders and alcopops.

Why? Because they are, in a nutshell, more profitable and a lot less trouble to keep than cellars full of local cask ale.

This depressing state of affairs has come about through a curious series of events, starting with an unlikely alliance between CAMRA and then Prime Minister Margaret Thatcher at the end of the eighties. Eager to break up the brewers' monopoly on pub ownership, the Monopolies and Mergers Commission ruled that no brewer could own more than 2,000 pubs. The plan was to derail the brewers' gravy train, while encouraging smaller brewers, providing more choice for drinkers.[6] What actually happened was that the brewers outmanouevred the government and created stand-alone pubcos which, because they didn't actually brew beer themselves, were exempt from the legislation; their distance from the brewers allowing them to act with only one guiding principle: the balance sheet.

To find out more we'll have to head back to the future...

---

6. One other result was that young chefs found they could buy their own pub and go it alone, sparking the gastropub revolution.

CLOCKING ON AT THE FUN FACTORY

Paul Moody

I t's 9 p.m. and the clocks are ticking backwards. I'm in an eighties theme bar called Reflex, close to Cannon Street station, and with each step down the circular staircase the years are vanishing faster than wrinkles after Botox. At the bar, there's a rolling sea of flushed faces. Next, New Look and the Lynx effect. City shakers, groovy bankers and antsy account executives jostle for space, girls in sparkling gold and silver shouting over drinks orders to the bar-top front line amid a bitchy breeze of office gossip. *Two Becks. WKD Blue. Sam wants a Shot-tail!*

By the entrance, a girl in a scarlet asymmetrical dress and silver clutch bag asks which of the VIP seating areas is reserved for her. It's a reasonable request: there are so many cordoned-off areas in the upstairs bar it looks like a crime scene; each tagged with a printed A4 description: 'Naomi's Party'; 'Craig', 'Lisa's Leaving Do'. I make the mistake of perching on the edge of one blood-red booth to scribble some thoughts, and am pounced on by two girls who are waiting for the rest of their party to arrive. 'This is reserved for us, clear off!' snarls one, while the other puckers her lips and puts her hand to her forehead in an 'L' shape: loser. Did people do that in the eighties? Probably.

On the dancefloor, an entire wall of TV screens runs eighties films as silent movies. When I arrive, it's the orgasm scene from *When Harry Met Sally*. I'm wondering how long it will be before I see Gordon Gekko mouthing 'greed is good', when it occurs to me that everything about Reflex screams excess apart from the prices.

Sex on the Beach (the tide is high with Smirnoff, peach schnapps, orange and cranberry juice) or a Strawberry Woo Woo (a strawberry train crash: Smirnoff, peach schnapps and strawberry puree with cranberry and raspberry juice) come in at just £3.50 (or £1.99 on Thursday, 'Ladies Night'). Alternatively, there are 'shot-tails': the Tongue Curler (apple and Sourz cherry) or the Glitter Bomb (Goldschlager with Red Bull). Another concoction seems to feature crushed Skittles in the bottom, and glows luminous under the club's retina-frazzling UV lights.

Most people opt for 'Sharers': huge cocktail glasses filled to the brim with brightly coloured liquid (turquoise, scarlet orange) complete with plastic umbrellas. Squint and it almost feels like a low-budget remake of *Cocktail*, sadly minus Bryan Brown's poetically cynical barman Coughlin, able to 'make things with juice and froth/The pink squirrel and the three-toed sloth'. Not that he'd be able to keep up with the routines.

Whenever the frantic pace drops, the bar staff continue the drip-feed insulin of nostalgia by breaking out in dance moves from *Dirty Dancing* or *Fame*. The mood is frantic, manic almost; and so deafening that you can hardly hear yourself think.

But then this isn't a place to discover yourself. It's a place to dance yourself dizzy and, indisputably, get paralytically drunk. 'You should see the state of some of the people here at two o'clock in the morning,' says one staff member who should probably stay nameless. 'It's cheap and it's cheesy. By the end they're literally crawling up the stairs.'

I saw it all in my mind's eye: hundreds of chronic eighties addicts, all of them sweating and drooling, stumbling back up the stairs to the 21st century where they'd be greeted with an *Evening Standard* headline reading: 'Think-tank forecasts bleak years ahead for Britain'.

Across the UK, the same thing is taking place. Not one-off club nights or parties to celebrate a birthday or an engagement but exact replicas designed to cater for a crowd market research has proved likes this sort of thing.

In Glasgow, Sheffield, Liverpool and 26 other bars across the country, branches of Reflex offer exactly the same 'authentic' eighties themed fun night out. For those inclined towards the seventies, there are Flares bars where, on student nights, patrons are invited to 'dance in your pants' while a third option, Babylon, strikes a more sober note, aimed at those still too young to treat their youth ironically. Instead, drinkers are lured in with a logo based on the film version of Irvine Welsh's *Trainspotting* and the promise of 'early evening relaxing beats'. When one generation becomes immune to *Saturday Night Fever*, the bar is simply revamped to cater for a crowd who'd rather 'walk like an Egyptian' (a classic example being Cleethorpes, where an ailing Flares bar was successfully reopened as a Reflex).

Which begs the question: can such cynical reworkings of our collective history be healthy? It's not as if the craving for a nostalgia fix is anything new. For generations people have gathered to play music and celebrate a shared past together. But at Reflex, seeing a room full of strangers singing along to Tiffany's 'I Think We're Alone Now' as *Bladerunner* fills the screens feels a bit like the aural equivalent of all those *I Love the '70s* shows, where someone who patently doesn't remember watches a clip and goes, 'Oh yeah, I really loved *Trumpton*.' Does anyone really recall this song fondly, or is it an implanted memory, worthy of Philip K. Dick? And if so, are we becoming the android sheep?

Originally part of the Mitchells & Butlers pub company, the Reflex, Flares and Babylon bars were sold as part of a group of 333 pubs in November 2010 to the Stonegate Pub Company for £373 million. In June 2011 Stonegate then merged with the Town and City Pub Company Limited (whose largest shareholders are Icelandic bank Kaupthing and Commerzbank, the second largest bank in Germany). This added a further 230 pubs to its estate, including the Yates's and Slug and Lettuce brands, all of whom are now owned by a company called TDR Capital. On announcement of the merger, plans were unveiled to 'evolve' the Flares and Reflex brands, while in June 2010 Stonegate chairman Ian Payne unveiled a 'limitless' bonus scheme for the company's 180 assistant managers, stating: 'I am delighted that you are grasping the opportunities to increase sales in your businesses.'

So who are TDR Capital? On their website, full of views of the London skyline reminiscent of *The Apprentice*, they describe themselves as: 'a highly selective private equity firm with a track record of investing in firms that have delivered excellent returns for investors'. Founded in 2002, their history goes back to 1999 when the company's founders Manjit Patel and Stephen Roberston acquired 1,428 pubs from Bass plc and formed Punch Taverns, with the aim of 'using the business on lease conversions and on growing revenues and EBITDA' (Earnings Before Interest, Tax, Depreciation and Amortisation, commonly used to indicate the ability of a company to service debt). TDR currently manage funds worth £2.6 billion and have completed transactions worth £15 billion.

Fair enough, you might think. But TDR also owns the majority stake in VPS Holdings who describe themselves as 'the worldwide leader in the protection and management of void properties'. As Hayley Brennan, a lead organiser at the GMB Union, put it on news of the merger: 'I say to the staff in these 333 pubs: "be afraid – be very afraid".'

So, what do we have? Booming private equity companies, stock-market-floated pub companies and chain bars which are little more than cynically marketed business enterprises, designed to make money: fun factories. Suddenly it all feels a very long way from 'Frankie Say Arm the Unemployed'.

This is just the tip of the iceberg when you take into account the size and scale of the pub companies and their rapacious desire for profits. Punch Taverns, the biggest of the major pub companies, announced half-year profits of £61 million in May 2011, down from £66 million a year earlier. Enterprise Inns, who own 6,600 pubs, announced in August 2011 they had made net proceeds of £69 million from the disposal of 335 pubs and expected to dispose of 500 pubs by the end of the year, netting £110 million. Both, however, are mired in debt due to policies of aggressive securitisation which have floundered with the stock market crash (Punch's debt in June 2010 stood at £3.2 billion). This wheeler-dealer nature has, unsurprisingly enough, failed to endear the pubcos to the average pub landlord, many of whom are struggling to make ends meet despite putting in 60-hour weeks.

In recent years, Enterprise Inn's founder and chief executive Ted Tuppen has become an online hate figure for landlords because of 'the tie'; an arrangement where landlords buying leases from the company agree to buy their beer from the company as well as pay rent.

A 59-year-old former accountant, who, according to an interview in *The Times* in 2008, spends his spare time 'skiing, shooting, racing cars, playing golf and walking the dog', Tuppen seems less like Lucifer than a very astute businessman.

While 'the tie' worked reasonably well as the pub companies and the pubs enjoyed the benefits of an economic boom – any debts offset against rising share prices – the economic squeeze has seen share prices plummet, causing a massive increase in pubs being sold off. Consequently, landlords argue that the pubcos are bleeding them dry with inflated rents, high beer prices and broken promises, all the while luring in naïve landlords, who plough their life savings into deals where the odds are stacked against them.

Tuppen's response is that these licensees 'freely entered' the contract and therefore have only themselves to blame. In fairness, Tuppen claims that Enterprise's policy of placing orders with small brewers has also kept many afloat during the recession, a notable example being Cornwall brewer Sharps, whose Doom Bar has boomed thanks to Enterprise. Nonetheless, landlords argue that the dramatic fall in pub numbers is at least partly attributable to the pubcos' willingness to sell off underperforming pubs rather than nursing them through the lean times.

Trawling the internet, these mind-numbing facts and figures come to life, flesh and bones provided by the stories of landlords struggling to make ends meet.

Steve Scarff, landlord of popular Plymouth pub The Mermaid in Eggbuckland, quit the industry suddenly in 2010 after nearly two decades, finally throwing in the (beer) towel having remortgaged his house and spent £200,000 of his own cash propping up the business, blaming, among other things, the conditions slapped on 'tied' pubs.

The White Horse in Edinburgh, the oldest pub on the Royal Mile and established in 1742, closed in June 2010 when 62-year-old landlady Kath Will quit, blaming Punch Taverns for soaring rent and beer prices. 'Punch Taverns was putting the rent up and the price of beer, which we had to buy from them. The prices were extortionate and we were just getting ourselves deeper into debt,' explained Mrs Will to the *Scotsman*, with Ellen Lindsay, 68, a regular for 30 years adding: 'I'm devastated and most of the regulars are disappointed. It was a family-oriented pub and you just knew everyone. You could go in there and you were safe, nobody bothered you.'

Some stories are heartbreaking for other reasons: at The Talbot Inn in Cheadle, landlord of 23 years John Bailey, 61, who was born in a pub and followed his parents into the trade, told website thisismoney.co.uk in March 2011 that despite working long hours carrying out a multitude of jobs – from handyman to decorator, entertainment organiser to accountant, counsellor to sommelier – he makes a profit of just 40 pence an hour for a ten-hour day. All this while the company that rents the pub to him, Punch Taverns, has made millions for its investors, and spent millions more paying corporate advisers such as Goldman Sachs and Citigroup.

So is it really all as black and white as it seems, the pubcos tormenting our quivering publicans like slavering Goliaths?

Brigid Simmonds, OBE, has had a busy couple of weeks. Meetings have been cancelled at a moment's notice, diary schedules rewritten with undue haste, scribbles of red ink scrawled across long-standing entries such as 'Pub Book – interview?' by her harassed PR, Neil. A fortnight ago, she was part of a panel addressing the Business, Innovation and Skills Committee to answer questions about pub company practices along with, among others, Ted Tuppen. Last week, she was appointed chairman of the Tourism Alliance, championing the industry's role during trifling events such as the Queen's Diamond Jubilee and the Olympics in 2012.

Today, however, she is back behind her desk on the seventh floor of a tower overlooking the Thames at Vauxhall. Because as CEO of the British Beer and Pub Association, she is charged with representing the interests of the BBPA's 64 members (including both Punch and Enterprise) in their dealings with both the public and parliament. Her previous job as chief executive at Business in Sport and Leisure, earned Brigid a reputation for getting things done. Headhunted by the BBPA, she has a brief to make those in power sit up and listen.

I had already heard her in action, providing a defence of pubco policy concerning 'the tie' on a phone-in on Radio Five Live. The voice was plummy, the tone robust. I pictured pearls, power dressing and a lady not for turning.

'The first thing which needs to be said is that the pub remains one of our proudest institutions,' she says. 'When the French president came here and he was asked, "What's the thing you would most like to take back to France," he said, "The British pub."'

Brigid in the flesh is warmer than the steely impression I'd formed over the airwaves. The daughter of a clergyman raised in Leicestershire, she's a keen runner (she's run the London Marathon twice) who approaches her job with a military rigour acquired during six years in the army.

Her good humour only dissipates when talk moves directly onto the role of her paymasters. Then, the arms fold and the tone gets sterner, and you're reminded of your own insignificance; a lowly drone daring to poke a stick between the wheels of industry.

'I learned that pubs had a central role in the community from my father,' she says, aware that she hasn't the typical pub trade background. 'However, I was heavily involved in the Licensing Act in my last job. I can't say I know a lot about beer but that doesn't mean I can't promote it as a product.'

Her views on pubs are equally forthright. The facts come thick and fast, delivered with the force of a prep school headmistress. 'Not only is beer a British drink, but ninety-five per cent of what we drink in this country is produced in this country,' she says. 'That's not true for any other form of alcohol. Whisky is an export market, all our wine and most of our spirits come from abroad. And fifty per cent of what is sold in pubs is still beer.'

The way Brigid sees it, it's not the pubcos who are to blame for pub closures, but the politicians. 'Closures are currently at twenty-five a week and it's really worrying. I don't think the government's really done anything to help us. The biggest problem we have is beer taxation which has gone up and up and up. No business can sustain a thirty-five per cent increase in duty since March 2008, and we're paying the price, I'm afraid.'

She explains that at the start of 2011 the BBPA commissioned a study from number-crunching experts Oxford Economics to outline quite how important the pub trade is to the UK economy. The results showed that it employs 980,000 people and adds over £21 billion to the UK economy every year. Brigid used it as a ruler to thwack the Chancellor over the head in the run-up to the budget, but no dice: despite high-level meetings, beer tax still went up 7.4 per cent (the average cost of a pint has gone up from £2.41 in 2008 to £3.05 in 2011). Her frustration is obvious.

'I've had meetings with the special advisers to the Chancellor, and regular meetings with senior ministers at the Treasury. We'll probably need to take it one step further and have one-to-one meetings with the Chancellor and the Prime Minister. The clear message we've got is that the arguments we are putting forward are the right ones, but in the economic climate we're in, they're saying the hatches are down and we're not making any concessions on anything. All we can do is to continue to remind them that we have a lot of public support and that this is something which will help them connect with the community. The average pub employs ten people, and you don't require a vast amount of qualifications to do it. So we say to the government, look we've got a lot of young people unemployed. We could help with that but you've got to help us the other way, which is by not taxing us so hard.'

As for the suggestion that 'the tie' is the root cause of most pub closures: poppycock. 'That's simply not true,' she says. 'The major-ity of closures aren't those connected to the pub companies. In actual fact the tied pubs are getting two hundred and fifty million a year being put into them to support them, because they've got someone to go to. If you're a freehold, it's just like having a shop. You go to the owner and say: "I can't afford to pay my rent" and they say "bye-bye".'

So why do so many landlords feel as though help isn't there for them? 'We get publicans writing to us and we've introduced various systems through the British Institute of Inn Keeping to help them, so that there is now a low cost appeal system where they can go now and argue about their rent. The BII are doing a lot more work involving individual complaints in that area. But my view is that the way the tied pub system works is that you pay less fixed rent and more for your beer. Now that's a variable. Who would want to pay more fixed rent because there's nothing you can do about it? At least if you've got "wet" rent, then if you don't sell as much, then you don't pay as much for it. So I think the tied system is a good one and should be allowed to continue. I won't say we've got there entirely, but I think we've moved an awfully long way with the behaviour, and are making it a much more transparent system.'

This 'behaviour', notably by Enterprise Inns, was the cause of Brigid's visit to the House of Commons to sit in front of the Business Innovation and Skills Committee who were looking into abuses of the tied system.

'Select Committees will say what they want to say,' she says. 'The question is, are the government going to regulate in any form whatsoever? But at the end of the day we have taken steps to make sure, particularly with new licensees, that they have a much greater understanding of the business they are entering into. One of the real concerns I have about pubs is that people think that it's a lifestyle option. They have no real business experience but say they want to go and run a pub in their retirement. As a consequence there is no doubt that we have a lot of people running pubs who possibly should never have got there. Now they have time to take training and go through various hoops before they can take over a pub.'

But won't that see the death of the character landlord? After all, they've always managed to survive thus far. 'Well firstly you could argue we've got too many pubs,' she says. 'And it is a lifestyle change as well. People are choosing to stay at home nowadays. They don't go out quite as much. When we had a manufacturing industry, people went to the pub in the evening to replace the liquid, as much as anything else. We've moved onto a service economy where that requirement isn't as great. So I think it's a lifestyle change as much as economics, the smoking ban and everything else.'

Is she not concerned that the pubcos' interest solely in profits might be helping to destroy our pub culture? 'I think that's completely irrelevant,' she says sternly. 'I don't see that at all. The pubcos do not want pubs that are not doing well closing. That damages their balance sheet, and it is not in the interests for their pub estates to fail.'

But they do whatever needs to happen to make them more profitable? 'Yes, but being profitable is having well-run pubs that take in more people. They will sell to people in a different way. Anyway, the numbers are reducing. There are fifty-two thousand pubs left and the two big pub companies, Punch and Enterprise, now only own about twelve thousand of them, so that number is coming down. The market will take care of it, and make sure the pubs are moved on.'

Brigid explains that the introduction of a new Localism Bill intends to give local residents the chance to put pubs on a 'risk register'. 'The pub will still go to the highest bidder, but whoever gets it must run it as a pub. And of course, if a community wants to save a pub they have to make sure they're in there supporting it.'

Brigid does concede, however, that the control of our pubs by foreign interests isn't ideal. 'I would argue that the Beer Orders of 1989 were a real mistake. What it did is stop British companies running British pubs, and opened the door to a lot of international companies to come and take them. You look at the four big brewing companies, Heineken, Molson Coors, Carlsberg and InBev, they've all got foreign ownership.'

Can she encourage them to do the right thing? 'A lot of those CEOs I meet on a regular basis. I can encourage them to support pubs through brewery loans, but in the end it's the government which should support the British brewing sector. They don't recognise it and they need to wake up.'

My interest in this gradual dismantling of our cultural landscape by big business was brought into sharp focus reading Paul Kingsnorth's utterly absorbing book *Real England: The Battle Against the Bland*. An impassioned polemic on the state of the nation, it finds Kingsnorth travelling around England talking to people (pub landlords, farmers, market traders), meeting those making heroic last stands against the globalising forces that he believes are draining our towns and cities of their lifeblood.

Along the way he confirms it isn't just the creeping paranoia of middle age that tells you our high streets are becoming unrecognisable, the cherished haunts of our youth (small book shops, independent record stores) replaced by impersonal structures of steel and glass. As he writes: 'All over England, the things that make our towns, villages, cities and landscapes different, distinctive or special are being eroded, replaced by things which would be familiar anywhere. The small, the ancient, the indefinable, the unprofitable, the meaningful, the interesting and the quirky are being scoured out and bulldozed to make way for the clean, the sophisticated, the alien, the progressive, the corporate.'

Kingsnorth isn't your average green theorist. His CV includes stints working in an orang-utan rehabilitation centre in Borneo, as a peace observer in the rebel Zapatista villages of Mexico and, far more unnerving, as a floor sweeper in McDonald's. I'd been eager to meet him at home, in Ulverston, Cumbria, but time restraints mean we eventually arrange to do the interview over the phone. He explains that he's been busy campaigning: there are plans for a huge superstore to be built on the site of the local brewery, Robinson's. This is doubly ironic, he explains, because Ulveston once had the highest ratio of pubs to population in the country: it now stands to have the highest ratio of supermarkets to population instead.

It seems like a sign the country is at a tipping point between old and new, personal and corporate, and it's one he describes as a battle to 'save the soul' of the country. Even down the wires there's a clarity to his thinking which has me hanging on his every word.

We start by talking about the fact that pub closures have, at least, slowed to around 25 a week. Nonetheless, in any other industry this would still be seen as disastrous. Is he surprised, as Brigid Simmonds had been, by the seeming lack of interest from the powers-that-be?

'I *really* understand it,' he says. 'I think it's something about the people who run this country. They're not interested in this sort of low-level culture. If you go to France, Italy or Spain it seems to be woven much closer into people's everyday lives. They make a huge fuss in France if a vineyard comes under threat, there's debates in parliament and the rest of it. To be honest, I'm not sure what it is. It's probably a class thing. We've got a ruling class who don't have much connection with this sort of stuff. Pubs are associated with working-class culture and there's a sense that you're somehow supposed to rise above all that and move on – be "upwardly mobile", whatever that means.'

I mention Orwell's comment about the intelligensia in 'The Lion and the Unicorn', that 'England is perhaps the only great country whose intellectuals are ashamed of their own nationality… it is a duty to snigger at every English institution, from horse-racing to suet puddings.'

'Yes, there's something in that, definitely. The media aren't very interested in pub closures either and that's why we don't hear more about it.'

Paul explains that the only really strong interest for his book came, ironically, from the *Daily Mail*, who wanted to serialise parts of it. As a former deputy editor of the *Ecologist* strongly aligned with the anti-globalisation movement, he was loathe to sanction it, fearing that the paper's right-wing readership may get the wrong end of the stick. 'I was slightly reluctant to do it at first, but I got a lot of really nice responses. I was steeling myself for letters saying, "Why haven't you blamed the immigrants?" but I didn't get any like that. In fact, they were really quite sweet and sympathetic. They understood it, far more than the so called sophisticates.'

I'm not sure how, but we start talking about how puritanical the world seems to be at the moment. Not only is pub-going in general frowned upon, but the health issues related to pubs are constantly flagged up, too. I tell him about an article I'd read in *The Times* about a character from *Doctor Who* being dropped from an audio adaptation as he was drunk, through fear it could encourage children to hit the bottle. The character was instead described as being 'merry and cheerful'.

'I was thinking about this recently,' he says. 'English culture seems to go through these waves of puritanism to licentiousness then back again. It's the ruling class trying to crack down on the appetites of the masses. If you read about what the streets of

London were like in the eighteenth century almost everyone was pissed all the time, there were people having sex in the streets, the depravity is there to see in Hogarth's image of *Gin Lane*. Then the Victorians come along and within a hundred years there's this most incredible crackdown. And suddenly you've got these hugely repressed upper and middle-class people strutting around the world controlling everybody's appetites, or trying to.

'It's strange at the moment because you've got this middle-class puritanism stalking the land, where everything's terrible, and people should cut back on drinking, when, of course, half of the government are probably pissed every night on red wine. At the same time, everyone else is pissed on this incredibly cheap stuff they've bought from the supermarket, so that if you go out onto any high street on a Saturday night, it's like a fucking warzone.'

Do these increasing regulations and the all-seeing eye of CCTV add up to one thing: a fear of individuality?

'Without a doubt. They want everyone to fit into these little boxes that they've got, and they don't like it when you don't meekly comply. The thing to realise is that corporatisation in general wants everything to be homogenous. Individuality, character and quirkiness represent everything it's against. It's the way the machine works. You can't afford to have lots of people doing their own thing, it has to be controlled from the centre. On a macro level, we're living in an age where everything is a business, the business mentality has infiltrated everything. You listen to the news and it's all about economics and money as if that's the only thing we should consider. You hear these political leaders, so called statesmen, actually referring to UK PLC with a straight face. That's all you need to know about their values right there.'

He explains that his wife is a doctor and that 'half her life' is spent in marketing meetings when she could be helping patients.

It feels like time to broach another topic which has been nagging away at me: that somehow caring about the fate of our pubs casts you, as, at best, a romantic, and at worst, a flag-waving reactionary.

'I get the same thing,' he says. 'Personally, I believe that anyone who says that shows a complete lack of attachment to our history and what it means. There are breweries closing down which have been part of local communities for generations. There's the one in Ulverston I mentioned in my email. It's a great big old Victorian tower which they want to knock down and build a supermarket instead. Half the town is against it and the rest are saying we want a supermarket, but it ends up being polarised into an argument where one side say, "We want cheap food and you're a load of romantics," and then there's us on the other side saying it's something different, to do with the fabric of the town and its history. The trouble is, there's this automatic assumption that it doesn't really matter if it goes. People forget that breweries like this used to be in every town, each with its own history, producing beer which was culturally specific to that place and time. They were part of the town, generations of families worked there, and most of them have got really interesting architecture. Now, they just get ripped out and replaced with supermarkets or shoddy flats which will fall down in twenty years, which are completely meaningless and have no cultural depth. It's getting to the point where people aren't aware of their own past, and that brings a whole set of other problems.'

This neatly brings us to the subject of the pub closures. While the closures themselves are the result of a perfect storm of conflicting interests, it's hard to escape the feeling that with each 'For Sale' sign another link to the past gets lost, another pipette's worth of the crystal spirit is drained away.

'The problems really started when the brewers became separated from the pubs they supply with the 1989 Beer Orders. Obviously brewing and selling beer has always been a business but it was once a different kind of business. If you've got a local brewer who is part of the town you've got a network of obligations which aren't just financial ones. It's paternalist, and so they have to weigh things up. They want to make money, but they don't want to just do that to the exclusion of everything else. Now we've got an economic system which has unmoored itself from people and places, and profit is all that matters.'

I put to him that, as humble pub goers, our frustration stems from the fact that, fundamentally, we don't even see the pub *as* a business.

'Exactly. The public house itself stems from the idea that once it was just someone inviting you into their house for a beer and getting a couple of pennies to cover it. The pub is also the last space where people gather for fun in a way which isn't dictated by commerce. Running a pub won't make you rich, but you'll earn a living from it and participate in a healthy way in society. Obviously, that's no use to big companies, because they're constantly looking for increased profit.'

Anyone hoping for a change, however, shouldn't hold their breath.

'Broadly speaking it's a Tory government and they like big companies. They'd have to turn government upside down and give away a lot of power. It's the same as The Big Society. On paper it sounds like a good idea, but it won't happen because it requires a huge shift of power from the top to the bottom. The only way things will change is when things start falling apart. It will change from the bottom up. We can't rely on politicians to change things.'

Part of the problem, as Paul sees it, is what he calls 'the myth of progress'.

'When I was writing the book I heard the same expression a lot: "you can't stop progress". The people who say it haven't thought it through. Progress is supposed to be a process of improvement. If something's getting worse, it's not progress. It's change, which isn't always good. It seems to be used in a resigned way in England. It's just something that happens to you, which you have no control over or say in. It's a complete sense of powerlessness, at a local and national level. People think there's absolutely nothing they can do. They think of it as a done deal. If someone wants to build a supermarket they'll build it. If someone wants to close a pub down, they'll close it. There's a feeling that the councils are corrupt, the politicians are corrupt, nobody trusts anybody to do their job properly. It's a real shoulder-shrugging sense of "we can't do anything", which is quite sad to see because if people don't do anything then it becomes self-fulfilling.'

So where did this malaise all start?

'Oh, I think the English have been powerless for a long time. You can date it back to the Industrial Revolution. The fact that we had our land enclosed and taken away before anyone else, we were shoved into cities and turned into cogs in the machine before anyone else. For a couple of hundred years most people in this country have had no real agency in anything. We've not had power at a local level, we've not owned any land. We just have to work for other people and hope that they're nice to us. For the last fifty years we've had a culture floating on money, which was all based on debt, as it turned out, but when things are going well people aren't fussy. It's like the gilded age, a plastic culture can survive. But when it all starts falling apart, people want something real.'

I tell him about my experience at Reflex, and the strange feeling of being brainwashed; having your own memories sold back to you but without any of the personal baggage.

'Well I think what's so horrible about that is that it's indicative of everything now. If it was just a few people having a laugh and everything else was fine and healthy it wouldn't seem so bad. But because all the real pubs are dying and our high streets are being taken over by big corporations, those places become harder to stomach. Personally, I think it's the sign of a dying culture. It's a corporation creating Groundhog Day-style bars which are completely divorced from most people's everyday reality. You're having fun to someone else's tune, in an ironic way, but it's detached and unreal and everyone knows it.'

There's then one of those odd pauses in conversation you sometimes get during phone interviews when you try to change tack without seeming too obvious, and in the middle of it Paul says: 'People don't leave their doors open any more.'

I'm surprised to hear the expression being used by someone in their thirties, and say so.

'Well, exactly. Whenever you start talking about this stuff people immediately start saying: "Oh you're just being romantic." But it's almost as if you're not allowed to suggest things might have been better in the past. It makes people nervous. They panic because they don't like to think things are getting worse. But the fact is that there are some things which have measurably been lost when a pub goes. You can't necessarily put them into numbers but you can see there's less community spirit in that area. It's only when you go to other countries you can see that a piece of the social jigsaw is missing. In somewhere like Greece or Italy you'll see old guys sitting around in bars every evening in the way they used to here fifty years ago.'

I hear him give a heavy sigh. 'I don't know how we've let it happen, this takeover of our culture by business, but it's happened within our own lifetime. Everybody knows that it's crap, really, but they don't feel as though there's much they can do about it. Even people who oppose it feel they have to talk the language of economics in order to be taken seriously. I'm secretly hoping that the global economy will collapse and it will give us a reason to start doing things differently. Because it's getting to the point now where you can't live any other way.'

His voice gets a little quieter and I can sense he's reaching to tie up all these conversational loose ends. 'Historically, we're in a very interesting place. People know they're being screwed from a great height but they don't really know how, and so there's this real sense of "what the hell is going on?" And of course everyone is to blame to some degree. People say they want healthy high streets, but they all go to supermarkets. They say they don't like the pub companies but they still drink in the chain pubs. We've all been doing it. So we're sort of complicit, and that makes us feel even more frustrated.'

The obvious question, then: what can we do about it? Paul explains that over the years he's been involved in countless environmental campaigns. The ones involving boycotts and negative campaigning usually proved counter-productive, offering little more than self-denial.

'What works is when people show it's possible to do other things. If you can create something which shows people what they've lost then you start inspiring people. People are depressed and they want someone to give them some hope. No matter how miserable you are, if you meet one incredibly inspiring person who's doing something really brilliant, even at a very small level, it gives you hope. It makes you think, "Yes, it can be done."'

I suggest that this boils down to one thing which seems to be lacking in most corporate organisations: authenticity.

'It's about authenticity, integrity, character and independence. If someone set up a pub tomorrow which has got all those four things then it's really good. It's a living place, which makes it far better than some two-hundred-year-old pub which is owned by the National Trust but which is actually a massive fake. It's about individual people following their star, even if it's just a grumpy old landlord in a village pub. Their character comes out and fills the place and you can tell that it's real. And right now, there's a war against the real going on. It's almost as if people are scared of connecting on an emotional level, they need to surround themselves with artifice and escapism.'

Back in Reflex, Debbie Harry is singing 'Roll me in designer sheets'. It's the best offer I've had all night. It's followed by Phil Collins's 'Easy Lover'. In a bid to stem the flow, I ask the DJ if he's got any 'rock'. Half an hour later he plays U2's 'I Still Haven't Found What I'm Looking For'.

I try and enjoy the irony of it all while the plastic party melts into a sticky mess of bodies around me on the Day-Glo dancefloor, but my heart's not in it. Besides, Michael Douglas is staring down from the TV screens now, hamming his way through eighties romcom *Romancing the Stone*. He flies headlong down a mudslide and ends up with his face between the legs of a startled Kathleen Turner. Time to go.

On the train home I start wondering where it will all end. Our pubs will disappear, replaced by cloned bars with imitation fittings and temporary staff. All music will be controlled by Cowell Industries, who will drip-feed us ersatz soul ballads, novelty acts and corporate rock. We will work for companies on vast retail parks and be regularly tested for alcohol and drugs, with all complaints dealt with by synthetically voiced options on a central switchboard. We will live in smoke-free homes and eat pre-packaged food delivered by Tesco where silent children disappear into virtual worlds, enslaved by Facebook. All on the Planet Starbucks, in the Microsoft Galaxy, in the Walmart Stratosphere. And we will be happy.

In a bid to stop my mind running wild with these nightmarish visions, when I get home I start reading a paperback copy of G.K. Chesterton's comic novel *The Flying Inn*. Published in 1914, it tells the tale of Humphrey Pump, landlord of an ancient pub, The Old Ship, situated next to an apple orchard and a bowling green in the tiny village of Pebbleswick-on-Sea. A man of 'incorruptible kindliness' Pump is forced to close his premises when the British government, led by the faddish Cabinet minister Lord Ivywood, imposes a blanket ban on the sale of alcohol. In retaliation, Pump and his compatriots uproot their pub sign and, taking a barrel of beer and a large cheese with them, set off around the country like boozy resistance fighters, every so often coming out of hiding to erect the sign and spread good cheer, vanishing before the authorities can catch up with them.

It's a light-hearted tale of British pluck, but it's also a reminder, as Paul Kingsnorth suggested, that sometimes the time comes when you need to do more than just shrug your shoulders and admit defeat. That every now and then you have to stand up and be counted.

There's only one place to go next: Parliament.

YES, MINISTER

Paul Moody

G erry Sutcliffe passes by where Sir Thomas More was tried for treason in 1535, nips gingerly beyond the exact spot Guy Fawkes was sentenced in 1606 and rubs a polished brogue over the gold plate commemorating where Winston Churchill lay in state on his death in 1965. Mr Sutcliffe and I are standing in Westminster Hall, and history isn't so much all around us as seeping through the cracks in the masonry.

'You see that spot there,' he says, pointing to a spidery fissure in the stonework above an impressive Gothic archway, 'that was the nearest the IRA ever got to disrupting the work of the House – a mortar bomb attack in 1974.'

In continuous use for over 900 years, Westminster Hall is the sort of building American tourists will happily tolerate a three-hour wait outside St Stephen's Gate and our creaking public transport system for. Completed by William Rufus in 1099, and home of the first elected English Parliament, summoned by Simon de Montfort in 1265, its sheer scale alone is enough to silence noisy school parties.

'I've been coming here for twenty-four years and I still get a thrill every time I walk through the place,' Gerry says, as we pause at the top of the stairs where the Queen, Nelson Mandela and, more recently, Barack Obama addressed the two houses. 'Anyway, let's go to the bar, shall we?'

It's December 2009. The original plan had been to meet Mr Sutcliffe in his private offices at the House of Commons. I had pictured comfy chesterfield sofas, walnut desks and red correspondence boxes, Sutcliffe parroting government policy over the tinkle of china tea cups until we both glazed over. But it's a quiet Tuesday afternoon and I had the agreeable impression Gerry Sutcliffe understood the appeal of the occasional mid-afternoon pint.

A bluff 56-year-old in a charcoal-grey suit, tortoiseshell glasses and a devilish twinkle in his eye, he could be any prosperous northern businessman ambling through the Commons as part of a trade delegation were it not for the constant nods, winks and grins being directed his way. Because in his triple-barrelled role as government minister for Licensing, Gambling and Sport, Sutcliffe has an almost unlimited capacity to make people happy.

In the marble-stoned grandeur of the central hall, Terry Rooney (MP for Bradford North) affords him a hearty handshake. In the exterior courtyard, a frozen-looking policeman brightens visibly as he approaches and shares a joke. In the subterranean corridor linking the two Houses with Portcullis House, a flustered lobbyist makes a point of introducing Sutcliffe to a cheerful black man in a shiny suit. 'That was the vice-president of Kenya,' says Sutcliffe as we thread our way along what is clearly a fully functioning corridor of power.

* * *

Strangers Bar has a wood panelled interior and a bottle-green carpet, a veneer of pub authenticity provided by a patchwork of beer mats pinned above the oak bar. There's a whiff of Mr Sheen about the place, and it seems more functional than conspiratorial, a venue for low-level grumbles rather than high-octane power-broking. It's also strangely characterless, and I'm reminded of Jeremy Paxman's comment in *The Political Animal*: 'The life of a mule harnessed to a wheel can have more excitement than that of the Government backbencher in Parliament.'

A TV monitor of the debating chamber glows silently in one corner, presumably as an early warning system for imminent votes, and the bar is empty apart from another MP in a dark suit and black slip-ons, deep in conversation with a young woman in a pale blue dress. Through the bay windows, a terraced area overlooks the Thames. 'The Terrace Pavilion is open for champagne, wine and Pimm's' reads a sign on the double doors, a raffish reminder of New Labour's salad years, and a riverboat chugs by full of tourists from Arizona to Zagreb. A phalanx of black binoculars catch the sunlight as they turn in our direction, hoping to glimpse a miracle in progress. And in a way they do: a round costs £2.45.

Thanks to the Commons' reduced drinks tariffs, two and a half pints of beer (for me, Gerry, and his PR, Kirsty) costs extraordinarily little, and I begin to see Strangers Bar's attractions. We settle into a corner seat and Gerry explains he's been hanging around in pubs for as long as he can remember.

'My dad used to run The Kings Arms in Bradford when I was a kid, so I grew up in them. It meant that I saw how pubs work from the other side of the bar before I ever went in them for fun. So I know how much hard work it is. Believe me, it's a tough business. From the moment you wake up in the morning you're taking in deliveries, then getting everything ready for opening time, it's non-stop. Then you have to look after people right up until the end of the night. If you're doing it right, it's like constantly throwing a party.'

This can have its ups and downs, he explains. 'This was back in the days when kids weren't allowed in pubs, so in one way it was quite exciting. But because you're living on the premises, or nearby, there's no escape. It was tough. The arguments between those two [his parents] would usually be about the hours they were working. On occasions it was great, because all the customers would make a fuss of you, but I also saw the negative side, the pressure the licensees are under.'

As for underage drinking, Gerry explains that he's in no position to talk. 'I first went to the pub was when I was fourteen,' he admits with a grin. 'Me and a few mates tried to get into a pub called The Horse and Trumpet in Bradford. Our school uniform was grey suits so we all thought we looked older than we were. I'll always remember going to the bar and ordering six halves of Heineken. And just as the guy was filling the glasses I looked over to the Tap Room and my dad was sitting there.'

He chuckles at the memory, and can't resist a swift diversion down memory lane. 'That was when there were twenty pubs along Manchester Road leading to the town centre. The trick was to have a half in each pub but I don't think anyone ever made it. Or if they said they did, they were lying.'

These disarmingly gentle deliveries prove of little use when I switch to googlies regarding government policy. The stance changes, the posture more businesslike and Gerry Sutcliffe responds with the conversational equivalent of the forward defensive. Yes, he is aware that pub closures are a 'very serious matter' and yes, there is a clear need for 'something to be done'. And while he appreciates my concerns over pub closures, he also explains that he is doing everything within his power to help.

As a member of the All Party Beer Group he explains that he has just this week told the Institute for Public Policy Research of the need for pubs to receive added protection, faced as they are by a three-way squeeze from cheap supermarket beer sales, the smoking ban and the Treasury's need for tax receipts. 'There are lots of competing views on this, as you can imagine,' he says, easing through the gears from affable bloke to government minister. 'Alcohol Concern are very strong on the need for alcohol consumption being vastly reduced. The Home Office are looking at the problem from a community safety angle and also in terms of business development. And then there's my department, who as champions of the industry are there saying that any measures which might affect the pubs have to be pro rata and don't overstep the mark.'

Gerry concedes that, as far as he's concerned, a lot of the problems can be traced to 'the tie'. Efforts to unravel it began in earnest in April 2009, when a House of Commons report by the Business and Enterprise Committee urged the government to refer the matter to the Competition Commission. According to a leaked article published in *Private Eye* the same year (headlined 'All tied and emotional'), the committee commissioned its own independent survey to see if the feelings of frustration among landlords were typical, only to discover that 64 per cent of lessees believed the pubcos didn't add value to their business, a fifth were in some form of dispute, and that only 18 per cent were satisfied with their lot. The committee were also shocked to discover that for all their efforts on the pub front line, 67 per cent of lessees surveyed earned less than £15,000 p.a., and over 50 per cent of lessees who had a turnover of more than £500,000 p.a. earned less than £15,000 (a 3 per cent rate of return). In other words, while the landlords shared the risk with the pubco, they didn't share the benefits. And all with the caveat that, if the business failed, they would lose their home as well as their business. *Private Eye* concluded that the committee's findings had 'at last shed light on an industry in freefall. Pubcos are essentially greedy property companies with a cuddly name – and they own nearly half the country's pub freeholds.'

This was followed by a CAMRA 'super-complaint', which forced the Office of Fair Trading to investigate the matter within 90 days. However, the subsequent OFT report, published in October 2009, controversially cleared the pubcos industry of behaving in any way that could cause damage to consumers.

'This is a phenomenally poor decision by the OFT,' said Greg Mulholland, chairman of the All Party Parliamentary Save the Pub Group, on hearing the decision, which in Westminster-speak is the equivalent of a single raised digit. 'Pub companies have just been given the all clear to carry on exploiting tenants, over-charging them for goods and exposing them to punitive levels of rent.' Share prices for the pub companies duly soared; investors were delighted.

So what did Gerry Sutcliffe make of the decision? It's obvious this is one he wants to crack into the off-field, but he resists the temptation. 'It wasn't the result we, or I should say, a lot of people within the industry wanted. People are very upset about it. We had a meeting the other week about the state of the pub trade and pretty much all the anger was centred around "the tie" and the effect it's having. I've been looking at it and it needs to be addressed, because most of the pubs that are closing are within that sector. At the same time, the successful managers are saying we've had enough of "the tie" because they're being penalised for being successful, so it's a no-win situation.'

There seems little point in banging our heads against a brick wall so we move onto the 2003 Licensing Act, which allowed licensed premises to open 24 hours a day. While it only brought us into line with the rest of Europe, this legislation, if you believe the tabloids, is also the root cause of so-called 'Binge Britain'.

'The Licensing Act gets blamed for a lot of things,' says Gerry, now with the air of a man experiencing a very dull déjà vu. 'I personally think the act has worked okay. When it was brought in it was largely seen as an enlightened piece of legislation. There was lots of consultation around the act, and when it first came in most people welcomed it. It gave power to the Magistrates Court, it gave power to local government and it streamlined bureaucracy. It's now getting blamed for things which are nothing to do with it. This idea that there's suddenly a culture of twenty-four-hour drinking is totally wrong. It's only about one per cent of premises using the full extent of the licence, and most of those are hotels. The national average is that people are drinking for an extra twenty-one minutes.'

Gerry takes a sip of his pint and I suddenly realise how audience members on *Question Time* must feel, disarmed by the dark arts of the debating chamber.

'It's simply a case of pubs using more flexible hours. People forget that in the old days pubs would have lock-ins, so they'd be serving until late anyway. People have been drinking after hours for a long, long time. And at the end of the day it's all about whatever is comfortable for the licensee.'

What is a major concern for the government, however, is the increase in 'preloading'.

'There's a real age profile to all this,' he says, warming to his theme. 'Some of these kids causing havoc are smashed before they even go out into town for the night. And if you look at youngsters now and the things they require from a night out, they're totally different from what someone from the older generation might want. The pub doesn't really supply what they're after any more.'

I suggest that there has always been a rich cultural tradition of kids drinking cider in the park. 'Yes, that's true, but they weren't drinking as much as they are now. These days you've got kids who are carrying bottles of vodka around with them. So when they get to a pub and the landlord says you're not coming in, that's when the problems start.'

I ask him whether these problems are a ticking time bomb, and he defuses it in an instant. 'We need a little perspective on this,' he says. 'We're sixteenth in the world league when it comes to alcohol abuse, so we aren't the runaway league champions. Crime numbers have come down. So things aren't as bad as they're sometimes made out to be. The only real problems in terms of alcohol and disorder are between 3 a.m. and 6 a.m. Before the act, what people used to do was drink three or four pints at half past ten, then at half past eleven the streets would be full of people. Now it's staggered, if you'll excuse the pun.'

Conscious of the need to cover all bases, he explains that there are 42 different police authorities, providing 42 different views on how to tackle the problems. The police, however, are 'generally happy' with the situation now.

As for the long-term future of the pub, Gerry sees it involving diversification. 'I think in terms of pub numbers we've been over capacity for a long time. It's now finding its level. We've got community pubs which are doubling up as shops and post offices, and are still at the heart of the local community. I went to see one in Chesterfield recently which is running sewing classes and meals on wheels. In many ways, that's the way forward. There are also new small breweries emerging too, which we're supporting. So there are shoots of growth.'

Policy questions out of the way, Sutcliffe reveals that his own Moon Under Water is situated far from the power politics of Westminster. 'I suppose my perfect pub would have to be my local, The Glen in Gilstead. I try and get back every week. I usually manage to get in at ten o'clock on a Thursday night. My mates look after me there. We have a couple of pints and put the world to rights. We don't talk about politics, except, of course, now they know I'm Licensing Minister they'll give me stick about something they've seen in the *Morning Advertiser*.'

We share the standard joke about this being one pub which never needs a late licence, and it strikes me that Gerry Sutcliffe is an honourable man stuck with (three) impossible jobs, frantically spinning plates conscious that the slightest policy wobble might spoil the whole dinner party. He makes it look easy though, and his ability to take the sting out of the subject means my protests about the unfairness of the smoking ban are all but snuffed out until we're joined by Marsha Singh.

As Labour representative for Bradford West, Marsha shares Gerry's enthusiasms for the area's pubs, but, crucially, is able to talk without Sutcliffe's ministerial responsibilities. 'Pubs have always been at the heart of British life,' he says, pulling up a chair. 'When I was growing up my dad used to say he would go to the pub because that was where everything happened. In those days that was where you got a job, or a plumber, or met people. It was a central part of people's social life. And I think that was certainly the case for most working-class families. And the smoking ban has really hit the working men's clubs. I'm sure the Department of Health would tell you there's health benefits to the ban, but if you ran the world on polls and referendums the minorities always get squeezed out. [Is he really saying what I think he's saying?] Maybe we went a bit too far in not having the provision for separate smoking rooms with proper ventilation in the act. I think we probably did.'

There's an awkward silence, and I get the impression that even if this is Gerry's opinion too, he isn't about to let on. 'I must quickly point out that's the view from the back benches, and not the government's position,' he says quickly, catching the china as it falls.

Back in the medieval grandeur of Westminster Hall I can't help mulling over how much of history has turned on a sixpence. If the Spanish Armada hadn't encountered a freak storm off the cost of Scotland in September 1588, the mural of Sir Francis Drake being knighted by Queen Elizabeth might show a portrait of Philip II of Spain. If on 10 May 1941, firemen hadn't battled all night to save the burning roof of Westminster Hall, waist deep in water pumped from the Thames, it would have burned to the ground, a totemic victim of Nazi incendiary bombs.

In comparison, the legislative knock-on effects of the Licensing Act and the smoking ban seem like microscopic details, but important ones nonetheless. How many pubs would still be in business had the ban not come into place? And how many ideas had been hatched, friendships won and lost, or even babies made as a consequence of those extra 21 minutes of drinking time?

Barely five months after our conversation the Labour Party were out of office after 13 years in power, Gerry's tri-ministerial post sliced up into two separate positions, with Jeremy Hunt as Minister for Culture, Olympics, Media and Sport and John

Penrose covering licensing and gambling as part of his role as Minister for Tourism and Heritage. In retrospect, it explained a lot: his affable, last-day-of-term manner and informal chit-chat all part of an acute awareness that he wouldn't be in the post to enjoy, say, the Olympic opening ceremony from the posh seats (although I'd like to think he was there somewhere).

Support for the pub in Parliament in 2013 is most vocally expressed by the Liberal Democrat MP Greg Mulholland, responsible for that broadside at the OFT decision back in October 2009. As part of the Con-Dem coalition (and parliamentary representative for Leeds North West), he has already tabled a cross-party motion highlighting the importance of community pubs and won some minor victories: in November 2010 David Cameron visited The Bernard Arms in Buckinghamshire to show his support for the newly created British Pub Week.

We meet at the Portcullis House entrance of the House of Commons as opposed to the grandeur of Westminster Hall, and it seems symbolic: the 'out with the old, in with the new' policy writ large. The presentational differences are stark, too.

Whereas Gerry Sutcliffe had the easy manner of the political old stager, Greg Mulholland possesses, if not quite Barack Obama's fierce urgency of now, then at least, an undue haste.

A youthful 44, with an MA in public administration and a background in marketing, he is every inch the 21st-century politician: steady eye contact and firm handshake matched by a brisk manner and conversation peppered with buzzword expressions like 'new politics', 'big challenges' and an urgent need to 'get things done'. It suggests empathy and understanding, but after the clubbable chit-chat of Gerry Sutcliffe it feels oddly contrived. We order pints at the bar and as he sits down I notice his suit is a slightly lighter shade of grey.

Greg starts by explaining that these are not easy times for the pubs and that we need to protect them. The emphasis, he explains, should be on maintaining 'real community pubs' where people can 'enjoy alcohol responsibly'. These thoughts come in fully formed paragraphs and it feels like I should be taking notes when he explains he has co-signed an early day motion calling for a freeze on beer tax.

His opposition to the takeover of the Tetley's brewery in Leeds, however, is total. Having been home to Tetley's Cask Ales for 189 years, owners Carlsberg announced plans to close it down in November 2008, with the loss of 140 jobs. This sparked a 'Boycott Carslberg' campaign which has Mulholland's full support.

'This is an appalling decision by Carlsberg which unnecessarily brings to an end more than 180 years of history. They have betrayed Tetley's and Leeds and especially the 140 people who will lose their jobs having given service to the city. It's a decision made purely in the interest of corporate greed and with no regard for Tetley's as a famous Leeds beer.' Greg explains that he has tabled a parliamentary motion condemning the decision, but for all the dynamism, and his genuine passion for the local brewery at Otley, it's hard to shake the notion that he's operating within the same strict grid system as Gerry Sutcliffe.

Maybe I'm developing some form of immunity, but an hour later, back out amid the rush-hour traffic outside Portcullis House, it feels a bit like I've been run over by a party political broadcast. Was Greg Mulholland simply a very busy man who had made time in his diary to talk about the future of pubs? Probably. But without a ministerial role, his ability to effect change seemed minimal. Tetley's duly closed down in June 2011 and it reminded me of a conversation I'd had with the poet Simon Armitage.

He'd grown up in Marsden, near Huddersfield and explained that the first time he ever visited a pub, much like Gerry Sutcliffe, he found himself staring in horror at his dad across the bar. Armitage explained that his dad had given him a straight choice: drink a full pint of Tetley's Mild or return home with his tail between his legs. I suggested this rite of passage must have proved challenging to his teenage tastebuds. 'On the contrary,' he said. 'It tasted beautiful.'

Would future generations say the same thing about their first pint of Tetley's 'Smoothflow', made at the Molson Coors brewery in Tadcaster?

After all the talk it's refreshing to feel the chill of the winter air, and I find myself next to St Stephen's Gate, where there's a statue of Richard the Lionheart in the courtyard, astride his horse, sword held high in triumph. Widely seen as one of our most noble kings, Richard was, in fact, French, could barely speak English and occupied his time with murderous crusades.

Another example of history being cynically rewritten through the ages? Or just proof we're all sometimes suckers for a fairy tale? With that in mind, it's time, as Jim Hacker might say, to leave the world of government watchdogs, sub-committees, OFT decisions, and supra-complainants and get back to the source. Or I should say, the sauce. Because, what, exactly, are we drinking?

AFTER THE FLOOD

Robin Turner

I n its heavily embossed pint pot, it looked perfectly quaffable. Split by light, it glows golden as bubbles spin recklessly upwards, forming a thin white foam as they try and fail to exit the glass. Dependent on your personal view of the UK's best selling beer since the 1970s, the sight either represents something close to a deep hit of a long, lost summer's day captured in liquid form or 568 ml of piss.

On closer inspection – glass to mouth – the smell isn't anything too overpowering, nothing to leave much of an impression. After a slurp, one deep and lingering enough to allow the taste buds to do their work and digest any hidden depths, and the overall flavour is hard to put my finger on. Almost a nothingness, possibly like fizzy mineral water with a vague kick of alcohol, a little brackish with a bitter, metallic afterglow. Maybe I am detecting the subtle hint of burned cigarette ash floating in liquid. The thought of going in for another sip doesn't exactly set the heart racing but this was an experiment that I really needed to see through.

I was drinking my first pint of cooking lager in over a decade to see what all the fuss was about. It really wasn't leaving very much of an impression.

Anyone looking at the state of pubs in Britain would be wise to cast a glance at what is being poured into the country's pint glasses. We have become a lager nation, taken by stealth by a grab bag of continental invaders. The bars of pubs all around the country are dominated by an ever-evolving selection of European brands. One glance at the average high street boozer reveals this year's models as Italian Peroni, Dutch Heineken and Spanish San Miguel (brewed in Northampton by the Danish company Carlsberg).

When Orwell wrote 'The Moon Under Water', we were a proud, tired nation that had earned the right to sit back quietly and sup its ales. Nowadays, the common perception – from our media and from abroad – is that we are a nation that binges on fizzy lager... or worse. It doesn't help matters that we have adopted a fickle, shuffle-control mindset that means that drinks change fashion almost as often as pubs do. This year's Magners is last year's Hooch. Blue alcopops are still on sale across the country at the time of writing.

The Moon Under Water was conceived in far less scattershot times. If nothing else, the war had made sure of that. In the immediate peacetime period, rationing had as much of a debilitating effect on brewing as it did with the food industry. The pub that Orwell mused on was one of the 'ten per cent of London pubs' that served a wistful sounding 'creamy sort of stout'. In H.A. Monckton's 1966 book, *A History of English Ale and Beer*, he notes that the strength of beer declined steadily between the wars due to shortages of ingredients and the need to keep munitions workers half sane in the daytimes. A comparable stout such as Guinness in 2012 is now weaker than the average bitter was in 1910 and around half the strength of the average stout from the same period.

Just a year or so after peace had been declared and Orwell's pint was suffering the indignity of a downgrade. At least he didn't have to drink today's versions.

In 1946 lager was comparatively unknown in this country. Although already having been brewed in the UK by then, it had yet to make any sizeable impact; it certainly hadn't bothered Orwell as he sat smoking in the backstreet pubs of Islington dreaming up his perfect getaway. Britain's first lager was brewed in 1882 by the Austro Bavarian Lager Beer Company. It hailed from just a few miles north of Orwell's stomping ground of London in Tottenham by an all German brewing staff. Glasgow's Wellpark Brewery went on to create the Scottish staple Tennant's Lager three years later.

Soon after the war, pubs began moving away from the standards (milds, porters and stouts) and began to look towards a future of bottled pale ales and, eventually, keg beers. Kegs – as opposed to casks – left the brewery ready to drink. They were pasteurised which made them sterile and came served with the addition of an ebullient kick of carbon dioxide. Live ales from casks were like any natural food product – they would go off with time and thus needed to be consumed quickly once tapped for serving. In the early sixties, consumption of pasteurised keg beers grew steadily. Although available since the thirties when Watneys introduced their Red Barrel, kegs would became more and more popular in the post-war period due to the convenience of not having to physically pull pints and the long lifespan of the contents.

The spearhead of lager's invasion force didn't come from the drink's spiritual home of Germany but instead from a brewery in Canada that had been set up by an ex-pat Yorkshireman. Thomas Carling settled in London, Ontario in 1818 and built an eponymous, family-run business that was eventually sold to Canadian Breweries in 1930. The Grand Union Brewery's History of Lager website documents the North American beer's first footsteps in the UK market. 'There were those who believed that lager could succeed among the British. One was E.P. "Eddie" Taylor, chairman of Canadian Breweries. His leading product was Carling Black Label. Taylor was determined to crack the British market with Carling and signed an agreement with Hop and Anchor Breweries of Sheffield to brew Carling under licence.'

Carling Black Label got off to a slower start in the UK than Taylor had anticipated. His solution to the problem of non-saturation was to take matters into his own hands. After forging a succession of acquisitions and conglomerations with other breweries, he created what was then the UK's biggest producer – United Breweries. By 1960, through United, Taylor was well on the way to the kind of market domination that would see Carling take centre stage in the vast majority of the UK's pubs.

United's growth was steady and clearly profitable enough to encourage more brewers to turn to keg lager. From Guinness came Harp; from Allied Breweries Skol; Whitbread began to brew a weaker version of the Dutch super-brand Heineken under licence while Watney partnered with the Danish brewer Carlsberg. Add to a now saturated market a series of unseasonably hot summers in the UK in the mid-seventies and lager had its perfect storm situation. In Richard Boston's classic 1976 text *Beer and Skittles*, he stated that lager had 'gone from virtually nothing in the early 1960s to 18 per cent [of the market] in 1975'. By 1986 that number was at 43.5 per cent. In 2010, lager still made up 74.3 per cent of the UK's £17 billion draught beer market.

While lager's determined rise wasn't going unnoticed by the chattering classes (in *Everyday Drinking*, Kingsley Amis described the tipple as 'an exit application from the human race if ever there was one'), the drink's most resilient enemy was CAMRA. When the beer industry pressure group came together in 1971, it was with the express intention of railing against the fast-rising tide of keg beer they saw as flooding the country. Like a bunch of bearded, beery Canutes, they attempted what most would see as the impossible – to buck trends and change the tastes of a nation. As well as trying to make sure every pint was full, they wanted to make sure that what went into every discerning drinker's glass was of the highest possible quality. As more and more rallied to their cause – both in front of and behind the bar – sales of their annual listings publication *The Good Beer Guide* grew tangentially.

CAMRA's membership has swollen to over 100,000 in the 40 years since inception. Their spokesman Iain Loe explains what all those people had signed up to fight for. 'Pasteurisation ruins beer. It might give a longer shelf life but the end product is bland, gassy and metallic. As well as producing an inferior product, large-scale brewing in the UK is deceitful. When will lagers like Carlsberg stop trying to fool people that their beer comes from Denmark when it all comes from Northampton?'

Although lager still dominates our pubs (and – in turn – our supermarkets), traditional ales have found themselves resurgent after long periods in the doldrums. A large part of this was down to CAMRA's dogged work. Another factor was the creation of a new ale type by someone with precision perception at Somerset's oldest brewery.

In 1986, Exmoor Brewery set out specifically to design a pint that would take on some of the characteristics of the then best-selling lager in the country. Exmoor Gold was widely regarded as the first modern Golden Ale. The brewers themselves described it as 'a counter-balance to the traditional view of beer – which had to be as brown as an old sideboard or as coal black as Irish Dry Stout. Exmoor Gold, instead, was the colour of Chardonnay or Carling, sparkling in the glass and appealing to both ale drinkers and lager lovers.' By invoking the dreaded Black Label, Exmoor had torn up the rules and redrawn the blueprints, creating a style that would be copied endlessly. Golden Ales soon become a hand-pull mainstay the country over, the jumping-in point for anyone bored of gassy lager but terrified of anything that looked like it would give you wind just by sniffing it.

To ale drinkers, lager had long been the great Satan. For lager drinkers though, their choice of pint poured from the tap satisfied a whole set of attendant aspirations. There had been a deluge of lagers launched in the UK since 'Eddie' Taylor had pushed Carling on an unsuspecting public. Increasingly behind each launch, marketing teams and the financial might of huge brewing corporations were never far from view. But the real breakthrough came with the introduction of the ring-pull can in 1967. By 1969 sales had exploded to 490,000,000 cans per year.

Lager went hand in hand with that other breakout hit of the 1970s – colour television. The perfect medium to present products to the nation, flashy 30-second adverts sold thirsty viewers lifestyles, however crass. From the pseudo-Nordic Skol with its rampaging Viking mascot Hagar the Horrible through to Hofmeister's trilby-wearing, wisecracking, irritant bear George; Paul Hogan's no-nonsense, outback philosophy for Foster's through to Budweiser's demented 'Wassup' phone pranks; Carlsberg's skewed Loaded-goes-HD vision of a perfect world (the eventual result of a campaign slogan dreamt up by the Saatchis in 1973) through to Stella Artois' 'reassuringly expensive' aspirational sales patter; wherever you looked, it was purely about basking in the reflected glow of your chosen brand.

Carling's absolute dominance of the market hit home to me in the mid-nineties when their sponsorship of the Reading and Leeds Festivals – a festival that had previously held a special place in my heart being the first one I'd ever been to after finishing school back in 1989 – saw them rebranded as the Carling Festivals. In the years after Carling's putsch, the overbearing influence of sponsorship would dictate many of the terms on which the music industry would run. When the digital revolution came at the start of the new millennium, record companies, bands and promoters were left with few places left to turn. But that's a whole different story.

After a couple of decades as a dedicated lager drinker, I switched to ale in 2004 aged 34. My paternal grandmother was dying and I found myself spending most of my time back in Wales trying to do whatever I could to help or at the very least offer moral support to my father. Each visit to the hospice she was staying in was followed by a trip to The Pelican, just outside Bridgend, the best pub on the silent drive home. A much needed mood enhancer, we'd sit there quietly staring into our pint pots, waiting for something – anything – to jumpstart a different set of emotions. As my grandmother became more ill, I found the ability to choose a drink at the bar both impossible and pointless given the attendant circumstances. Before long, I'd just ask Dad to get me whatever he was having.

Wye Valley's Hereford Pale Ale was truly an epiphany. When Dad placed it in front of me, I probably even thought it was lager. It looked that way, only visibly less gassy. After the first mouthful, it fair glided down. And glide was the right word. It had none of the gassy delay one got from pint after pint of lager, none of the heaviness. Somewhere above my head, it was as if a pint-glass-shaped light bulb had flicked on; I'd found my perfect drink. From there, I began the exploration into the myriad different ales of our isles.

Over the following weeks, our pub visits carried on, eventually becoming reminiscences, before finally, the wake. In the years since, I've often wondered whether it was a final act of bonding with my father or just a case of the right pint at the right time. Either way, it stuck. I felt like I'd left a certain part of my youth behind – I no longer hankered after the same pint I'd drunk since my teenage years, its appeal had faded to almost nothing.

As my own tastes changed, my Moon Under Water also underwent a mental refurbishment. Gone were the gleaming chrome taps left pouring ice-cold flaxen liquid day and night. They were now replaced by a row of hand pumps that each stood firm, proudly displaying descriptive clips to entice the thirsty visitor onwards. Behind the bar was someone who loved beer and wanted to impart their lifelong knowledge, someone who took an interest in the drinker's choices and wasn't content to foist mass-produced, mass-marketed beer in their direction.

Interlude: Daytripping in the Magic Kingdom

Robin Turner

'Can I take this as proof that we don't buy beer, we only rent it?' slurs the man stood penis in hand at the urinal to no one in particular. Behind him, a queue of 50 or so blokes trail out of the door, each one desperate to empty his bladder and ease the pain. It is the reverse of the toilet situation at pretty much every gig I've ever been to. There are no queues for the ladies, just legions of gents nervously stepping foot to foot, forming lines for the conveniences. This scene is being repeated in all of the toilets in the venue. I am halfway down the line and already making mental pacts with God to increase the speed.

It is a little past two in the afternoon at the Great British Beer Festival at Earls Court.

Like great expos the world over, the Great British Beer Festival offers the public a rare chance to bask in the glow emanating from the heart of an industry. As well as a showcase for new product ranges and classics alike, the expo allows punters a rare chance to test and to covet, to tick off wants from personal wish lists. Whether viewing a riot of soft furnishing and triple glazing options at the Ideal Home Show (Glastonbury Festival for *Daily Mail* readers) or witnessing the annual firing up of the hype machine at Apple's Mac World, these super-sized trade shows give the public the chance to peer behind the curtain and visualise the very people operating the machine.

The annual shindig for British beer is no different. In the morning's *Guardian* Sam Jones writes, 'The Campaign for Real Ale's annual homage to the UK's national drink is unashamedly passionate and evangelical when it comes to matters hoppy, malty and wheaty.' The Great British Beer Festival has been around since CAMRA held their first official shindig in Alexandra Palace in 1977. The brewers mingle with the landlords and the punters, awards are given and eagerly taken – previously obscure breweries can walk away as the nation's most wanted pint.

The festival lays lofty claim to be the 'biggest pub in the world'. The daytime trappings are certainly pub-esque: a thousand differ-ent beers, an admirably eccentric (predominantly male) cross section of society, the gently rising hubbub of boozy conversation and more cross-legged blokes than you can possibly imagine; it has the makings of the perfect lost afternoon. More than a pub though, the scale of the Great British Beer Festival means it is to the average town-centre pub what the Monsters of Rock festival is to downstairs at The Hope and Anchor on a wet Monday night, such is its jaw-dropping scale.

Setting off for an early start, I start to sense a change in the demographic somewhere around Embankment station. On the hottest day of the year, a Tube that had been full of well-to-do ladies desperately fanning themselves begins to cross-fade into a wholly different picture. From the edges moving inwards with every stop, men of a certain type appear. The average age raises drastically; haircuts become more brutal – less Vidal Sassoon, more Mr Toppers. One man stands staring madly into the middle distance decked out in loose-fitting militaria. Another nervous-looking fellow sits counting the stops while wearing a black T-shirt with 'Back to the Boozer' (fashioned proudly in the *Back to the Future* logo). As the District Line rumbles towards the Real Ale Xanadu through superheated tunnels, the clientele of the 'biggest pub in the world' grows and grows. Slowly but surely, a distinct feeling of CAMRA-derie has taken over the 1 p.m. to Richmond. By the time I alight and stride to the ticket gate, I've become at one with them. For one day only, they are going to be my people.

I'd last been to Earls Court to see Bruce Springsteen play a sanity-testing marathon to 18,000 people, each of them emoting wild-eyed at the stage. I spent much of it in the bar clock-watching, hopelessly praying for 'Dancing in the Dark' to start up so I could pretend to get involved. Now Boss-free the venue is a wholly different prospect though. Although teeming with people – healthy amounts each of retirees and skivers – the room bears no resemblance to any monster gig the venue has seen before. A mercifully mellow gathering, it feels more boozy village fete than rock'n'roll rally.

I find myself following a strange geography as I wander the aisles; one where beers are arranged into bars listed alphabetically by county. Devon and Dorset happily border East Yorkshire and Edinburgh and Lothians; a crunched-up country where local distinctiveness blurs away from bar to bar and any petty provincial rivalries could be sorted out in a sup. Here, we are one nation under the bar; a sozzled society drinking our way across the British Isles one foaming nut-brown ale at a time. For the beer drinker this festival is Nirvana; somewhere where you can drink your way around the whole of the British Isles without ever leaving the exhibition centre.

'What can I get you?' asks a heroically bearded Gandalf-alike behind a bar whose constituency includes start-ups from as far afield as Manchester and Orkney. It is hard to force a decision; a glance in any direction throws up untold liquid temptation. From titanic presences like Fuller's and Greene King through to relative unknowns (to me at least) like Nottingham's Blue Monkey or Goose Eye from West Yorkshire, the list of breweries representing themselves here is staggering. When ordering I find that, more often than not, an idiot xenophobia of pot luck and regional bias dictates. My predisposition to small Welsh breweries takes me to Cwrw Glaslyn, a fruit-nosed bitter dreamt up by Purple Moose, an award-winning operation on the borders of Snowdonia national park.

Thankfully, food options are an altogether different story. As is so often the case at any respectable pub without ideas above its station – food is a reassuring means to an end. Pasties and pork scratchings, biltong and burgers, everything is purely stomach lining (actually I can't honestly say that there isn't a tripe stall somewhere); a double drop Gaviscon incident just waiting to happen.

On the day I visit – as with any decent city centre pub on any given daytime – Earls Court is a predominantly male domain. And for every beer gut there is a stick-thin counterpart. For every lowbrow T-shirt slogan ('98% Drinker, 2% Twat', 'The Liver Is Evil And Must Be Punished' being two fine examples) there's someone who looks like they've walked in to drown their sorrows straight after being fired from Lord Sugar's boardroom. That said, eccentricity sometimes heats into a bubbling cauldron of madness, notably the couple who are wandering around dressed in Victorian bed wear carrying babies' bottles and dummies. Although admirably trying to raise money for charity, it is more than a little discomfiting to hear a constant babble of baby talk coming from a bearded man in his fifties. The demented duo work the room mercilessly; after several beers, his croaky mumble of 'Mama, mama' and her vacant stare become the thing of horror movies. Behind them, respect is due to a man on stilts dressed as the Cowardly Lion who valiantly tried to down a pint.

No one ever really explains beer festival etiquette to you before you step through the gates; it just seems to be something learned solely by hard drinking experience. On the way in, you either buy or rent a glass. The novices (like myself) head straight for the pint pot while the stalwarts – wily with their practical knowledge worn like Scout badges – all shell out for the halves. Many of the calmest and most collected (surely the festival's equivalent of a Masonic sect) are even imbibing in thirds of pints.

After a couple of hours of drinking – at first leisurely and considered before a little more random and fever pitched – my early rooky mistake becomes apparent when I realise I have only tried four of the thousand-odd beers, yet I am already heading for the urinals every 15 minutes clutching the walls like they are in perpetual motion. Meanwhile, there are the stalwarts, working their way patiently around the venue; eyeing up obscure breweries with magpie-like fascination, ticking the names off pre-prepared printed sheets. Like trainspotters cluttering up the ends of station platforms the length of the country, the task in hand doesn't appear to be a whole load of fun. Well, it certainly doesn't to the kind of idiot who is busy working through Earls Court in pint measurements.

If the Great British Beer Festival is the 'biggest pub in the world', it certainly doesn't resemble any I've been to in the 21st century. It is far more like stepping back to another age; visiting a cryogenically preserved pub nation that had been dusted down from the early seventies. Those were places for serious drinking; places where drinking was taken seriously even. They were the places that sat quietly on street corners back before the age of flat screens and karaoke machines, before alcopops and draught wine, back when children could reliably be seen and not heard.

I found myself wondering if CAMRA in their commendably valiant efforts weren't all that different from historical re-enactment societies up and down the land, only making painstaking efforts to preserve elements of a rosy past when the unions were still welcome at No. 10 and event TV was the *Morecambe & Wise Christmas Special*. As much as I entered the room feeling like I belonged, I knew socialisation and conditioning had pushed me in a different direction. I loved exploring new beers but so many of the lone drinkers at the festival made it look somehow so solitary, like a task to be mastered. After all, like it or not, beer does get you pissed eventually – it should be fun.

By now acting a little too much like a poster boy for that last statement, I decide it's time to leave. On the way to the exit, I stop off to browse at the t-shirt stall. There, masters by Escher and Hogarth are reworked into visual paeans to the psychedelic effect of too much loony soup; a whole section is reserved for the requisite Olly Reed display (the unrepentant pisshead's leisurewear of choice – sizes running small to XXX-Large). There, I talk to Craig, an accountant from Hartlepool. He had booked into a nearby B&B in a valiant effort to throw himself headlong into the whole three days of the festival. He explains his mission as he forces down a bag of chips.

'This isn't like anything we get back home, there's nothing else in the world on this scale. The whole country's in this here pint glass,' he slurs, eyes kaleidoscopic and bloodshot from the previous day's drinking. 'I'm trying to have half a pint from every county in the British Isles that's represented. I'm just trying to stay on top of it all. You have to look at it like you're running a marathon.' A casual glance would have told anyone that 26 yards would pose something of a challenge to Craig; that said, here was a dreamer having the time of his life.

I wish him the best of British as he marches off towards a bar representing Lancashire, Lincolnshire and London. Craig's final stop, should he complete the honorable, sprawling, demented nationwide trip is – by my reckoning – Worcestershire. He still has a long way to go before he's home and dry.

HAUNTED DANCEHALLS

Robin Turner

I t has been drizzling for hours, raining down the kind of insidious damp that permeates everything and rises over you like a creeping flu. I am walking around Camden Town with a friend, trying to pinpoint a couple of pubs that aren't there any more; a hunt for ghostly snug bars and former gig venues now peopled only by spectral drinkers. My friend is giving his liver respite from another winter season; I am the designated drinker.

The historical fact-finding mission we are attempting is a small effort to piece together the muddled-up jigsaw pieces of memory. By retracing steps and heading back to old haunts that I'd formed liquid attachments to, I am trying to work out what makes certain pubs stick in the memory long after their taps had run dry and after last orders had been called for the final time. Pounding the streets and wearing out a healthy amount of shoe leather seems the best way to reacquaint myself with the memories of a couple of pubs in particular.

When I moved to London, Camden quickly became the centre of my universe. As a penniless and unmotivated student I could never afford to live there, yet still it was the place me and my friends went to hang around and to make pints last as long as possible while watching hotly tipped bands. Looking at the listings for The Black Horse or The Falcon, we would invariably choose a couple of nights worthy of spending a tenner (including the £3 entry). Unbeknown to me at the time, those listings were compiled by Jeff Barrett, founder of Heavenly Recordings and one-time gig promoter.

I didn't know Jeff when I was at the door unfurling crumpled notes that had been mercilessly chipped out of my student grant. In the years since though, Jeff became someone with whom I had plotted numerous daft schemes – and the occasional genius one. I had drunk myself insane then sober again with him in more pubs than either of us would care to remember. We had propped up bars while the cleaning staff mopped up around us. Jeff was one of the world's greatest pub people – a born raconteur who would always, without fail, be the first person to get a round in. Originally from Nottingham, Jeff moved to London in the mid-eighties to work at the nascent Creation Records after stints running various record shops in Plymouth and Bristol.

After standing outside what was once The Falcon paying our respects, we repair to the nearby Hawley Arms to talk. Built in 1900, The Hawley has become this current generation's club-house of choice. A sturdy pub just off the main drag of Camden High Street, it's the kind of place where both punter and landlord discretion has meant that the beautiful people – those regularly seen tumbling headlong towards the pavement in the tabloids – can drink without fear of being pestered. More importantly, The Hawley is a prime example of how resilient the spirit(s) of a great pub can be. On 9 February 2008, a blaze swept across Camden market, gutting the pub and depriving skinny-jeaned teens of their favourite watering hole. Picking up and dusting off, eight months later The Hawley was rebuilt and reborn with a nip and a tuck and some shiny new toilets.

Possibly it's no coincidence that the pub's most famous barfly,

Amy Winehouse, chose that same period when The Hawley was shut to relocate to St Lucia in the Caribbean; such was her attachment to the place. According to the *Independent* (19 July 2007) Winehouse once temporarily left a drink and drugs clinic in Essex on the pretence that she had to go home and pick up a guitar. In reality she was checking into her local. According to that paper, of the pubs glamorous clientele – branded the Hawley Arms Set – 'Winehouse, 23, is such a regular she could be made its honorary life president.' Winehouse's untimely death robbed The Hawley of a spiritual figurehead. Her presence there was now as ethereal as Dylan Thomas at the bar in Browns Hotel, Laugharne, or the wheelchair-bound spectre of Jeffrey Bernard, still angrily banging on the doors of The Coach and Horses at five-to-opening time.

For Jeff and myself, The Hawley is an escape from the afternoon's depressing, dirt-streaked weather. As I settle into a restorative IPA, Jeff begins to talk about London pubs in the days before rock 'n' roll – at least the version I remembered.

'When I moved up from Plymouth in 1985, pubs hadn't yet undergone that big reconstruction period. Creation [Record's] offices were in Clerkenwell but this was still a few years away from The Eagle being opened and the whole advent of the gastropub. Working around that area and seeing that pub have its transformation was very odd. You were seeing an experiment; the beginning of that change in the way that people saw and used pubs. I used to drink piss lager back then so I didn't really care about the quality of what was coming to the taps or out of the kitchen.'

In the mid-eighties, a cash-strapped Barrett had decided to utilise the growing phone book he'd built through years of working with bands by starting to promote gigs. He was determined to promote in pubs away from the London's more established gig circuit.

'I needed to supplement my income as I was on a crappy Enterprise Allowance Scheme that didn't provide much money. I was a DJ and club runner before I moved to London. It was natural for me to try and get something going. I wanted to put groups on but I wanted to avoid all the usual circuit venues so I started hunting out pubs with a copy of *Time Out*, scanning the gay listings and the folk listings. By avoiding the rock venues I figured that I could find somewhere that younger gig goers wouldn't have stepped foot in. There was a massive resurgence in the underground with a guitar scene going on for the first time since punk. There was a massive amount of DIY bands that had sprung up out of fanzine culture but there weren't a lot of venues for them to play. I thought if I started a club it could be a place where all these people could come to sell fanzines, write them, see bands, meet like-minded souls.

'The first place I found was The Black Horse,' he continues. 'It was a very traditional working-class pub in a pretty unscrubbed-up part of Camden Town. Looking at the area even now, it's still more boarded up than tarted up. It's always been a mad busy road and it was like The Black Horse was an estate pub that somehow managed to creep away from where it should have been. Finding it was a joy – it was exactly what I wanted; a perfect fit. It was no-frills but it wasn't in any way dodgy. It was springtime when I first saw it. In the upstairs room they still had the Christmas decorations up which was just brilliant.

'The upstairs room in the pub held seventy people at most... that included a few peering in from the landing too. As more people got to know the place, more people really liked our nights. The music was good and it felt a bit like a scene. If you were an *NME* reader or a Peel listener, more than likely you'd like the rest of the people there even if you didn't like the particular band that was playing that night. The pub itself offered a safe environment – for both boys and girls.'

Within a couple of years, the tiny upstairs room at The Black Horse played host to early gigs by the likes of The Weather Prophets, My Bloody Valentine and Felt as well as the first London headline shows by a bunch of loose-limbed Mancunians who would go on to twist and bend popular music.

'We put Happy Mondays on twice. The first time was on a Sunday evening. I remember a Transit van turning up outside the venue. When they pulled up, the back doors opened and about ten people fell out. This wasn't a minibus, this was a proper white-van-man van. So out rolled this gang with a load of empty tins and plastic cider bottles and a fug of smoke that you could smell from miles away. Immediately they were different. They looked different to anyone in London – different to any other group around really. All of the mates they brought with them dressed the same too so the line between band and audience was totally blurred. When they got in the venue, Shaun (Ryder) was asking where the stage was. I told him there wasn't one – they were playing on the carpet in front of the mantelpiece where there was a crap stuffed heron in a glass box. Straight after, his dad – their roadie throughout the band's career – came over and said, "He hasn't just asked you for acid has he?" I said no and asked why would he. "He will," he replied. "And when he does don't fucking give him any." I don't think I've ever been asked that before or since anywhere! That was the first time I got an inkling of how inclined they were – there was no culture of that in the scene in London, it was much more innocent at that point.'

The massive success of The Black Horse became its eventual downfall. As bands broke and crowds got bigger, so the neighbours complaints got louder and louder.

'We were putting on the three bands two or three times a week,' says Jeff, 'and the residents were threatening to lynch the landlord. They'd gone from having a dead pub in the backstreets between Kentish Town and Camden to having My Bloody Valentine at full volume on Wednesday night; the natives were obviously going to get a little restless. The House of Love properly broke out of that venue. Gigs by them would have been our busiest kind of night. That usually meant a load of furious phone calls and at least a couple of visits from local crazies looking to try to shut things down.'

The Black Horse called time on Barrett's nights just as the scene he was promoting started properly snowballing. But even though he'd lost one perfect venue, he didn't have to venture too far to find the replacement.

'We ended up moving across the road to The Falcon. On the day that we agreed to finish, I came out of there a bit despondent and noticed a pub I'd honestly never seen before – The Falcon – pretty much opposite The Black Horse. I went in and loved it straight away. It was about one in the afternoon and there was a mad-looking pissed-up bloke behind the bar smoking fags, a right miserable face on him. I asked him what was out the back. "Why do you wanna fucking know?" I told him I used to promote at The Black Horse and he said we could have the room if we wanted. Word obviously travelled fast round those parts. The room was ace. It had a stage, it was bigger and it had terrible surrealist paintings on the walls. It was a proper garage sale of décor, it was just perfect.

'I stayed and got drunk with the miserable bloke for the rest of the day. I asked if they ever put on bands in there. "Nah, strippers." Have you got a licence for bands? "Nah. Not got one for strippers either." His name was Pat, he was brilliant. He ended up buying speed off my mates every week. It didn't take him too long to work out what was what.'

Back before I'd ever met Jeff, The Falcon had been the first place in London where I regularly went to watch gigs. Sometimes I'd even go just to hang out at the bar. It was the centre of gravity for indie kids in the late eighties and early nineties; the place where bands would hang out and people would want to be seen in the gritty, ill-fed years before the champagne socialism of Britpop. I can remember Pat. He was an actual ogre, a bleached-out Shrek. He would spend most of the night – most nights too – screaming at people for no reason, his face straight out of a Hammer Horror, all the blood vessels straining to contain themselves beneath the surface of his pasty lock-in skin. There was a six-month period – possibly longer – where he wore his arm in a cast. This was almost inevitably due to a boozing accident or fighting or a combination of the two. Back then he terrified me in a way I'm not really sure anyone could nowadays. Jeff recalls the venue and its eccentric staff with massive fondness two and a half decades later.

'We started booking bands at The Falcon straight after The

Black Horse and immediately it was really successful. People loved it. It was a proper pub with a lot of character. There really weren't any themed pubs around back then. Places had remained unchanged for years, they were all still decorated in what ever mad style the landlord fancied. Pubs then were still all about smoking, sitting, drinking, spitting, fucking and fighting. No one cared about trying to make pubs glamorous or aspirational. The jukebox was always one or two top forty records and a load of Irish rebel songs. The Falcon was a really great music venue. I wasn't always into the groups we put on but I always loved being there to see gigs. I do think what we had there wasn't just a pub with some bands out the back; it was a destination and hang-out for people regardless of who was playing. It was out of the way enough to make it feel a bit exotic as well. Well, if a mad Irish boozer in the backstreets of Camden can ever really be considered exotic.'

Jeff's interest in The Falcon and in promoting in general waned as the music scene mutated and venues hidden away down misty side streets south of the river became more and more important.

'I knocked The Falcon on the head in 1989 because a mate told me about the clubs down on Clink Street by London Bridge. I was spending far more time enjoying myself at acid house nights than dealing with daft bands. One of my last gigs was the Inspiral Carpets, which was packed to the rafters. Everyone seemed to know that they were going to be huge but I just didn't get it. My head was elsewhere already.'

Whatever circumstances led to Jeff leaving The Falcon behind, his fond memories of the place and that time have never faded.

'The Falcon was a really good boozer – a really good boozer's boozer – because it had the bohemia and it had the lock-ins. It had a mattress upstairs for when the landlord would go, "You're not going like that, you pissed twat!" I liked all that. You'd wake up in the room in the morning and find Pat on the mattress next to you going, "I'll sort out some breakfast then." The whole thing was so bloody funny. It was a particular period of barfly-dom in my life which I enjoyed a hell of a lot.'

Bukowski by way of Belsize Park, I suggest. 'That kind of thing, yeah!'

Later on that week, a quick internet search for The Falcon reveals a planning application to convert the building into two residential properties. The extension – the back room that had played host to the great, the good and the grot of the rock stratosphere – had already been demolished to make way for 11 flats all but hidden from street view.

The Falcon and The Black Horse both stopped tap for the last time before the turn of the millennium. Neither pub would ever bask in the blue plaque glory they so deserve. Maybe one day they'll be listed, rightly lauded as the first places where people saw the likes of everyone from Blur to Coldplay, the Sundays to the Mondays, but that seems unlikely anytime soon. After all, it took the former site of The 2 i's on Old Compton Street – the actual birth place of British rock 'n' roll – some 40 years to gain any form of permanent memorial outside.

The fate of those pubs is symptomatic of what's already happening all over the capital, a creeping trend for redevelopment with no replacement. For Barrett, the current parlous state of the capital's drinking venues has not gone unnoticed.

'I heard that there are six pubs a day closing in London and the south-east. That is plainly our culture disappearing. It's nothing to be glib about – it's something that needs to stop. We're not going to get them back once they've been badly carved up and converted into flats. These places are the community – whether for locals or for tribes of kids looking for a point to it all. Take away smoking and watch people taking advantage of cheap piss in the supermarkets and it all falls away. I keep asking myself, "What replaces a boozer?" What takes its place at the centre of the community? Sadly though, the way I see is it that if people don't use these places – for gigs, for darts teams or film nights or Women's Institute meetings or knitting circles or whatever – then who can we really blame when they shut down but ourselves?'

* * *

Leaving Jeff at the Tube, I brave the rain and headed southwards in the direction of the Post Office Tower. Rushing down Camden High Street, I pass The Elephant's Head, a time-warped pub where a rocket-powered jukebox howls out the hits of the fifties to a clientele of greased-back roadhog bikers, all of them stuck in slow motion at the pulsing heart of a gridlocked city. Uphill onto Parkway, past the pub that kick-started the career of local heroes Madness (The Dublin Castle). At the top, another building block in Chef Ramsay's empire – The York and Albany. An enormous white-tiled gastro-dome that chimes to the sound of chinking wine glasses and high-heeled laughter, in its current guise it seems a million miles removed from the reassuring sound of solitary pint pots thudding dead on the bar. The York and Albany's arrival symbolised the final phase of Camden's slink towards becoming the sort of moneyed playground that would seem as fantastical as it was ludicrous back in the days of Pat and The Falcon.

Pubs have changed stylistically several times round here over the last 20 years or so. Property developers leapt on dead sites while councils turned a blind eye. Those local pubs that had given up the ghost – the crumbled cornerstones of the communities – were gutted and converted with no regard for what they had actually offered to the locals. The few that survived either had their rough edges smoothed by pub companies or their insides spruced up to join the gastro revolution. Arguably all of this was progress. What's unarguable though is that a little piece of our history had been whitewashed away.

It was easy to forget that for a while (certainly all through my formative drinking years), all pubs were like The Falcon – throwbacks to a post-war world where pubs simply weren't family friendly. Most of the time, they weren't even people friendly. They were, as Jeff puts it, all about the 'smoking, sitting, drinking, spitting, fucking and fighting'. They were staid, locked in a time where the only food on offer was a stale bag of ready salted and the beer was – at best – alcoholic brown water. Although not exactly the first boozers you'd hanker after, they are that piece of pub history that's been all but wiped out. And where all the mid-afternoon boozehounds who used to frequent them – bloodshot eyes and hair like bleached straw – were shipped off to really is anyone's guess.

Remembering these dead pubs now is a lot like reminiscing over long-gone relatives. When you summon up these memories more often than not your recollections have warped completely. The bad bits – all the family arguments and youthful tantrums, hissy fits and bored afternoons in bad weather – have been glossed over, leaving you with a rose-tinted vision of yesteryear.

The younger me loved those pubs – probably more than the older me loves most of the pubs I frequent these days. In the case of The Falcon and The Black Horse, they represented something indelible – an attitude, a badge of honour, a code of conduct. A crude tattoo inked with a group of mates after way too many beers. They were the places in which you felt part of an in-crowd. To be shouted at by Pat added a certain swagger to your trip home.

In that respect, every boarded-up public house was once someone's Moon Under Water. In the dusty vaults of memory, everywhere always served the perfect pint and provided the perfect night out. Memory doesn't send you back to those furious kicking-out times or to the fifth visit to the rancid toilets, paint peeling from the walls and splattered piss all over the floors. No, the glowing mist of memory always sends you back to that first sip from your second pint – that perfect moment where the last rays of sun break through the grubby windows and hit the golden liquid in your glass. That superlative moment where everything seems possible.

CIGARETTES & ALCOHOL

Paul Moody

'Rules and regulations are everywhere,' says Josie Appleton, draining a drink constituting two-sevenths of her recommended weekly intake. 'Please hold the handrail. Caution Bench May Be Wet. Please Wash Your Hands. They're treating us like children.' Josie's doll-like features break into a grimace. 'A hundred years ago this pub would have been buzzing with real life. Prostitutes, dealing, gaming, deals being done, people having affairs, a sense of intensity and illicitness. Now it's all polite after-office chats, quiet drinks. It doesn't feel very real or very exciting.'

We are sitting in the nicotine-averse, music-free environs of The Sir John Oldcastle in Farringdon, London. Outside, Community Support Officers prowl the streets, clamping down on space invasion and litter louts. On the table, *Metro* is open at a story about a new government initiative to combat binge drinking:

the third of a pint glass.

As the convener of The Manifesto Club, a worldwide body dedicated to 'campaigning against the hyper-regulation of every-day life', Josie explains she spends her time helping those blinded by bureaucracy or bound up in red tape. She does not, however, go along with the opinions held by some libertarian groups that the average person in the street is a 'Starbucks-swilling zombie' who follows corporate orders. 'It's really condescending. The truth is, most people are concerned about the way things are going but they don't know what to do about it.'

In Josie's opinion, the erosion of civil liberties is impacting directly on how we enjoy ourselves. In 2010, she took part in the Provocation Picnic in London's Hyde Park, defying new restrictions on public drinking. 'It was a protest at the fact you now can't have a drink in the park without having your beer confiscated. It's very important, because if you're having a picnic with your friends, someone is now within his rights to come along and pour your drink into the grass. That's a huge violation.'

The raft of legislation in the last few years has, among other things, robbed the pub of its identity. No longer autonomous, it has become a slave of the state; scrubbed clean, much like the pub backrooms of Camden where, even in living memory, bands would play in unregulated bliss; screaming amps and dripping candles flickering next to exposed cables.

'I think we all remember the way pubs were fondly. As a sixth-former in Nottingham I was always impressed by the effect it had on people. Some of my friends would behave outrageously at house parties, but in the pub they couldn't get away with it. They had to follow the codes: buying a round, not drawing attention to themselves. It made you feel protected, because it was its own republic, and you were a citizen.'

Once the pub was the one place where we could go to unleash our wilder, more Byronic side. Where as Liam Gallagher sang in 'Cigarettes & Alcohol', we could find 'something worth living for'.

Here's Dickens's description of The Three Cripples in *Oliver*

Twist: 'The place was so full of dense tobacco smoke that at first it was scarcely possible to discern anything more; by degrees there appeared to be a numerous company, male and female, crowded around a long table, exhibiting cunning, ferocity and drunkenness in all its stages.'

These days, Josie explains, the merest hint of bumfluff on a patron's upper lip could see the place closed down. 'The clamp-down on underage drinking is ridiculous. The penalties which pubs face if they serve a seventeen-year-old drinker are astonishing. It's like it was child abuse. They can lose their licence over it. There's this idea that on the stroke of your eighteenth birthday you're an adult and you can drink. But adulthood is a process of assuming responsibility. Between sixteen and eighteen, the pub provided a probation period. If you behaved yourself, you could stay. Now, underage kids can't get in, so they buy spirits from the off licence and hang out on street corners, or pile down to Newquay. So the result is much worse.'

With younger teenagers barred, the pub's rock 'n' roll credentials took a further hit with the 2003 Licensing Act. This cast a dead hand on small-scale events across the country, meaning that you needed a licence for anything from a solo guitarist strumming away in a pub to a poetry reading or even a village fete. Paperwork was also made mandatory for the use of a piano ('facilities for making music') or a dancefloor ('facilities for dancing'). The result of all this unnecessary legislation? A weakening of social bonds, with potentially disastrous results.

'It leads to a breakdown of socialisation which is damaging all aspects of society, from the classroom up. Essentially adults are now less confident with each other and the younger generation, because they're being told they can't do anything off the cuff; they have to abide by official sanctions. So if a kid smashes something up in the street, no one will intervene. There's an atomisation of society. Everyone thinks that it's not their responsibility.'

Like Paul Kingsnorth, Josie traces this to changes in society over the last 20 years. 'I grew up quite close to the pit villages in Nottinghamshire and after the miners strike they were really broken, demoralised. The old structures and sense of identity went. The Labour Party lost its identity and became something else, and in a bid to assert itself New Labour attempted to supplant what had gone before, replacing social regulation with official regulation. The irony is, I think a lot of these laws are very fragile in terms of their authority. Whenever I debate with politicians they're always very apologetic, they say: "I take on your concerns." It's kind of an authorless totalitarianism. It's not like a big strong man or machine is behind all this, it's something else. Basically the state is asserting itself almost with a negative justification. It's not "we're making this or building that", it's "we're carrying out a work assessment". There's no will, no centre to it. No one's responsible for it. Yet it seeps through the cracks and affects our lives.'

For a second I'm suddenly back in Strangers Bar with Marsha Singh and Gerry Sutcliffe. Because for a lot of pub goers it was the legislation implemented on 1 July 2007 which was the most damaging of all. Putting health issues to one side, it's hard not to argue that the result has seen pubs lose a lot of their magic.

The artist David Hockney expressed this notion far better than I ever could in an article in the *Evening Standard* in May 2011 headlined 'Light up and laugh at the anti-smoking killjoys'. 'Bohemia has been banned,' he wrote, 'my little corner of Bohemia has now been reduced to my house, where free spirits are welcome and I try to keep the dreary and the boring away. I have a large sign that points out "Death awaits you even if you do not smoke". I like to enjoy Now, as there is only now. Longevity as an aim in life seems to me to be life-denying. The prohibitionists can feel sorry for me all they want; I am just going to laugh at their smallness.'

Did the ban do anybody any good? In an article in the *Publican* in July 2010, journalist Peter Robinson outlined how the count-less millions of 'new' non-smoking customers the industry had promised would flock to their newly fumigated premises (dubbed 'New Breed') simply failed to materialise. Instead, pub numbers began dropping like a stone almost immediately, proving that the demand for universally smoke-free pubs simply never existed. The result? Widespread closures, and as Robinson sees it, a 'pub holocaust' which won't end until half are wiped from the landscape by 2017, leaving us with a nation of chain-managed, town-centre food pubs-come-coffee-houses, totalling around 12,000.

'Future generations may try to recreate the atmosphere of the British pub,' wrote Robinson, 'but we'll never recapture that quintessential time-honoured character that made British pubs unique – the envy of the world. We lost something very special the day we allowed the state behind the bar.'

In the ozone brightness of a Soho afternoon, Joe Jackson is sitting outside a central London pub. The sky is that faint, smoky-turquoise big city colour, largely thanks to the American Spirit Medium slowly burning in his right hand.

A Grammy-nominated singer and composer, he's still best known here for 'Is She Really Going Out With Him?', 3 minutes, 33 seconds of teen-angst which catapulted him from the pub rock fringes to pop stardom. Now living between London and Berlin, Joe's a vociferous opponent of the smoking ban. Like almost everyone else we've talked to, he started going to pubs in his teens, and was playing gigs at 16.

'I loved pubs as a kid not only because they were the natural habitat of musicians, but because they were a neutral space where people could relax, talk, and feel free,' he says, recollections of heady nights flooding back. 'It could get pretty wild. At one pub gig the landlady could be persuaded to get up on a table and do a striptease after a few gin and tonics. One night, an army marine did the same thing. The table collapsed, beer sprayed everywhere, and the naked marine found out his mates had hidden his clothes somewhere. It was all sorted out "in-house", so to speak, and it was great fun in a way that is hard to imagine now.'

I want to reassure myself we're not slipping into misty-eyed reminiscences, and Joe seems to sense it too. 'I'm aware of the temptations of nostalgia, and it's true that a lot of pubs back then were pretty sad, dingy places,' he says. 'Pubs now are cleaner and have better food and better wine. But otherwise, I can't find much to celebrate. Too many good pubs have been demolished or turned into nasty "theme" bars or bland family eateries. The staff are less friendly; the only part of the evening they actually seem to enjoy is chucking you out. We also now have CCTV cameras, bouncers on the door, very little live music and no smoking. Even if pubs still had pianos, budding musicians like me wouldn't be able to get a gig without a special permit. They're being strangled by mean-spiritedness. The only way to save them, I believe, is by loosening things up, but that doesn't look like happening any time soon.'

The reason, Joe explains, is simple: too much legislation, weighted in favour of the killjoys. 'I was living in London when the licensing laws changed. My local pub was in a very central location with a lot of cinemas and theatres nearby, and every night I would see people running in after shows and being refused a drink because it was 11:02 p.m. Many of them were tourists who would walk away not just disappointed but utterly baffled. Then I got a letter from the local council, saying that this pub had applied for later hours, and that as a local resident I was entitled to object if I wanted. A few weeks later, I had a chat with the landlord. The council had said no, and he was furious, because in fifteen years, he hadn't had one complaint about noise or disturbance. Now, about fifty people had objected. But you can always get fifty people to object to anything, if you encourage them. Why pander to them, the landlord wondered, rather than local residents who'd like a late drink, or the fifty tourists he sometimes turned away in one night?'

Joe explains that when the weather improved, this same land-lord put two tables outside. He'd done this the previous year, with no problems at all, but this year he was informed by the council that he must apply for permission. He did so, and once again, was refused, on the grounds of 'possible obstruction to pedestrians'. All despite the fact there was plenty of space for people to get past.

'Unfortunately, these are typical examples of the way things are done in Britain today. If something can be even suspected of causing potential harm, or even potential offence, to someone, somewhere, then it must be banned, and to hell with the rest of us, and the quality of our lives. Everything seems to be increasingly dictated by soulless nannies and prigs whose only pleasure in life seems to come from saying, "No."'

As for the smoking ban itself, Joe sees it as politically motivated. 'Anyone who thinks the ban is about "health" is naïve. It is intended to make smokers look and feel bad, to make certain kinds of politicians and busybodies feel good, and to placate the extravagantly funded health and pharmaceutical lobbies who are currently having such a great time demonising and stigmatising tobacco. I've done years of research on all this, and I have no doubt whatsoever that the potential risks of smoking are grossly exaggerated, and that so-called "second-hand smoke" hurts no one. There is not one documented case of death, anywhere in the world, proven to be caused by SHS – not one. There are just computer projections based on dubious statistics from carefully selected studies. The majority of studies, including the biggest and best, show that SHS either has no effect at all, or is actually beneficial. Anti-smokers are fearmongers, taking advantage of people's ignorance of basic scientific facts.

'For instance, a poster promoting the smoking ban says that tobacco smoke contains arsenic and benzene. But there is benzene in your coffee and arsenic in your tap water. The quantities of "nasty" chemicals are always too low to hurt anyone. Or to look at it another way: if there was proof of harmful levels, don't you think they'd say so?'

Joe explains that, if you extended the logic behind the smoking ban, you'd also have to ban the cooking of food (which produces carcinogens), candles and incense in churches, bonfires, and barbecues. 'And we should certainly ban music, since it might get too loud and damage someone's hearing.'

Perhaps the worst aspect of the ban, Joe says, is how mean-spirited it is. 'If the authorities were to encourage a spirit of toler-ance, there would be no problem. Smokers and non-smokers could relax together just as we've done for hundreds of years. But the anti-smoking movement specifically promotes intolerance.

Fundamentally, this should be sorted out by the free market. The anti-smoking movement, for all its money and power, is terri-fied of this idea. That's why no one, anywhere in the world, has been given any choice about smoking bans. The New Labour government passed the most draconian ban in Europe despite (a) promising in their election manifesto to ban smoking only in places serving food, and (b) the fact that their own Office for National Statistics showed sixty-eight per cent of the population were opposed to a total ban. Adult citizens are being banned from enjoying a legal (and highly taxed) pleasure in places which are actually private property. This sets a terrible precedent. Politicians are blurring the boundary between public and private, and claim-ing the right to ban and regulate everything, everywhere, so long as they use the magic word "health". Smoking bans are not only anti-social, but anti-business, anti-science and anti-democratic.'

Back in Farringdon, Josie explains that Spanish opposition to the smoking ban is employing a smart strategy. With a total ban in no way representative of the popular mood, an organised and politi-cally astute opposition have mounted a shrewd defence.

Tired of being ordered about, the slogan of the Spanish anti-smoking ban movement is '*Prohibido prohibir*' ('Ban the Bans').

Instead of the authorities being allowed to convince the popula-tion it is working in their interests, columnists and agitators have pointed out that it is, in fact, a breach of far more long-standing traditions of tolerance and a 'live-and-let-live' broadmindedness.

'The health lobby will always tell you they are operating for the greater good,' she says. 'But essentially what they're saying is that one person's enjoyment is less important than that of some amorphous whole. So you get to the point where enjoyment is seen as being anti-social. It's a very selfish attitude. I don't smoke, but I can see the pleasure it gives to other people. Spain won't be the same country any more, because all the guys over sixty hang out at bars all day and smoke. Now that culture is being killed off, purely for the sake of it. If all the smokers are in a bar together, what harm are they doing to anyone else?'

Is it worth pointing out that in Germany, where smoking was frowned upon by the Nazis (I'm not saying anything), a blanket ban was overturned in 2008, and deemed unconstitutional by the courts after two small bars claimed their business had been affected by the ban? Perhaps.

It feels like one battle which has already been lost though. In May 2011 New York, a trailblazer in anti-smoking legislation, initiated a ban on smoking in outdoor areas including the city's 1,700 parks and its iconic heart, Times Square. It makes me think of that student bedroom perennial: Dennis Stock's image of a young James Dean trudging through the rain, his body reflected in a puddle, shoulders hunched, cigarette dangling from his lips.

How long until Piccadilly Circus and the streets of our major cities go the same way? Farewell, Bohemia.

GOING FOUR ROUNDS WITH THE KING OF BEER

Robin Turner

When would I ever learn? I had committed a schoolboy error of epic proportions. The night before I was due to meet arguably the country's foremost beer writer, I'd gone to the pub 'for research purposes' with the express intention of having just the one. Five hours later I was completely legless at home nursing a bag of chips like a hot-water bottle while trying to follow the events of the week on *Newsnight*. Within minutes, I had passed out to the sounds of Paxman.

The lion's share of the next day is spent wasted on the same sofa I'd collapsed into, feeling like death. Eventually, after throwing a couple of Nurofen down my throat, I cycle to meet Pete Brown in The Jolly Butchers in Stoke Newington. Wrestling a chronic beer shame that makes me fear a judgemental stripping down, I sheepishly walk into the bar to try to find the man described by no less than *The Times Literary Supplement* as 'the beer drinker's Bill Bryson'. Luckily it quickly transpires that Pete has stood in very similar shoes to mine on more than a few occasions.

Starting his first shift behind the handpumps, Lee, an affable Manc, takes our order in what had become – in just over a year since opening – one of north London's finest ale pubs. As he scans the bar to find Pete's chosen tipple (Dark Star American Pale Ale), the barman shakes his head, incredulous at the turn of events. 'The first pint I ever pull and it's for the king of beer.'

'Why do I think the pub is such an iconic part of British life?' Pete ponders the question as the pub begins to bustle with after-work imbibers, a cross-generational, multi-racial mix of men and women all seemingly getting stuck into pints. 'I've spent a long time wondering about that and, really, there's no simple answer. Part of it is down to the British climate, the way that British society evolved in terms of how we lived with much of the year spent indoors. I'd add to that a little bit of amateur psychology and say that we need a bit of alcohol to fuel conversation and interaction. Those things have combined to make the pub the focus of the community in this country for the past thousand years. In medieval times, many other countries had similar community hubs but that all seemed to fall away.

'Personally, what I think characterises the British pub is the sense of shared ownership; there's a sense of "I've got more of a stake in this place than I have in my local bakers or supermarket or coffee shop." The whole notion of regulars having a pint of the usual, that kind of thing adds to that sense. I think culturally we came to depend on it here many years ago. Other countries can promote a café culture where you sit around outside – here it's dull and rainy for long periods of time across huge parts of the country. For most of history our homes were smoky dark hovels where you just went to put your head down. The pub was something of a haven, somewhere to spend your leisure time. I think every single aspect of the pub is designed to facilitate human interaction. Us Brits just aren't that sociable without some form of encouragement. The British are famous for queuing but the pub doesn't encourage a queue, it's much less formal. The fact that in order to drink someone has to get up and go to the bar, to start a conversation, to mingle. That very action forces that interaction.'

Pausing to savour his pint, Pete references the spirits guide himself. 'Orwell nailed it better than most. In *The Lion and the Unicorn* he said that all the greatest pleasures in Britain are informal. We're a nation of stamp collectors, gardeners, hobbyists. The draw of the pub becomes about moving away from the prying eye of the state to somewhere to relax.[7] Somewhere we leave our pretensions at the door. In our depressingly class-ridden society, we can be different in the pub to anywhere else. Inside, everyone's money is the same. Class used to rule the pub, thankfully it doesn't any more. All those factors mix in and make the pub – well, a good pub – something of a social release valve from all the idiosyncrasies and pressures of British society. The pub allows us to get rid of them. And that release makes for a very welcoming, informal, fun environment.'

Pete Brown wrote *Man Walks into a Pub*, his 2002 'sociable history of beer', out of necessity. Up until that point, there was no definitive text on the evolution of beer as social glue in Britain. Pete – a man at that point happily working in the advertising industry – found it inexplicable that there wasn't a book that documented the 'life' of those magical 568 millilitres that bind so many of us together. So he set out to 'write' that wrong. That book – and its follow-ups *Three Sheets to the Wind* and *Hops and Glory* served to make Pete one of the country's most important writers on beer

---

7. '...*another English characteristic which is so much a part of us that we barely notice it, and that is the addiction to hobbies and spare-time occupations, the privateness of English life. We are a nation of flower-lovers, but also a nation of stamp-collectors, pigeon-fanciers, amateur carpenters, coupon-snippers, darts-players, crossword-puzzle fans. All the culture that is most truly native centres round things which even when they are communal are not official – the pub, the football match, the back garden, the fireside and the "nice cup of tea".*' The Lion and the Unicorn, 1940

and, importantly, the culture surrounding it.

In just under a decade since his first book was published, Pete has become – as the barman effused – the 'king of beer'. And people recognise him as such; it is a role that he has eased into (a chance meeting with him at the Great British Beer Festival a month or so after we met in Stoke Newington saw him happily press flesh with a steady stream of well-wishers and picture-takers). He spoke to a post-CAMRA generation, one that didn't carry round like a tombstone a set of moral codes about what represented an accept-able pint. He is also as interested in the reasons why we choose one pub over another as much as why we choose a certain beer to fill our glasses.

It is strange to think no one had written that book about beer and its cohesive nature as it clearly filters through almost every circumstance of everyday British life. From those nervous first underage pints in the one pub in town that never cared about checking ID through to boozy, tearful wakes in the nearest pub to the crematorium. Births, exam results, hirings, firings, weddings, retirements and deaths – invariably for most people the pub is the venue and beer the lubrication.

'I still see a lot of pubs as community pubs,' continues Pete. 'This place we're in is a community pub. I definitely think that the pub often sits right at the heart of the community and I think it's rediscovering that role in certain places as well; places where it's dropped away over the years. Places like this – what people are calling craft beer pubs, pubs where there are no mainstream brands on the bar and where someone is so confident in their knowledge of beer and the ability to attract the right audience that they can even take Guinness off – were previously a failed pub, somewhere that had closed down, boarded up. There's a pub called The Cask in Pimlico that's a good example. They had tried everything with that site and failed. They'd tried it as a sports pub, a gastropub, a kara-oke theme pub. I think it had been a strippers' pub at some point too. Everything failed. The landlords were desperate. And some bright spark comes along and says, "What about making it a beer pub?" and suddenly you've got people travelling from St Albans and Kent specifically to drink in there. That's a community, it's one built around beer.

'I was researching for a piece last year about community pubs and I heard the same story everywhere I went. In each place, people were saying that the decline of the pub is invariably down to publicans who don't understand the business or – more often than not – publicans who just don't understand people. They start seeing business disappearing to the supermarkets so they put bigger fonts in, they'll put fluorescent stars in the window with cut price booze offers, they'll turn the jukebox up to ear-splitting volume thinking that'll create more atmosphere. They put up more screens to show even more sport. Before too long you're in a pub that's loud, brightly lit, eye-wateringly fluorescent. There's constant banging, discordant music that's jarring with the *Sky News*. All these things serve to wind you up, to make you fractious and irrit-able which – let's face it – completely contradicts all the reasons why you'd go to a pub in the first place. When you do that, you get more and more desperate so you do more of it. The next thing people are staying away in droves and the pub closes. The idea is a pub serving real beer with real conversation. What you find happening is that people from the local community would all start going back in. These were people who hadn't been seen in the pubs for five years or so. And often they couldn't remember why they stopped going in the first place, it was as if something subliminal had stopped them walking through the doors for years and years. Looking back it's all of those factors mentioned. The reinvention of the local pub ends up bringing them back in as customers.'

Returning to the table with a second round (Camden Town Brewery Pale Ale), I wondered what made people form attach-ments to certain pubs so much so that they blank out everywhere else around. After all, you can stand outside the Butchers and – with a good aim and a lull in the traffic – throw stones through the windows of at least three other pubs (the Rochester Castle, the Three Crowns and the Coach and Horses). Yet here we are, regulars in one particular boozer above all others. At this point Pete admits to a psychological dilemma.

'I really see the relationship between a regular and their local as being like a marriage. My problem is that I'm a bigamist at the moment. I've got here (The Jolly Butchers) and just down the road, I've got The White Hart. When I first moved to Stoke Newington and walked into The White Hart, the pub seemed to speak to me quietly. I honestly felt it was saying, "You're home now." I couldn't tell you what it is about it though. It's not the big screens or the way the music is chosen to suit the time of day. It's not the Sunday lunch, which could be better but I still like it, and it's not the range of beers, which is solid if not that interesting. It's not the beer garden… it's all of that and none of that. I remember when I found my first local, back when I was at university in St Andrews. It was a place called The Niblick. Me and a group of mates started going there because it was where all the second-year students were drinking. About six weeks into my first term, I walked in and Tony the barman looked over all the people stood at the bar and said, "All right, Pete, the usual?" And with that phrase he had me. For the next five years. Before long I was working behind the bar. Bigamy aside, that feeling of finding a proper local that you love – for whatever personal reasons – it's like nothing else.

'The one thing I can't stand in any passionate community – and the beer community is more passionate than most – is the need to define what's best. We don't have to define everything. Why not just relax? Different pubs can suit different needs for the same person. The two pubs I'm torn between – the White Hart and the Butchers – are very different to each other but I love them both. It'd be extremely boring if everything were the same. If it was decided by committee that the perfect pub was deigned to be four hand pumps of guest beers, this kind of décor, that kind of jukebox – if all pubs in Britain were going to follow that path, it'd be really shit.'

Above and beyond an undying love of beer, Pete seems to truly believe that a well-run, thought-through pub is a force for good. And I can't disagree. I've felt the hop-scented tractor beam draw me towards watering holes that I love (and a few that I am at best ambivalent about) almost daily throughout my adult life and I know the faces and occasionally the names of others who seem to be driven by the same impulses. I bang the drum for the great, the good and occasionally the grot if they capture my heart with that magic, rare essence; that thing that maybe even your mates don't quite understand. That same idea had got Pete thinking.

'I've started to wonder whether a pub has a soul. We talk about places being soulless all the time; I think a proper pub has a soul. I'm researching a book about one pub in particular – The George, in Southwark. It's been there for 500 years; the current building being around 350 years old. Really, it's like a creature. I'm picking up stories from people who work there now and they're practically the same things that HV Morton [the journalist and travel writer] said when he spent the night there in 1926. They talk about how the building feels, about how it seems to watch you, to judge you almost. So I do think a pub has a soul. A proper pub rings with echoes of footfall after footfall from people having the time of their lives. Some of that stays in the place and gets into the furniture. And it's something that people want to cling onto even after a pub goes for ever. There's a few places between here and Islington where pubs have been converted into flats yet people still keep the pub sign up outside. I did once try to walk into someone's front room because it still looked so much like a working pub. Why do people keep that? People – developers or landlords or residents – they want the bricks and mortar to retain some of the spirit that it had back when it was a pub.'

I think back to my walk through the backstreets of Camden with Jeff Barrett earlier in the year where I'd noticed the very same archival advertising. The Black Horse sign still swung as buses sped past, representing nothing more than a boozy blue plaque; a symbolic nod to the fact that once upon a not long ago behind this newly renovated façade people whiled away hours propping up a now junked bar. Behind the triple-glazed Everest windows, locals told tall tales and wasted away the hours daydreaming, courting, laughing and living. It seems a hollow gesture – a badge of honour to tell the community that you and your fellow residents doff your cap to a past when the plush central London conversion you now live in was a cornerstone of local life. It is more than a little ironic that the sign itself is cleaner and more well kept than any of the actual pub signs in the area, seemingly repelling the weather, both foul and bleaching.

Third round (Camden Pale again) and I wonder aloud what the elements that would constitute the perfect pub would be. Pete takes no time in answering a question he has clearly mused over time and time again.

'For me, it's all comes down to atmosphere. It's got to feel welcoming. Not too fussy with its decoration but not too shabby. It would be somewhere anyone could feel at home. Drinks-wise, it'd be craft beers, ciders, wines, spirits. Not just premium, top-end brands; good, well-chosen stuff. Good food but I'd be more interested in bar snacks than I would in full meals. Different spaces. The vogue now is for knocking pubs through into one space. I think it has to be different rooms. One that's loud, one that's quiet. You've got a place where you sit with the wife and somewhere different that you stand with your mates.'

I laugh at the idea of reinstating the snug and lounge set-up that the majority of modernised pubs have razed in favour of bright, clean, open-plan spaces; he is clearly right though. Too many pubs have fallen prey to design by committee; design by what-worked-somewhere-else-must-work-here. Pete continues to sketch out his mental map of the perfect pub.

'The lounge bar would have a telly showing sports, snug wouldn't. I was doing some market research in a pub recently and all the guys who were coming in for the focus groups kept looking around wide-eyed saying, "Oh you could bring the wife here." And I was asking what they meant by that. They all saw it as you could go to the pub more often that way. You could go with mates one night and with the wife the next. Then they'd backtrack apologetically, saying, "I'm not saying I would though!" What it was really was an attempt by a group of proper blokes trying to talk about how much they liked the décor of the pub. They can't come out and say they appreciate a vase of flowers in the window or some nice soft furnishings; they have to say that it's "wife friendly".

'Personally, perfect pub-wise, it's all about looking at what the enduring things are, specifically those things that endure for a reason. With so many pubs coming and going, it always seems the ones that stay are the ones that nail a kind of unpretentious comfort and welcome. I used to live in Notting Hill and there was a pub called The Eagle up on Ladbroke Grove with beautiful old black and white tiles on the outside. I walked past everyday for two years and the G in Eagle had been hanging off the whole time. I'd walk past and think if you can't be bothered to take ten minutes to fix that then I'm imagining that your toilets are covered in shit, they stink of piss, your pipes aren't clean and your food's shit. Just on that one little letter, I made all those assumptions about that pub. I used to fantasise about taking over that pub and paying the cleaners a couple of quid above the going rate but getting the place gleaming – all the brasswork, the toilets… just sparkling and bright. I had this idea that I wanted to take over a place like that and get all of the staff to have a stake in the place, to be proud of every single element of it. And if not, fuck off. I had this idea that bar staff would know all the beers, that when you got guest ales in you'd get everyone to try it so they'd understand each one. You'd talk people through where they were from, why you'd got them in. You'd hire staff based on enthusiasm, on interest in beer. So I suppose I was even dreaming of pretty much my perfect pub back then.'

Is Pete's perfect pub, one with knowledgeable staff and a sense of community and all the letters lined up the right way in the signage, just what Orwell had been talking about all those years back? The place where the barmaid calls you 'dear', one where you can walk in and the barman asks if you want your 'usual'? We finish our pints and survey the bar. Standing room only by 7 p.m.

'What I love most about this place,' says Pete, 'is that if you order cask ale, they serve it in a dimpled jug. Now you look around. There's a lot of dimpled jugs on the go. Some belong to ordinary middle-aged blokes. Some to East End hipsters. Some to women. Some to the people who resemble that clichéd picture of a typical CAMRA member. Those groups of people might not even notice the other; they exist in their own spaces and don't bother each other, just give way to the other on the way back from the bar. That to me is the sign of a good pub. Not just a good one, a brilliant one.'

I turn off the Dictaphone and contemplate the bike ride home. A nag at the back of the head reminds me of something I'd seen in the Butchers on a previous visit. Tucked away behind the bar in the fridges is a row of bottles of a beer labelled Avery, Brown, Dredge. A hefty 7.5% ABV 'Imperial Pilsner' collaboration between three beer writers (Zak Avery - aka the Beer Boy, Pete and a young beer blogger called Mark Dredge) and the Scottish brewery BrewDog. As I'm sat with the 'king of beer', surely it would be churlish not to drink a bottle of something he's actually had a hand in brewing?

I hand Pete his bottle and he cracks a smile as he pours it into a glass. 'We started brewing so late in the day I had to get a flight back to London. I ended up choosing the colour of the label. I wanted it to have that same classic lager look as Carlsberg and Heineken; the major difference being that the beer inside the bottle would pack a hell of a punch. And, of course, at the end of the day, the colour of the label is the most important part of the process!'

The beer is a knockout. It is lager elevated to Olympian heights; full flavoured, hoppy and delicious. And drinking it seems to signal the first point of the day where I've felt truly fantastic. It's a reminder that our national drink was once a holy brew. Not long after I've wobbled the bike back home, Kirsty Wark is talking softly in the background as I doze off in a cloud of vinegar fumes.

BETTER THE DEVIL YOU KNOW

Paul Moody

The devil can take many forms. For the Aguaruna tribes of the Amazon, he can be any white man with a camera. In Buddhism, he is known as Mara, a tempter who lures his victims from the spiritual life by making the mundane seem alluring and the negative seem positive. Today, however, he comes in the form of Steve Brown, a retired policeman from Duddington in Northamptonshire. 'I've been coming here for thirty years,' he says, trident in hand, a pair of plastic horns perched on his fore-head. 'In a funny way, I feel like I belong here...'

We are standing in the courtyard of The Bricklayers Arms in Whittlesey near Peterborough on a chilly January evening. To the untrained eye it might seem an unlikely place to catch el Diablo quaffing a pint from a silver tankard, but for one weekend of the year, this ancient Fenland market town becomes a place where anything seems possible.

Ghoulish figures appear from out of nowhere, middle-aged men in Victorian bonnets lurk on street corners like cross-dressing time travellers and a sense of convention being turned on its head is as perceptible as the fog creeping in from the River Nene.

Held on the weekend closest to Plough Monday, Straw Bear is unique among the traditional festival dates on the British calendar. Because unlike everything from the harvest celebrations to Glastonbury; from the solstices to the annual cheese rolling event in Brockworth, Gloucestershire – it doesn't revolve around the changing of the seasons or a bumper crop. It's about something else altogether: drinking.

A local custom dating back to the start of the 19th century, Straw Bear's origins can be traced to the outlying villages around Cambridge. Locals, known as molly dancers, would blacken their faces with soot, disguise themselves as anything from Native Indians to the plain bizarre (one reveller at Little Downham in 1932 was spotted wearing a pink coat, racing goggles, a top hat and a long white pigtail) and go from pub to pub, singing and dancing all the way with a fiddle, concertina or dulcimer as accompaniment. The climax of the festivities would see them converge on the centre of Cambridge for a spot of binge drinking, where they would wreak havoc, their elaborate outfits acting as a handy disguise. The aim, essentially, was to fight back against the sheer drudgery of the post-Christmas slump, and get royally smashed in the process.

'There are local festivals all over the country in one form or other but Straw Bear is unique to the Fens,' explains Steve Williams, affable chairman of the Peterborough branch of CAMRA, and a Straw Bear regular since the mid-eighties. 'In Ludlow they do a sausage festival; there's black pudding throwing in Lancashire. Basically, people just want an excuse to go to the pub.'

Banned by the authorities, the practice lay dormant for almost a hundred years until its revival in 1980. In 2010, 400 dancers from 35 teams from around the country have braved the elements to take part, including exotic ensembles ranging from Cat the Whip to the nightmarish Pig Dyke Molly. All weekend they will partake in outdoor dancing, play stomping, hearty folk music and drink copious amounts of Straw Beer, a hoppy ale produced especially for the weekend by locals brewers Elgood's.

By mid-morning Whittlesey appears to have been invaded by a New Orleans Death March, auditions for *Kiss: the Musical* and the cross-dressing cast of *The French Lieutenant's Woman*. In the main square a middle-aged drummer wearing a tweed suit and a maharajah's turban thumps out a rhythmic beat. As he does, a man dressed up as a nine-foot Straw Bear jigs from foot to foot on the cobblestones like some awkward, rural cousin of the yeti.

Looking to escape this faintly disturbing vision, I turn a corner only to chance upon a group of men re-enacting a play dating back to 1740. 'This is the season of epiphany which proclaims the coming of our Lord,' bellows one, dressed in top hat and tails, to a crowd of bemused shoppers. 'So kindle a fire of kindness and fill the jug with strong beer. And brush away all thought of sadness for the Midwinter Mummers are here!'

As the various dance groups go about their business, curious images abound. In the main square, toddlers hug tightly to their mothers' skirts as a group of teenagers decked out in white fright wigs loiter outside Starbucks. At Sue's Chippy, a man with a blackened face carrying a large wooden stave buys a battered sausage. And all the while, the bells, the bells: like some form of medieval tagging device, most of the morris dancers can be heard before they're seen, leg bells a-jingling as a drummer announces their arrival.

Seeing the morris dancers going about their slightly surreal business, it's easy to see parallels with the plight of the pub itself. Once an essential part of rural life – records date its origins in Britain back to 1448 – morris dancing is now widely seen as an archaic anomaly rather than something of cultural worth. In Whittlesey you don't have to look far to see evidence of the pub's decline. In the main square The George, an inn dating back to 1770, shut down in 2009, meaning that the festival's traditional climax, the ceremonial burning of the nine-foot Straw Bear, will take place in front of a boarded-up building.

'It's terrible,' says Steve Williams. 'You've got a festival going on which attracts people from all over the world and the main pub in the market place has closed down. Most of the people in Whittlesey are absolutely ashamed of the market square now. It was the heart and soul of the town.'

Sadly, it's not just Whittlesey where last orders are regularly being rung. In the last ten years, Peterborough has lost a number of traditional pubs while a new drinking centre in the middle of town – The Broadway – has risen up to cater for younger drinkers.

'Twenty years ago there were no bars at all in the town centre,' explains Williams. 'It was pub-free. There was a library, shops and a cinema. Then the cinema closed down, and Wetherspoon's opened up in what used to be a technical college.' Despite a number of excellent local breweries in the area – Elgood's in Wisbech and Oakham Ales in Peterborough – there's a sense that without a thriving infrastructure of good local pubs, in time, they won't have anyone to supply.

'I'm an optimist,' says Steve. 'I believe that if a pub is well run it's going to last. But they're not safe in the hands of large companies who see them simply as a way of making money. Putting a spotty teenager in plimsolls in charge and calling them a master innkeeper isn't going to work, is it?'

He takes a thoughtful draught on his pint. 'Locally, the problem is not so much the pubs closing, as them reopening with temporary managers. People get fed up with paying £3.20 for a pint of beer when they don't know if the same staff are going to be there the next week. People don't like change. A great example of how a pub should be is my local, The Coalheavers. It's the perfect pub as far as I'm concerned. Most people know each other, and the landlord,

Tom Beran, is in every night. That's the attraction as much as the beer, people know what they're going to get. George Orwell might have wanted ten specific things, but if a pub is friendly and the beer's okay, I'm happy.'

In the courtyard of a pub called The Ram, I'm chatting with a group of pagan dancers called The Witchmen. Black-faced, and wearing top hats festooned with animal skulls and pheasant feathers, they're about as far from the stereotypical idea of morris men as you can get.

Their de facto leader is a gregarious ex-biker called Terry Dix. Bearded and bursting with bonhomie he has the sage-like countenance you'd expect of someone who has already cheated death: while performing a dance called – spookily enough – the Grim Reaper in 2007, he suffered acute chest pains which turned out to be a heart attack. 'They call us the Motörhead of morris,' he says, fixing me with a crooked grin. 'Our dancing has been known to make Bibles spontaneously combust.'

Today The Witchmen are having the morris equivalent of a 'dance off' in a pub courtyard against a team called Red Leicester. A strapping bunch decked out in multicoloured coats and bright red faces, they engage in light-hearted banter then look on, stony-faced, while The Witchmen launch into a little satanic square-bashing. 'Top that, Gorgonzolas!' yells one of them as they troop off to the bar.

Further investigation reveals that The Witchmen's ranks include everything from a qualified hypnotherapist to a car salesman, but they also boast an undeniable edge which comes from having a largely biker background. 'There's definitely a rock 'n' roll aspect to The Witchmen,' admits a wiry fellow called John, silver tankard dangling from his belt. 'Morris dancing is traditionally very happy and associated with the beginning of summer, but we're a reminder of the dark side. We touch on something deep in people's souls.'

He explains that The Witchmen were formed as a reaction to the rules and regulations of conventional morris dancing. 'We all wear black top hats but we're allowed to dress them individually. The feathers on mine come from the local hunt, and the skull is a crow which died near me, so it's living on. Quite a few of us were part of the Cotswold morris dancers before we joined The Witchmen but we got tired of the politics. They said we couldn't bring our girlfriends, it's men only. It seemed a bit mad to us. We bring the wives and kids with us, it's a family event.'

For all their good spirits, The Witchmen have already felt the chill wind of local pub closures. 'The way the country's pubs are closing down without any help from government is tragic,' continues John. 'It's all forgotten now, but morris dancing traditionally was about the poor working-class people who used to dance in the pub in exchange for beer. Now because all the pubs are licensed to breweries they can't spare you any beer because it all has to be accounted for. Rules and regulations. It's only ever when we're at a freehouse they might say "here's a jug of beer for you". It's frustrating because drinking is integral to what we do, it goes with the dancing.'

He shrugs his shoulders. 'It's not as if these morris dancers ever end up in mass brawls. It's good-natured rivalry which ends in a drinking session. But the powers-that-be are scared of people getting together and enjoying themselves.'

If The Witchmen are the most outwardly anti-establishment group present, by far the oddest are the Pig Dyke Molly. Dressed up to resemble harlequin-themed look-alikes for *The League Of Gentleman's* Papa Lazarou, they're as outlandish as anything seen on the streets of Cambridge at the turn of the last century.

'For us, Pig Dyke Molly is a challenge to the accepted order,' explains their leader, an affable type called Tony Forster. 'Traditionally Straw Bear happened at this time of year because of the ancient festival of Saturnalia. It's to do with the Lord of Misrule and extends over the twelve days of Christmas, and there's a long tradition of turning things upside down at this time of year. Geographically, the Fens are very isolated, too. It's quite a hostile environment, and people can be very stroppy in this part of the world. The Iceni tribe were based here and the Romans never fully conquered the area. Hereward the Wake led the local resistance to William the Conqueror after the Norman invasion, and he was only defeated when he was betrayed. Then there's the Peasants Revolt, the sabotage of the drainage system, the Littleport Riots…'

By 7 p.m., the festival has finished for the day and the participants are getting down to the real business in hand: drinking. In The Bricklayers Arms, a woman in full-face balaclava, Victorian dress and a hat with a floor-length train of ivy models a jarring juxtaposition of Steeleye Span and the IRA. I'm wondering how I can get hold of Vivienne Westwood when I get chatting to a man called Ken, dressed in a ladies shawl with matching bonnet.

He tells me that, despite looking like a stunt double for the French Lieutenant's woman, his day to day wardrobe is much more sedate. During the week he works as a scientist at a government research laboratory. Today he is the leader of Old Glory, a molly dancing team from Suffolk. In this team, all the dancers are men while the musicians are all women, playing traditional instruments such as the four-stop melodeon.

'We met in the beer tent at the Towesey Folk Festival in 1994,' Ken says. 'We decided to revive a form of molly dancing particular to Suffolk at the end of the nineteenth century. This is a very busy time of year for us. We celebrate Plough Monday but we also celebrate on Boxing Day with a very ancient tradition called the Hunting of the Cutting Bread which is only recorded in Middlesea in Suffolk.'

Ken explains that Old Glory number about 35, an all-ages ensemble who often practice in a pub called The Buck in Bungay. 'It's a great little pub, one of the best in Suffolk. We even named one of our dances after it.'

By 9 p.m., The Bricklayers has become host to the sort of party it would have seen a hundred years ago. In the back room, a man in a black waistcoat starts playing an accordion and people from various different morris and molly teams start dancing together.

Young children wearing animal heads of pigs, horses and cows happily run through crowds of men dressed as women, women dressed as men, Gene Simmons lookalikes and Witchmen, faces still blackened with soot. All of whom are having a whale of a time, knocking back pints of Straw Beer and carousing, singing, chatting and dancing as the mood takes them.

Suddenly a reason for all this occurs to me. It's a local pub serving mostly local people with local beer. Is the answer to the pub's problems really that simple? Suddenly drink becomes not a means to a very messy end, but something to savour; a holy ale rather than a pint of, as Stella Artois is unfortunately nicknamed, 'wife beater'. It tells a story about who we are and what it means to come from somewhere, and with that comes civic pride.

Out in the courtyard, I come across Steve Brown. All day Steve and his fellow members of the Midwinter Mummers have been entertaining crowds, as they have done for the last 30 years.

'I'm always bloody Beelzebub,' he laughs, taking a long draught of Straw Beer, still dressed in his devil costume. He explains that mumming, and 'the mummers plays' came into being around 1740, with each play having a distinct connection with the region it was performed in. 'We think the term originates from the mystery plays from medieval times. At the end of the day they're about life, death and resurrection. I know that sounds corny. The one we've been performing today was discovered in the library in Whittlesey. It's very silly, with lots of stuff about "talking ipsy, tipsy, and falling down" but we add in lots of contemporary stuff ourselves about politicians expenses or *X Factor* or whatever. Everyone loves it, and we're keeping the tradition alive.'

Steve explains that Straw Bear taps into a feeling we can all relate to. 'Everyone feels the same after Christmas,' he says. 'You've been cooped up for a week, you're fed up, it's freezing cold and there's a whole year stretching out ahead. Straw Bear was originally a reaction to that, but it was frowned upon, because we're all meant to just knuckle down and get back to work. It gets sneered at when we should be celebrating it.'

We talk about the benefits of eating and drinking locally produced goods and Steve explains that most of the people involved in Straw Bear are living what the *Daily Mail* would call 'alternative lifestyles'. 'I've got my own smallholding and some people here are completely self-sufficient. A lot of us grow our own vegetables and keep animals, we're environmentalists. It's a very small community and there's a very strong pagan element, especially among the younger members.'

The devil shrugs. 'We come out and do our mummers plays in pubs and at festivals like Straw Bear to raise money for various charities. Basically, we're demanding money with menaces. And if you don't give us enough money, we'll do the play again.'

It feels good to be standing here in a pub courtyard, chewing the fat with Beelzebub, and I'm struck by the thought that it's doubtful there's a more life-affirming example of the crystal spirit taking place anywhere in the country, enveloped as it is in a blanket of post-Christmas gloom.

I tell Steve my background as a music journalist and get the feeling he's as surprised as I am that we're getting on so well. It occurs to me that if the pub really does have a role in the 21st century, maybe it's exactly this: to remind us how to talk to each other, one to one, when social networks like Facebook and Twitter encourage us to communicate only with people on our own wavelength, subconsciously reinforcing our own prejudices.

'It's also fun tonight because it's against the rules,' he grins, casting his gaze at the all-ages oddballs having the time of their lives. 'They want you to be miserable and going back to work, and this is our way of saying balls to all that. We come here and do this dozy play, people laugh, talk to each other and have a few drinks, and, well…'

He rocks back on the soles of his pointy boots, clearly content with his day's devilry. 'You can't knock it, can you?'

BLACK AND WHITE TOWN

Paul Moody

I t's just beginning to rain when the taxi pulls into the parking lot of The Percy Arms in Walbottle, just outside Newcastle. As I arrive, a fragile figure in his eighties slips out of the side exit, licks his lips and gazes curiously at the black Northumbrian afternoon.

Until three years ago, it's unlikely he would ever have seen this curious hinterland between lunchtime and evening, instead cocooned in a warm glow of cigarettes and alcohol. These days, however, like many others of his generation, he's forced to shuffle home during the afternoons to feed his nicotine addiction.

'It's heartbreaking,' says Richard Simpson, the pub's landlord, watching this unnamed soldier trudge off. 'One bloke I know is that fed up he's converted his garage into a den and all the lads go round there now. Others just sit in the house. Another guy, Little Brian, used to sit on the same seat every day, smoking away and getting through half a bottle of gin. Now, he's lost. He doesn't know what to do with himself.' He shrugs. 'It's like they've put a tax on fun.'

It's a grey Thursday afternoon in Newcastle and Richard Simpson is mulling over the strange twists and turns of a life dedicated to raising people's spirits. Dressed in jeans and a black t-shirt which reads: 'If Found Return To the Pub', he's a softly spoken fifty-something with the wrinkles which tells you that he's been there, done it and, quite clearly, bought the t-shirt.

I've come here to meet him because I'd read on the internet about his and his wife's efforts to keep open a pub called The Vallum, and was intrigued to see if his first-hand experiences of dealing with the pub companies tallied with the picture painted by either Brigid Simmonds or Paul Kingsnorth.

We're sitting in a corner booth in a bar dwarfed by a dining area where blood-red paper napkins are folded in perfect triangles in the middle of two dozen empty tables. At one end are five gleaming silver tureens. 'It's all you can eat curry for ten quid,' he says. 'We've only started it two weeks ago, but it's doing okay.'

In the other bar a fruit machine called 'Quid Vicious' bleeps away to itself in one corner where Slade's 'Gudbuy T'Jane' plays softly in the background. The pub gets new machines in every month. The most successful one was 'Deal Or No Deal', but people don't play them so often as they used to, because, as Richard explains: 'If they're going to spend their money, they'd rather blow it on the drinks.'

Shafts of sunlight pour through the windows, illuminating the dust motes like glitter, and Richard explains that he's been entertaining people all his life. Aged 11, when most kids are still obsessing over football stickers, Richard was making homemade beer with the aid of a friend, a keen amateur chemist. He started playing in groups at the same age, when his maths teacher, who taught him guitar, recruited him for his folk band.

During the seventies and eighties he travelled the country as half of Travis 'n' Allan, an acoustic duo specialising in close harmonies who were once described as 'the North East's answer to Simon & Garfunkel'. As he tells it, it was the traditional musician's life: non-stop gigs propping up the likes of Charlie Williams and Bernard Manning while strippers danced in front of spangly curtains in smoky working men's clubs.

In my mind's eye I picture his life at the time as a cross between *Phoenix Nights* and the *Confessions Of* films starring Robin Asquith, especially when he tells me about the rum goings-on in the duo's transport-cum-sleeping quarters: a converted ambulance.

Any lingering dreams of stardom, however, flat-lined one Christmas when their van was stolen at a gig one night, losing all their gear. Richard explains that after a 20-year hiatus they reformed in 2010, swallowing their pride and auditioning for the *X Factor* with their best song: a version of The Everly Brothers 'All I Have To Do Is Dream'. 'We did it perfectly,' he says. 'But they didna wanna know. They put through a fat bloke who slaughtered some opera song instead.'

The way Richard tells it, The Vallum in Dumpling Hall was the sort of pub where anyone was welcome. 'It wasn't an old place, it was an estate pub which they'd built in the seventies and which had grown with the estate. It's a poor area. There was another pub down the road called The Centurion which was always getting its windows put through, which closed down and The Vallum was on its uppers, too. One day the owners, Enterprise Inns, rang me up because they'd heard about what I'd done with other pubs and said, "Would you stop this pub from being boarded up?" So I went down there and looked at it one night and the place was totally dead. There was one bloke slumped on the counter serving and a TV on in the corner. They didn't serve food, the back room was never opened, the back garden was never used. The day I took over, the windows were even boarded up. So I walked in, put speakers everywhere, I got the music going, built a stage and stuck a chef in there cooking decent food. It cost me ten grand but within a month the place was buzzing.'

Supported by a loyal band of regulars who would drop in every night, The Vallum became the perfect example of a local pub catering for a close-knit clientele, raising local morale in the process. However, because the pub was already on Enterprise Inns' disposal list, none of it mattered: the pub had already been earmarked to be turned into a care home.

'Enterprise promised me a long lease,' says Richard ruefully. 'Then they turned around and said, "You've got a fortnight to get out, we've sold it." All their promises came to nothing.'

Where most people would have thrown in the towel, Richard carried on trading, only to find the might of the law coming down on him. 'I just came out of court yesterday,' he explains. 'Basically, when they gave me notice to quit I thought that was the end of my tenancy. But I'm being done for twenty-five grand's worth of fines and costs because I held out and carried on trading. What I should have done is buy the beer from them, because eighteen thousand of it is a fine for buying beer from elsewhere. They charged me rent up to that point, too, even though I thought I was squatting.'

The way Richard sees it, his eviction was another result of the trend for pub companies (in this case Enterprise Inns) to sell unprofitable pubs to the highest bidder.

'Ever since the three big pubcos, Trust Inns, Punch Taverns and Enterprise Inns split off into a monopoly, the trend has been to sell on pubs for profit,' he says. 'The difference with The Vallum is that Enterprise didn't recognise it was doing well, so it was already on a disposal list of pubs they were looking to get rid of, and they aren't interested in the human side of it.'

To draw attention to his plight, Richard and his wife Danni channelled their energies into a concerted campaign to keep the pub open. As well as a petition, he even recorded a single called 'Give Us Back

Our Boozers', an impassioned slab of pub rock including lines like: *'No more friends, no more chat, cos the pubs are all flat'* and *'What will we do when our social life's gone?'* complete with a YouTube video filmed in the pub.

'We got twelve hundred signatures on a petition, got local MPs and councillors to back us, and got the story in the press. It even hit the six o'clock news up here. There's a human interest element. I can fully understand if a pub closes down because it's not attended and it's run down, fair dos, it's knackered. But not a pub that's actually rocking and rolling and has got its regulars coming in. At Christmas and New Year we were at capacity, you couldn't move for people, it was choc-a-bloc.'

Since The Vallum's closure, the pub's darts, domino and football teams have relocated to his new pub, The Percy Arms. Occupying a corner site ten miles outside of Newcastle city centre, this local must once have been an impressive sight, a vanilla-coloured landmark dating to 1850, complete with strawberry-red chimney pots.

Today as the drizzle gets slowly heavier, and thunder ripples overhead, it reminds me of W.H. Auden's quote about his own faded looks: like a wedding cake left out in the rain.

Richard explains that whereas The Vallum was a thriving business, The Percy Arms is a closure waiting to happen. 'The locals don't come in here much. It's an ancient village and most people have lived here all their lives. They're too old to want to go out much any more. It used to be dead popular once upon a time, but now it struggles like mad.'

As we're talking it's obvious that for all his friendliness he's clearly distracted, and I sense there's a cloud over him darker even than the storm brewing outside. When his phone rings, it comes in an escalating cavalcade of electronic bleeps which I soon realise is the *Doctor Who* theme. It goes off constantly, but he says he doesn't want to answer. Why not? 'It's only going to be more bad news.'

Yesterday, he explains, the pub's gas supply was cut off due to an unpaid bill for £9,000. This morning, bailiffs arrived on the doorstep threatening him with closure.

On top of that, he tells me that he's just come off the phone to the PRS (Performing Rights Society), who had been demanding this year's money – £860. It feels like the straw that broke the camel's back. 'I had to tell them I haven't got it,' he says, more resigned than exasperated. 'It's just another nail in the coffin. They're killing their own industry by charging us so much.'

Last December, Richard admits, things got so bad he even had to cancel Christmas. 'We planned to have a big party but we only sold three tickets. It's got to the point where I wake up every morning wondering what the next bit of bad news will be. I'm getting deeper and deeper into debt. I'm just living day to day.

'The biggest problem is that the people who own these companies are relentless,' he says. 'Their whole philosophy is: "This is the rent that you're going to pay and we're not going to help you. The beer you have to buy through us and we're not going to give you any discount." If you're not hitting targets, they're on your back straight away. I got to the point where I said it's going to be cheaper for me to give you two and a half grand a month and live upstairs rather than open and lose more, and they said, we'll sue for breach of contract. So you've got to have the pub open to the public, whether you like it or not. But if you ask them for help it's like talking to a brick wall because the people at the top are just looking at the figures.'

To attract trade, Richard's been doing the same as he did at The Vallum, attempting to draw custom in with a range of events and entertainment. Next week, a 'psychic to the stars' is appearing, aiming to channel the spirits of John Lennon and Bob Marley in this genteel village in an upmarket corner of Newcastle. Last Saturday, meanwhile, a performance by a local comedian was a raging success. 'It was like a throwback to the old days,' he says wistfully. 'We had a turn on in the back room, we had the domino squad in one corner, the lads playing pool in another, a disco afterwards, everyone had a fantastic night.'

Hearing his enthusiasm for these boozy nights, with the whole community brought together in search of a good time, you can't help but think that, at their best, The Percy Arms and The Vallum are exactly the sort of pub Orwell would have loved. There are no pretensions here, no beer snobbery, simply a local pub doing what it does best – drawing local people together.

The last few years, however, have seen widespread closures locally. 'They're dropping out of the sky,' he laments. 'It's terrible to see it. I used to drink everywhere in the city: Wallsend, Byker, Scotswood, all the districts, and loads have shut down all over. The kids still want to go out, but they want to go to town now. It's three drinks for the price of one in Bigg Market. How can I compete with that? I can't blame the people running the bars down there, they're the same as us. They need to get people through the door. We've swallowed five or six beer price increases here just to keep people coming in. In town, the rents are so big, they have to get a crowd in. They don't want to sell drinks cheaply because it causes problems. People falling over sick, it can get nasty down there…'

As I'm leaving Richard tells me that he worked in the shipyards for ten years after leaving school. Every weekend a gang of 20 of them would go to town on a Friday night and drink at a German themed bar called The Hofbrau House. Twenty tables of lads and girls would drink big steins of beer prior to a trip to local night-spots Scamps or Tiffany's. It is good to hear about these long-lost port-of-calls, names to bring a smile to the lips of a generation of Geordies, and even Richard's tale has an upbeat ending. Later in our journey I'll discover that The Vallum has reopened its doors, and Richard is probably back behind the bar lifting spirits as we speak. Right now, however, it's time to go somewhere that's always been having it large.

'It's like Frankenstein's monster,' says the cab driver as we pull up in the city's notorious drinking zone Bigg Market. 'It sleeps all week but when it wakes up all hell breaks loose.' I'm mulling this over in The Beehive when a huge guy arrives, whips up his Newcastle shirt so that a rippling blancmange of flesh is resting, orb-like, on the bar and shouts: 'Fill her up!' Can this really be happening?

It turns out he's an affable giant called Jacko and this is just his flabby party piece. He tells me he's been drinking in Newcastle man and boy. It is, he says, 'the Geordie way'. At first I think he's joking, but he's older than he looks, closer to 40 than 20, and when I explain why I'm here he happily agrees to chat.

When he sits down, the black and white stripes of his shirt bulge, and it looks for all the world as though he's smuggling a consignment of Grecian urns under there. Mercifully, like most men staring down the barrel of middle age Jacko, like Richard Simpson, saw the drinking habits of his youth bathed in a golden glow.

'I like a drink but I'm nothing like the kids today,' he says. 'It was just beer and a few spirits back then, now it's about the drugs. They can't do one without the other.' How much does he drink on an average night out? 'About twelve pints will do me. On a good night, I can drink twenty.' Jacko explains that he once drove home after eight pints, was stopped by the 'red and whites' and still passed the breathalyser test.

I'm all for a slow descent into drunkenness, but bragging about an immunity to the effects of alcohol seems plain daft. And anyway, isn't it the way that with most other stimulants it's the one who feels their onset first who is seen as the most worldly? Nonetheless, it doesn't seem prudent to bring this theory up, and besides, Jacko is explaining that drinking is in his genes. Both his father and his grandfather worked at the Vickers-Armstrong munitions plant on Scotswood Road, and he tells me that each factory once had its own mini-social club opposite: The Gunmakers, the Forge Hammer Inn, The Hydraulic Crane. 'There were forty-four pubs along there at one time,' he says. 'There's only one left now, and that's a gay bar called Heroes.'

Two years ago, Jacko explains, a pub called The Globe reopened on Scotswood Road to cater for the influx of Eastern Europeans into the city. 'It was always a canny boozer, Alan Shearer's auntie used to run it, but these Polish fellas took it over, and did a great job. There were loads of Polish ales to try out. But they've all packed up and gone back to Poland now the euro's gone to shite.'

If any city is used to life on the economic rollercoaster, it's Newcastle. Its roots (presumably dyed blonde) go back as far as a Roman settlement called Pons Aelius situated at the eastern end of Hadrian's Wall, and although there's nothing left of the New Castle, built in 1080 under the auspices of William the Conqueror's son Robert Curthose, civic pride still runs deep.

While the coal trade fuelled shipbuilding and repairing on the River Tyne, it was the Industrial Revolution which put the city firmly on the map; its considerable muscles flexed in the direction of the railways, heavy engineering and armaments manufacture.

The subsequent economic decline is now a distant memory, and these days you'll struggle to find anyone with a bad word for the place, it's pick 'n' mix of neoclassical architecture, vibrant street markets and swish arcades given a royal seal of approval by Princess Eugenie, a student at Newcastle University, and much liked locally for her enthusiastic endorsement of the city's night life.

This successful civic face lift has, however, left some nasty scars. In 2009, The Cooperage, one of the city's oldest buildings and dating to the 15th century, closed its doors, and dozens of other pubs across the area have disappeared too, victims of the recessionary pinch.

For those locals of certain vintage, it's the loss of The Egypt Cottage which pulls at the heartstrings. Sited opposite the old Tyne Tees TV studios on City Road, the Egypt was once the haunt and unofficial 'green' room of the staff and guests at *The Tube*, locals often finding themselves propping up the bar next to everyone from Boy George to Miles Davis. Jools Holland even lent his weight to the campaign to save it, telling the *Newcastle Chronicle*: 'The public house is one of the most fragile parts of our heritage and they are closing at a terrifying rate. I'm a great believer in the idea that when a lot of great things have happened somewhere, the atmosphere is caught in the fabric of the place and everyone who came up to Newcastle for *The Tube* will have sat in that pub.'

* * *

I'm sitting in The New Bridge Inn with Richard Dollimore, chairman of the Newcastle and Northumbria Branch of CAMRA. An accountant by trade, with a local pub pedigree stretching back 20 years, he's an avuncular figure, and explains in the politest possible way that each pub closure should be taken on it merits.

'It's sad to see it go, but The Cooperage had been limping along for the last fifteen years,' he says. 'Anyone who lives here will tell you the same. It got taken over by a company who didn't appreciate its merits and tried to change it. The beer was shite. The whole Quayside area has changed and they tried to please everyone which was always doomed to failure. For a pub to succeed you've got to live and breathe it, and with a management company in charge, that won't happen.'

As for The Egypt Cottage, there were extenuating circumstances there, too. 'I was talking to [someone] the other day and he said they weren't really on the ball,' he says matter-of-factly. 'It's a real shame. Across the road from the Egypt was another great pub, The Rose and Crown, but that went too. It's all flats, car parks and offices over there now.'

The point Richard is making is that while pubs are closing at an insane rate – at the time we met, 50 a week – there's generally, as he puts it, a 'bloody good' reason.

'There's fifty-odd pubs a week closing, right, but there ain't fifty real ale pubs a week closing. Put it this way. It takes eighteen months to compile the *Beer Guide* for the pubs in our area, which is pretty large. It covers the whole of Newcastle and Northumbria. During that period, only three pubs have closed. The Holy Bush, The Tap and Spile in Hexham, and the other Tap and Spile in Morpeth. The Holy Bush is the one that Charles and Camilla once had a tipple in. Since then, that's reopened, and so has The Tap and Spile in Hexham. So in the last eighteen months we've lost one real ale pub. The point I'm making is that the good pubs, with good vibes and decent ale, will always do well.'

Richard explains that what he calls 'the real ale community' is, in fact, booming. The local branch boasts 850 members and last year there were 22 beer festivals in the region, well-attended events at idyllic-sounding venues such as the Stables Brewery and the Chesterlee St Cricket Club.

'Whisper it, but the microbreweries are making a lot of money,' he says. 'We have nine microbreweries in our region and they can't make enough beer.'

He rattles off a quick list of names: The Ship, run by Michael Hegarty, The Northumberland Brewery in Bellington, Mordue, Hadrian and Border, Big Lamp at Newburn, High House Farm, Hexhamshire, Dipton Mill, all, as he puts it, in 'rude health'.

'At the last count there were 711 microbrewries in the UK which is incredible in the light of the pub closures,' he says. 'It also suggests that there must be some pretty awful pubs out there.'

It's a spirited defence of real ale pubs in general, and one we've heard, to a lesser extent, whenever we've hooked up with local CAMRA representatives. Richard explains how a recent trip to Dipton Mill saw him sampling a pint of Wap Weasal. I feel obliged to tell him it's exactly the sort of anecdote that might put people off ever getting involved in real ale in the first place.

'Well, all the names have got their own story,' he responds good-naturedly. 'I think it's a name of a place rather than an animal. But there's a self-awareness too. Mordue recently brought out a series of beers named after footballers' haircuts. There was a Vinnie Jones. There was a Gazza. There was even a Keegan's Perm.' We muse on what a pint of Keegans's Perm might taste like: a fuzzy mix of hops, a dash of nutmeg, a hint of onion bag? All topped off with a quick splash of Brut?

In-joke or not, it's part of an image problem real ale drinkers are still saddled with and I'm eager to challenge it head-on. Because the one thing that has always put me, and, I suspect, many other pub goers, off beer appreciation societies like CAMRA is their blinkered refusal to care about any pubs other than those selling 'quality' ale. The New Bridge is a great example: I'm sure the beers are wonderful, but for my liking it's too bright, too antiseptic and so lacking in what Orwell called 'atmosphere' it may as well be on the moon.

Talking of which, I'm eager to get on with the task at hand, but he pre-empts the inevitable question by telling me about his favourite pub, which is also where we plan to go next: The Crown Posada.

The Crown, Richard explains, is a very old-fashioned kind of drinking emporium. 'It's an oasis of calm, really. The only music is from a record player they've got on the bar, and they only play records by people who are dead or over fifty years old. And there's a community of regulars, so you see the same people, but it never feels too cliquey.'

He explains how the pub's landlord, Keith, used to moonlight as a science teacher and would set up experiments on the bar that he was going to do in class the next day. Often punters would arrive to find bowls of hydrochloric acid in water and plumes of smoke everywhere, magnetic balls flying across the room. Health and Safety would no doubt have a fit, but it sounds almost too good to be true to me, and walking across the concrete walkways there's a nagging thought in my mind: could The Crown match up to the Moon Under Water?

When we get there, it doesn't matter. In fact, nothing really seems to matter. Known locally as The Coffin, it's a tiny building wedged like a safety deposit box into a narrow site on The Side, a street which plunges deeply down towards the Tyne. Entrance is via a wrought-iron gate set on a grey granite plinth and the interior is, frankly, enough to bring architects to orgasm, so we'll mention the fluted pilasters, swaged panels, entablature with a pulvinated frieze and leave the vintage design-porn there.

Before we know it, we're deep in conversation with all and sundry; a father and son from Düsseldorf, two girls in polka-dot dresses studying art at the university, an old fella called Mike, and others I've already forgotten and I'm sure they have too. I get chatting to a local poet called Keith Armstrong who explains that he started coming to The Crown when he started drinking 'seriously':

in 1970. 'I can't say it's changed much apart from occasional gentle refurbishment, which I suppose is its strength. But I've never dared ask to put any music on. Even when it's non-stop Frank Sinatra. I'm a bit like Oscar Wilde and his Paris hotel when it comes to this place. One of us has to go – it's either me or the wallpaper and I think it's going to be me!'

There are other pubs I've vowed to go to tonight – The Cumberland Arms, The Free Trade, The Bridge Hotel, The Bacchus, The Bodega, to name but a few, but like all good pubs The Crown Posada whisks you away with it, and there's not a lot you can do but hold on tight and enjoy the ride.

The next morning I do what you never should do: I go back. I've returned to swot up on a few facts about the interior and I've bought a vinyl record with me too, picked up at a great little second-hand shop near the station. I'm eager, basically, to test out The Crown's legendarily tough music policy. The album is only 45 years old, and neither of the musicians who made it are dead, but seeing as the pub's empty apart from me and the barman, he shrugs his shoulders and lets me put it on.

As the crackle and hiss gives way, the strains of The Everly Brothers' 'All I Have To Do Is Dream' float across the bar. It sounds great, and I decide to toast Richard Simpson's crystal spirit with a second pint. 'Fill her up,' I say at the bar.

It's the Geordie way.

HALFWAY HOUSE

Paul Moody

Guess what? I'm standing outside the archetypal London Pub. In fact, it's so archetypal, that's what it's called: 'London Pub'. It's a sunny day in central London, cloudless blue skies shimmering in the heat-haze, and it feels good to be back in the capital as hundreds of pubs and restaurants go about their business, steaming glasses and putting out tablecloths in preparation for the lunchtime rush.

I'm here because if my trip to Newcastle proved that things in pub world aren't as black and white as they seem, then it's time to examine another boozy truism: the pub's role as a symbol of British identity.

Part of the National Russell Hotel, a 1600-room magnet for foreign tour groups close to Russell Square tube station, London

Pub is also perfectly situated to cater for hundreds of thirsty sight-seers deposited outside daily by city-tour buses shuttling between Madame Tussauds and the London Eye. However, as clichés of the capital go, it is as bizarrely inaccurate as Dick Van Dyke's cockney accent in *Mary Poppins*.

Entrance through the smoked-glass doors reveals sturdy wooden furniture and, on the walls, black and white prints of Edwardian London evoking a bygone age of flat-capped commuters squeezed on to open-top buses and trams. The old world ambience dissipates, however, when you notice the dimmed disco spotlights. Which almost, but not quite, disguise mauve bench seating, where occasional rips in the fabric expose large bulges of pale yellow foam, like flashes of thigh under a too-tight skirt.

If I didn't know better I might easily be in a downmarket pole dancing club called Caligula's. That, at least, would explain the bored-looking barmaids gossiping in Polish, the overwhelming sense of lethargy and the banks of TVs pumping out non-stop bump'n'grind R&B (if not the inexplicable reek of chlorine in the corridor to the toilets). For the average visitor from Missouri it must be quite an eye-opener: having found out that the capital's streets are all but free of Routemaster buses, they then discover that our pubs are seemingly designed to evoke the mood of an underwater strip club.

Perhaps I'm being unkind. For all its faults, the London Pub is probably no better or worse than any number of nearby bars, and the American youths washing down their fried chicken wings with bottled beers seem happy enough in this strange neon noon.

It just seems emblematic of the pub's current position. While it's still, as Brigid Simmonds pointed out, a massively bankable cultural asset, the reality often feels very different from the promises made in the brochures. Interviewing foreign musicians over the years for the *NME*, I'd regularly been amazed at the huge reservoir of goodwill we seemed to have stored up through our cultural exports (primarily, pop music). This seemed to go hand in hand with an impression of the country which, even now, still accorded with its Hollywood stereotype, full of smiling bobbies and Hugh Grant types on every corner, apologising for the weather. Once, in San Francisco, I interviewed a band called Hot Hot Heat who had grown up in Victoria, British Columbia. A British sovereign state, Victoria boasts double-decker buses, red pillar boxes erected during the days of the Raj and, from the band's own account, a gentility reminiscent of a comatose Isle Of Wight. Growing up as staunch anglophiles, in awe of the mother country and its music (notably The Beatles, the Kinks and the Who) they couldn't wait for their debut UK tour and a visit to the local pubs. Their first date was on a bitterly cold Tuesday night in Middlesbrough. I can still picture the singer's doleful expression as he sighed: 'Put it this way, it wasn't quite how we imagined.' Do all visitors to these shores experience such a rude awakening?

As we reach the halfway point in our search, the London Pub also feels like a good place to take stock. We started out in search of Orwell's Moon Under Water and so far we've found that submerging ourselves in pub world has produced more than a few ripples of discontent. We've listened to activists and pub experts extolling the pub's role at the heart of the community, heard administrators blame central government for closures and listened to politicians saying all the right things. But are we getting any closer to finding out if the Moon Under Water actually exists?

Yes and no. If our travels so far have shed some light on the pub's history and current travails, they have also uncovered a whirlpool of cross currents (pub closures are bad; our heritage is under threat) which seem to be leading us towards the murky waters surrounding our own national identity.

While we are, of course, a glorious mongrel of a nation, a pick 'n' mix conjugation of every race and pigmentation under the sun dating back to the first Celtic and Pictish invaders from central Europe, it is also daft to pretend we don't share some common bonds, forged over the centuries.

As the writer Gavin Hills wrote in *The Face* in 1995, what unites us on these islands are 'the simple things', the same things people have wanted for years: 'peace, a right to diversity, fun and freedom'. But, he warned, if we 'don't give a toss about our fellow countrymen, we don't give a toss when hospitals get closed, when gangs rob cabbies, when Nazis bash Pakis, or when the rights of thousands are dismissed as expendable', then we will descend into a 'disparate land of paranoid people'.

I've been thinking about the notion of what it means to be English (or Welsh, or Scottish, or Irish) ever since I saw that pub sign rusting by Archway roundabout, and it's one that won't go away. As Pete Brown mentioned, Orwell's essay 'The Lion and the Unicorn' goes some way to explaining the strange umbilical cord linking pubs and our national identity. In the papers Damon Albarn is discussing his quasi-operatic piece about John Dee, alchemist and consultant to Queen Elizabeth I. Albarn examines the notion of Englishness, and his own mixed feelings on watching the royal wedding in April 2011. 'It was strange... I was moved. I'm not a monarchist. But I'm English. And I have an irrational emotion for my country.'

This, it seems to me, is the same feeling expressed by both Kate Burt and Paul Kingsnorth, among others: a determination that passion for this land and what it stands for shouldn't be mistaken for jingoism or, heaven forbid, some form of veiled, right-wing nostalgia kick.

A few months previously I'd met the journalist and author Iain Aitch on a bitterly cold January evening at a pub in Stratford called the Edward VII. Iain's latest book, *We're British, Innit*, examines the national character via a witty A-Z lexicon of British likes and behaviour ranging from alcopops to the *X Factor*. It's a light-hearted read, featuring the delights of everything from Ovaltine to Readers' Wives, but like all worthwhile endeavours it contains a grain of truth.

A government report into our own identity published in 2005 concluded: 'The French have a clear understanding of their values of liberty, equality and fraternity. America has a strong national perception of itself as "the land of the free". But there is a less clear sense among British citizens of the values that bind groups and communities who make up the body of the British people.'

This panic over the lack of social cohesion eventually resulted in the citizenship test, compulsory for anyone claiming citizenship. Ironically enough, this took on the form of a particularly dry pub quiz, asking questions such as the speed limit on a single carriageway (60 mph), the percentage of Brits who have tried illegal drugs (a third, apparently), and, splendidly the correct etiquette when buying a round in the pub. The absurdity of the whole idea was summed up by the failure of harrumphing *Daily Mail* journalist Dominic Sandbrook to pass, despite being, as he pointedly remarked, a British-born Oxford graduate with a Phd from Cambridge. Which, presumably, makes him more British than you or I.

It's a strange idea, reducing our collective personality to a multiple choice test, and Iain explains it was what inspired him to write the book in the first place.

'It made me think about what it actually means to be English,' he said, settled in the Edward VII's back room. 'We're not good at sticking up for things. St George's Day is probably the least celebrated national day in the world. There's this feeling that "they" don't allow it, when in actual fact we can celebrate it as much as we like if we want. Also, because we're not a Catholic country we don't do festivals well. In fact, we're not really good at happy or cheerful things, aside from music festivals, where we're allowed to get pissed.'

Iain explains that he grew up in Margate and, much like everyone else of his generation, he'd moved away because of college and his career. 'Within three generations, people have become segregated. We've moved further apart geographically. Families don't tend to live in the same areas quite so much these days because they meet people at university or college and end up staying there. My family all used to live close to each other in Kent, and that doesn't happen so much now. In the past people would work close to home and then go to the local pub together, and so there was a real local bond there.'

Have we lost something in the process?

'I think we have. But whenever there's a breakdown or a change in how society works there are advantages and disadvantages. You move somewhere nice, but you lose something else in the process. The way people work has changed too. In the past people would have gone to the pub on the way home. Now you're working in a shop or doing shift work, and so when you go out it will be after you've been home, and then you'll get ready for a big session. Socialising has also changed generally. People don't go out so much now, because television has provided them with home entertainment and the comforts they didn't have before.'

Walking from Stratford Tube station, a swish temple of chrome and glass built to impress visiting dignitaries turning up for the Olympics in 2012, I couldn't help but notice the area's vast cultural mix. Yet even though the pub was jammed to the rafters, there were very few non-white faces.

'In some areas the make-up of the population is changing and it would be daft to suggest otherwise,' says Iain. 'There are a lot of cultural knock-on effects which come with that. Pub culture doesn't necessarily appeal to some communities. Muslims don't drink full stop. So in those areas pubs are going to close because there's no demand. The thing to remember is that as a nation we're very adaptable to change. All the things which we think of as British are pretty much imports from abroad. Tea for instance. We have made it our own. Curries too. In a funny way we adopt these things and they become part of who we are. I think the same thing will happen with the pub. You might have a situation where your pub becomes your library or post office as well.'

We talked for a while longer about the things men do when they're sitting in the pub, and discovered we were both Spurs fans. I recalled how former Spurs striker Martin Chivers had once been landlord of a pub in Broxbourne, and how much fun it had been to go and see him in situ. Nowadays, footballers are shielded from reality by their wealth and fame, and another wire in the mainframe of local connectivity gets lost.

This indifference to our own identity, the distancing between the generations and increasing social divisions is seeing us drift into uncharted social waters. The more segregated we are, the less connected to each other we become. These days the middle classes quaff wine at home or in approved gastropubs while the lower classes buy cheap booze from the supermarket or drink in city centre bars run by large companies (themselves owned by large corporations with governmental connections).

Is it such a huge leap to see the comparison between this and the population of Oceania in *Nineteen Eighty-Four*? Where the Inner and Outer Party enjoy restaurant-standard food and fine wines while the Proles (85 per cent of the population) receive little education, live in poverty and are entertained by meaningless songs written by machines?

Back in London Pub, the ersatz-soul of Aloe Blacc's 'I Need A Dollar' blasts from the speakers. Far from being a penniless bluesman, Blacc was once an intern at megabucks business consultants Ernst & Young, and the song's mantra-like message of self-prioritisation has been an inescapable pub soundtrack as the recession rumbles on.

So, as belts tighten and we naturally become more insular, are we, as Gavin Hills predicted, turning into a 'disparate land of paranoid people'? And has the pub lost its ability to soak up the nation's spirit?

To find out, we must leave the comforts of Strangers Bar and the gleaming corporate offices; bid adieu to Stoke Newington and the smoky snug bars of Memory Lane. Because the pub's glass may be half empty, but it's also half full.

It's time to get down, and out of it.

PART TWO

THE PIER AT THE END OF THE UNIVERSE

Paul Moody

|I|t's a blustery July afternoon on Blackpool seafront and Lee from Macclesfield is in the process of pulverising his latest victim.

Thwack! A full-blooded uppercut sends his opponent reeling. Bam! A neat one-two combination triggers an inhuman noise, not unlike a punch-drunk fruit machine. Splash! A vicious final left hook connects with lightning speed, sending a Bacardi Breezer clattering to the floor, gloopy contents dribbling out onto the linoleum.

I'm in a bar called Brannigans, and Lee's adversary, an electronic boxing machine in a corner alcove, looks well beaten. It's been an unfair fight. He's 5ft 10in, 12 stone, at the point where teenage energy meets adult muscle, and he's still bobbing and weaving, trading with an invisible Ricky Hatton, when I persuade him to join me for a little verbal sparring.

I explain that I'm here looking for the perfect pub and I wonder if he has any thoughts. 'The perfect pub?' he says. 'That's easy. Anywhere with some decent tunes. And cheap drinks. And a few tasty-looking lasses.' Lee, he explains, likes KFC and the Foo Fighters ... and cheap drinks. All of which would sound entirely reasonable if not for one thing: he is also wearing a bright pink Power Rangers outfit.

It's the weekend of the annual Stan James World Matchplay darts tournament at the Winter Gardens and Blackpool's natural inclination for fancy dress appears to have gone to its head. At The Star, a group of men dressed in sombreros and Hawaiian shirts in honour of darts ace Wayne Mardle discuss bad habits with a couple of bruisers decked out as nuns. In The Sun Inn, a man in cloak and fangs in honour of Ted 'The Count' Hankey looks suitably deathly, while through the windows I even spot a group of cowboys going for an Indian.

Everywhere you go, darts mania has taken a grip. At my B&B, the landlord points to a bullet-headed man in a packed TV lounge where everyone is glued to the action. He tells me in a hushed whisper that he's England's number eight Andy Smith, who had been surprisingly knocked out in the first round the previous day. I ask Andy whether he might be up for a chat about pubs. 'Maybe later,' he says, eyes never leaving the screen.

'Blackpool is a big spangling beast of a town,' wrote J.B. Priestley when he visited in 1933, and more than 75 years on the place still screams a particularly shrill kind of hedonism, the result of a 100-year party where the concept of cramming a year's worth of fun into three days provokes suitably deranged results.

Originally a collection of small fishing villages along the Fylde coast, Blackpool's fate as a party destination was sealed by the construction of the Preston and Wyre Railway in 1840, its seaside location making it the perfect excursion for the milltown workers of industrial Lancashire to let off steam. At its peak in the 1930s

Blackpool played host to seven million pleasure seekers a year, a Victorian Las Vegas where visitors would chew on Sally Whatnots while being dazzled by attractions including Sharma Yogi's, the Five-Legged Cow and the Headless Woman, and where seafront 'sheikh machines' told fortunes against a background of T.E. Lawrence and the Sphinx. These days major draws such as the Girl in the Goldfish Bowl and Professor Baldwin's Parachuting Cat are, sadly, long gone, but the feel of a frontier town where the forces of work and responsibility have been roundly defeated remains.

Hen parties prowl the Golden Mile or lark about on the Pleasure Beach, and the seafront shops are defiant in their daftness; places where plastic comedy breasts are sold alongside replica firearms next to penis-shaped shot glasses labelled 'Spit' or 'Swallow'. The amusement arcades, too, come with an aggressive sense of fun. Crop-headed kids strapped into hi-tech star fighters, scythe the heads off alien warlords at deafening volume, and the regular clatter of the Penny Falls comes almost as a soothing balm amid the relentless thrum of mortal combat.

By night, however, Blackpool becomes plain camp. Drag queens mingle with the assembled devils, angels, cowgirls and escapees from St Trinian's and tassles still rotate at risqué cabaret club Funny Girls, where stag parties, old married couples and groups of lads sing along to acts lip-synching to show-tune chestnuts like 'Hey Big Spender'.

The town's singular appeal is probably best summed up by The Macc Ladds in their song 'Blackpool'. A tale of an impromptu trip down the M6 involving puking, picking up nubile hitchhikers and throwing cans out of the car window.

Sitting in The Ramsden Arms, Ian Ward confesses he doesn't know the song but acknowledges it's a pretty accurate description of the city's rough 'n' ready reputation. A local resident for 22 years who works in the town's planning department, he's also chairman of the Blackpool branch of CAMRA.

'It's always been a kiss me quick kind of town, and that even extends to what it looks like,' he says. 'The town made its reputation as a place which developed very fast, and it's still got that build it fast, knock it down even quicker ethos. With some very notable exceptions, such as the Winter Gardens, the Tower, the Grand Theatre and the piers, there are no buildings on the grand civic scale. Architecturally, the pubs are nothing to write home about. For instance, this pub, The Ramsden Arms is in the Tudorbethan style, with some impressive-looking chimneys, and in a Blackpool context it looks fairly remarkable. But if you transported it into Chester, you wouldn't give it a second glance. There's certainly no showcase pubs to rival The Philharmonic or The Vines in Liverpool.'

We talk about the city's history, and how the Promenade once thronged with visitors thirsty for the local ale. It all seems a far cry from today, despite the fancy dress convention for the darts.

'It's hard to imagine, isn't it?' he says. 'Back in those days the most famous local brewery was Catterall and Swarbrick, or C&S. From all accounts, the quality wasn't always reliable. Its local nickname was Come and Suffer because often it was very good but it could also be pretty ropey.'

Once, the powerhouses of northern brewing such as Boddingtons and Higsons would have met the demands of thirsty milltown workers, but all is not lost. Recent years have seen a resurgence in local brewing. 'We've got three local microbreweries within the branch area,' says Ian with a hint of pride. 'The Lytham Brewery, the Hart Brewery in Little Eccleston and Fuzzy Duck who are in Poulton, just outside Blackpool. They're microbreweries, but you can find Hart's beers in London. And Lytham have just got themselves a deal with one of the supermarket groups up here, which is great news.'

Despite the recession, Ian explains, CAMRA-approved pubs are managing to survive, much as they are in Newcastle. 'Pubs are feeling the pinch across the board, but the pubs that we support, places like The Saddle Inn or The Shovels out at Marton, The Lane's End Hotel and The Taps in Lytham are doing well because of the quality of the real ale they provide. They know their market and are confident that if they offer a quality product it helps them keep going. We cover a big area, from Fleetwood in the north to Lytham in the south and right over to the M6 in the east, and the message is the same: if a pub serves quality real ale it will attract a core of regulars who will keep the pub in business.'

From what I've seen of it, though, I suggest that the city centre isn't looking so promising. 'Well, the famous Yates' Wine Lodge burned down after an arson attack a couple of years ago, so that was a big loss,' Ian says. 'It's just a big hole in the ground now. But there are much bigger problems. I've been here for twenty-two years and the town centre has changed a lot. It now has a lot of licensed bars and nightclubs and the result is that it's gone seriously downmarket. They've sought to attract younger drinkers through cheap drinks promotions, which to an extent is a response to the downturn in visitor numbers. But that has always seemed to me like a very short-sighted move. Because if you go down-market, suddenly your market share becomes relatively small, so it only takes a minor downturn for your profits to suddenly start turning into a loss. Most of the pubs we promote are no longer in Blackpool town centre, it's pretty much a beer desert now in terms of quality ale. There's loads of nitro-fizz and rubbish, but if you want to drink a quality product you're struggling.'

But on a more positive note, he explains there are already plans afoot to reverse the trend. 'I get the impression that the council are keen to improve the town's image,' he says. 'The problems relating to vertical drinking venues have become political as much as anything else. The council is determined to bring back the idea that Blackpool is family friendly, and part of doing that is tightening up the licensing. So that if anyone opens up a bar they are under enormous pressure to provide a quality service. We all know it's a cheap and cheerful kind of place, but locally there's a recognition if it's going to be successful it has to get away from the cheap, tatty reputation it's got.'

Ian explains that one positive development is that Wetherspoon's have planned to take over a building on the Promenade close to Blackpool Tower. 'A lot of the town centre licensees are moaning like hell about Wetherspoon's,' he says. 'It's probably because they recognise it is real competition. It's not more of the same, and it will provide the seafront with a family friendly venue. They're claiming it will be dirt cheap with drunks falling out of there day and night, but I can't see that myself.'

Ian recounts how, 20 years ago, CAMRA's annual Christmas pub crawl would take in the pubs along Talbot Road, stopping off at The Wheatsheaf, The Kings Arms, The Ramsden and the New Road Inn. Only the latter two remain and The New Inn has seen better days. But, as Ian explains, Blackpool's role as the nation's party host means that it has never been averse to the occasional nip 'n' tuck to keep up appearances.

'Blackpool has never been the kind of place where traditional pubs like the one Orwell describes in "The Moon Under Water" ever thrived,' he says. 'By that I mean male-dominated, smoky places which don't do food. That notion doesn't really exist here. Maybe in Lytham there were once a few like that. There certainly hasn't been any pubs in Blackpool like that for thirty years. That's because it's always had to cater for both the residents and the visitors. Places have to diversify. There's an interesting pub in St Annes in an old Lloyds bank vault called Number Fifteen which is a very good example. The pubs which are prospering are the ones that adapted, and that provide good quality food at a reasonable price.'

I ask Ian what he thinks makes a great pub. 'It's all about the right pub for the right place,' he says. 'I think the ingredients Orwell talks about can make a great pub, but that pub has to be in the right location. It's also not about what you do but the way you do it. There's a great pub called Number 4 in Blackpool, a mile from where I live. It's a Thwaites pub, and it only serves real ale, and the beer is always in tip-top condition. It's got two rooms, and the couple who run it have insisted to the brewery that it be smart and they offer good pub grub, not fancy restaurant-type meals. Before they arrived Thwaites gave it a really plush makeover but it put the locals off, they weren't comfortable settling in there for a session. So they made it less showy, altered the menu to honest pub fare, and installed Sky Sports for big events. Now they've got the right mix for the location they're in. The same couple used to run The Pump and Truncheon which is just behind the Golden Mile. They insisted on good quality beers and refused to charge over the odds. You have to tailor the product to where it is. The key is realising that one size does not fit all. It's basic marketing at the end of the day.'

Like many other people we've spoken to, Ian places a lot of the pubs' problems on the one-size-fits-all policy pursued by the major pub companies. 'The pub companies have killed the goose that laid the golden egg,' he says. 'The big change came with the 1989 Beer Orders when breweries stopped owning the buildings that their product was being sold in. When the pub moved into the hands of property management companies rather than being pub owned by a brewery, the interest was severed, which is a huge shame. Rather than the pub being the showcase for the breweries' product, the people who own them now simply see them as a property investment. It was only very late in the day, two or three years ago, that central government recognised that pubs have always been a focal point for communities. Not so long ago there was something called Planning Policy Statement Number 4 regarding pubs which established that pubs are a place of value and should be protected in some way. It was to do with villages which have lost their pubs, but you could just as easily apply it to towns. They're losing their identity.'

On the seafront, a gale force wind whips in from the Irish Sea, sending spumes of foam crashing against the barnacled legs of the South Pier where waltzers, reverse bungee and white knuckle rides like the Skyscreamer cater for adrenaline junkies. On the pier, a pub called The Laughing Donkey offers cheap pints for the parents and sweets and ice creams for the kids, and the queue at the ticket office suggests that local comedian Joey Blower should have a full house for his performance tonight at the Merrie England Bar.

Not that it feels particularly merry. It's getting dark, and stag parties prowl the amusement arcades, killing the hours before the alcoholic onslaught begins. Behind a beaded curtain, Gypsy Petrulengo lures in customers with signed photos of George Michael, Madonna and, erm, Little and Large; tales from the tea leaves told for three pounds a pop. 'That were crap!' splutters one disgruntled punter as I pass, clearly not pleased with the family's fortunes.

As I move north, things get worse. Outside a sex shop I see a young baby in a pram abandoned in the doorway. As I approach The Crazy Scots Bar, there's a noticeable dip in temperature. 'Prick!' shouts a bloke in a Rangers shirt sitting outside as I walk in. He can only mean me, and his mates laugh with the sadistic pleasure that comes with someone eyeing their next victim. Nerves jangling, I slip out of a side exit and make my way back towards the centre of town.

I'm oddly pleased, then, when I arrive at Thors, a Viking-themed chippy near Blackpool Tower where chips come served in a bucket with a spade. I decide to take away and watch a few miserable-looking youths glumly riding on one of the city's oldest rides, Sir Hiram Maxim's Captive Flying Machine, dating to 1904. It's a tame affair, and it's sedate rattle 'n' hum seems wholly out of sorts with the brutal electro-slaughter going on across the road in the arcades. It seems like a metaphor for the way we approach our nightlife, too, and how the pub has been eclipsed by bar culture, younger drinkers seduced by the idea of more frenzied thrills. We now want our rides to go faster, the thrills higher, the impact harder. But what happens when you can't go any faster? You go spinning off the edge, pulped like matchwood as you crash blindly into the waves below.

In search of shelter from the wind, I head for a pub called Churchills on Topping Street. A traditional coaching inn, it's a Blackpool institution where a sign outside reads 'the Friendliest Little Pub in Blackpool' and, Blu-Tacked to the window, 'Tuesday – Boozy Bingo'.

At the bar a man with a milky eye and hair like windswept candy floss strikes up a conversation. 'In a good pub your feet should stick to the floor and your eyes should be glued to the barmaid,' he says, and we start chatting about the pubs in the area. He's called Stan and he tells me he can remember when the city centre pubs would be heaving, the smoke so thick you could slice it. 'All the manual labourers used to knock off on Thursday, and it would be packed by lunchtime.' He grins. 'You could drink ten pints then and still be able to walk home because the beer was a lot weaker then.'

The way Stan sees it, the pub's demise started long ago, in a blaze of flashing lights. 'It was the introduction of the breathalyser tests that really fucked it,' he says. 'Before that people would take the chance, but that killed the village pubs off round here. And town is all about the young 'uns now.'

He's on crutches, the result of a nasty fall the previous week, and tells me that apart from Churchills, he rarely stays for longer than one pint in any pub these days. 'The atmosphere's not the same,' he says. 'If you hang around on your own for too long you draw attention to yourself. So I like to keep moving.'

I tell him about Ian's concerns about the pub companies but he gives a heard-it-all-before shrug. 'Watneys tried the same thing in the seventies,' he says. 'It's still the same bastards up to their old tricks. They don't care about the working man.'

It feels like the sort of exchange Orwell might have had while researching *The Road to Wigan Pier*, but, mercifully, there's no time for socio-political analysis, as a man in a grey herringbone jacket takes to the stage, coughs into a microphone and says: 'Blackpool. We don't have much fun, but we have a laugh.' In the absence of local legend Frankie Whittle, the weekly karaoke is being hosted by a middle-aged man called John who has the camp air of Larry Grayson and a quip for every occasion. 'We're here until we shut,' he says, explaining that those willing to brave the ridicule should log in their requests on the machine on stage. 'If anyone wants to give us one, come up here,' he says, gesturing to the karaoke apparatus. 'I'll shove it in no problem.'

It's a typical Blackpool crowd. In one corner, a group of young lads dressed identically in black suits and white leather ties nurse pints of Carlsberg, while a muscular six-foot prop forward totters to the bar in a pair of blood-red six-inch high heels, fishnet tights and a tight leather skirt. John's eye, however, is drawn to a man in the front row dressed as a policewoman. 'Fuck me, it's Juliet Bravo!' he bellows to raucous cheers. 'Show us your truncheon, love. Don't worry about the handcuffs, I'll supply those.'

A group of hens in their thirties in matching pink cowboy hats urge one of their number to get up and sing her favourite song: Tori Amos' 'Happy Phantom'. She's tired and emotional, and as she totters back to her chair afterwards she almost falls over, sending a tsunami of vodka tonic across the table, revealing an eyeful of pink flesh and elastic as she falls.

'You know what I really want?' she says, pulling up a stool next to me. She's so close I can smell her breath: white wine and apricots. 'I want to lie on a piano in a red dress and sing "Fever" like Michelle Pfeiffer in *The Fabulous Baker Boys*. That's my dream.'

Laughing along to the good-humoured ribbing are a ten-strong stag party from Devizes sitting in the back booth. They're in their mid-thirties, and enjoying the freak show nature of it all as much as anyone. 'People said we should go to Krakow or Prague for the stag but that's bollocks compared to this,' grins a bloke addressed by everyone as Sarge. 'What are you gonna do? Spend a fortune and then talk pidgin English for three days? It's daft. My old man came up here for his stag do and we thought, why not. It's been a great laugh. And the girls are up for it, too.'

He says this in a way which suggests the girls in Devizes usually aren't. One of the lads goes up to perform a version of Razorlight's 'America'. It's dreadful, and Sarge and his mates can barely conceal their glee at the feeble smattering of applause. 'A little clap goes a long way,' says John. 'And I should know.'

In one last bid to see what makes Blackpool tick I head back down to the seafront. The daytime crowds have scattered now, and there's a vague menace in the sea air.

To get myself in the mood for the trip I'd been reading the memoirs of a character called Steve Sinclair called *Blackpool Rock: Guns, Gangs and Door Wars in Britain's Wildest Town*. A legendary figure in the city's nightlife, or at least that's what the promotional blurb said, I'd hoped that his tales of life behind the thin red rope might encourage me to plunge head first into the town's fleshpots and give myself up to the mysteries of the local nightlife. However, after 200 pages of split noses, broken bones, bungled bank jobs and enough Charlie to open a chocolate factory I'd reached the point where I never wanted to see another black suit or a plastic headset ever again.

In Brannigans, Binge Britain is in full swing. By the bar, I negotiate a couple of burly specimens who would have had Charles Darwin reaching for the Tipp-Ex and discover it is Happy Hour Thursday, meaning that shots can be bought at half price. I didn't realise earlier, but it's a vast shed of a place, the dancefloor area which was swathed in darkness earlier now a neon-lit heaving mass of bodies. In one corner a group of lads attempt an inebriated version of the haka, which seems a bit excessive for 9.30 p.m.

A group of girls gathered next to a separate bar called The Shooter Shack order double shots to add a splash of colour to the grey day outside. A group of lads from Tranmere come over to talk to them but they're not interested. One of them, called Emma, tells me her boyfriend is in Afghanistan. 'All these places and missions,' she says above the din. 'Wishtan, The Panther's Claw. It's just old men playing war games, using young lads to do the fighting.' A-ha's 'Take On Me' pounds from the speakers. 'I just want him back here, home with me.'

Wary of the lads doing the haka and the disgruntled Tranmere contingent, I head over the road to The Soul Suite where a chap calling himself Lionel Vinyl is whipping the crowd of assembled stags and hens into a frenzy. Wearing an afro wig and leopard-skin suit, his spiel is pitched somewhere between Barry White and Lenny Henry's Theophilus P. Wildebeeste, not so much cheesy as deep-fried gorgonzola.

'All you guys, you don't have to dress as good as me,' he booms over Sister Sledge's 'Lost In Music'. 'All you need is a pair of white socks.' I later find out he DJ-ed at Wayne Rooney's wedding, but it's lost on me.

At the bar I bump into Lee. I don't recognise him at first – he's been back to the hotel and changed into a shirt and trousers combo which, he explains with a grin, will secure him entry to places even his Power Rangers outfit couldn't. 'You're hanging with the Teenage Lords of Chaos!' he says, and tells me my luck could be in. He's already 'snogged the face off two birds' tonight and spent an enjoyable afternoon in Madame Tussauds, lured in by the life-size model of Del Boy's canary-yellow Robin Reliant outside. Lee shows me a photo of him in an eye-watering embrace with a waxwork of David Beckham. 'Take that, Goldenballs!' he beams, pupils dilated to the size of black saucers.

His mate Sully, however, seems less enthusiastic at my presence. I try to ask him some questions about why he likes bars more than pubs and he gives me an interrogated look which suggests he's seconds away from demanding a phone call to his lawyer. 'Are you paparazzi or pepperoni?' he says, words slurry and full of menace, and suddenly I feel very alone, a ghost or a ghoul, cramping up the dancefloor while Lionel puts the audience through its paces to 'Kung Fu Fighting'. It's time to leave before Sully sees it as a cue to try out the moves I'd seen him practising in Brannigans.

Back at the B&B, I try to make some sense of the last few hours. Rain drums on the windows and downstairs in the TV lounge late night coverage of the darts continues; the steady chinking of glasses suggests the party might just go on for ever. To drown out the noise I watch a trashy TV movie called, ironically enough, *The Party Never Stops: Diary of a Binge Drinker*. 'We had fun, we had a blast. We were on our own, and it felt like a dream. Not too fat, or too thin. For once we belonged,' goes the opening monologue.

The single bed feels like a trampoline and as the low rumble of approval for each dart builds into boozy audiowaves, I feel almost seasick. In a restless state my mind returns to *Nineteen Eighty-Four*, where orthodoxy is described as 'not needing to think... orthodoxy is unconsciousness'. Has Samuel Johnson's 'oblivion of care' been traded for oblivion itself?

Downstairs, a dart hits the bulls-eye and a cheer goes up.

Blackpool: they don't have much fun but they have a laugh.

CARDIFF AFTERLIFE

Robin Turner

'The place is a total time warp. Inside it's for ever 1975. The Brains beers are cheap, the toilets are outside in the rain and the bikers come down to drink every Saturday lunchtime. It's full of Cardiff history. It reflects the working-class maritime history of the city – the lives of people who worked on the docks before the city's regeneration – and it does so in a way you wouldn't ever see outside of a museum.' Cardiff-based writer John Williams is sat in a bar in London deep in thought about The Vulcan Hotel, a South Wales establishment that we'd each grown to love like a dear friend despite its fairly obvious faults. One of Brains' city centre pubs, The Vulcan had been on some public house death row or other for the last few years. Under threat from development - either from expansion of the university or from the supposed need for another overspill car park for the newly built John Lewis store - The Vulcan was a beleaguered boozer living on its knees on borrowed time. Local Liberal Democrat councillors had made the biggest noise in favour of saving the pub back when they had time on their hands before the manacles of government dragged them down.

'You could easily miss somewhere like The Vulcan,' continues John. 'It's a proper spit-and-sawdust pub. When you step inside, you see the details, the things that fill the room… there's bits of brass, nautical things… a dartboard with sawdust on the floor. But really they're all superfluous. What really makes a pub is the people behind the bar and the people in front of it. Take them out and it's just a room with some ornaments in it.'

John has been chronicling working-class life in South Wales in print for years, penning books like *Cardiff Dead* and *Five Pubs, Two Bars and a Nightclub*. He has also been drinking in The Vulcan for half a lifetime; organising informal drink-ups for the Welsh literary set at the pub for more than a decade ('We just drink beer and talk nonsense,' he modestly puts it). When the pub first faced closure, Williams and his fellow writers started to make a noise about the proposed fate of the 'sanctuary of ordinariness' – a perfect summation of this most functional of pubs. Looking across the bar as the typical Thursday night Soho rituals begin (mates pumping coins into the jukebox, blind dates eyeing each other for the first time), we sup average lager and contemplate the as-then-unknown fate of a spit-and-sawdust boozer 150-odd miles away. I ask John if he thinks pubs took on some kind of spiritual significance back in the Land of our Fathers.

'Well, I grew up in a village without a pub and my father is definitely not a pub man so I didn't experience the traditional view of the Welsh and their drinking habits as a youngster. Rather the reverse. But, I do see similar aspects to the local chapel and a pub like The Vulcan. I think that's a fair comparison. It's certainly been a place of refuge for the last survivors of a near vanished community.'

* * *

Alighting at Cardiff station, it is immediately obvious that the city is undergoing a monumental developmental growth spurt. Although I grew up within staggering distance of the capital and spent countless afternoons mooching around the shops and arcades, I hardly recognise the place. The 21st century had forcefully imposed itself – and not without some success. Cars sit bumper to bumper waiting for available parking space in the newly constructed John Lewis. Jamie Oliver and Antonio Carluccio offer rival visions of rustic Italian cooking, duking it out from opposite sides of the newly pedestrianised Hayes shopping centre. A very Welsh form of café culture prevails. Here on a bright but biting spring day spotting with sleety rain, men and women sit outside in shirtsleeves sucking cigarettes down to the stubs as if their very lives depend on it.

One fundamental change to the heart of the city has been the relocation of the Brains Brewery. Now a stone's throw away to the south of the centre, its cloying hoppy fug is a woozy, scented memory for an older generation. The resultant hole has been quickly rebranded as the Old Brewery Quarter, though – quaint name aside – the current tenants are the kind of ultra-slick operations seen on McHigh Streets all over the country. Snuck in besides the identikit branches of Hard Rock Café, Starbucks and Nando's is Brains' vision of 21st-century vertical drinking: The Yard Bar and Kitchen. A vision in marble and polished steel, after just a handful of years pulling pints the Brains website already refers to The Yard as an 'iconic Cardiff pub'. In an age of surgically enhanced celebrities filling glossy magazines week in week out, maybe they've got something of a point. It's ironic though that just five minutes around the corner lies The Vulcan Hotel, recently reprieved from demolition after concerted effort from a disparate bunch of locals determined to save one of the city centre's genuinely iconic boozers.

The Vulcan was first opened in 1853 to provide liquid refreshment for thirsty local dockworkers. Back then, Cardiff was a thriving port, the point where the only desirable export that the Valleys could muster up was hauled out to sea. While fashion might have dictated the colour of the walls from one decade to the next, the majority of The Vulcan's features – inside and out – remain reassuringly unchanged by the passing of time.

What has changed is the building's immediate surroundings. Approaching from the station, pretty quickly you can picture the plethora of development meetings that must have featured the pub on the agenda over the last decade. ('And now on to Point 15. The Vulcan. When the fuck can we knock this place down?') It stands there on its own, opposite a gleaming new university outbuilding, lonely on the edge of a car park overlooking Cardiff's restless post-millennial redevelopment. Up the road, another construction of The Vulcan's heritage looms – the local prison. The two buildings conjure up visions of another time, one that's all but been erased from history in town centres the country over. And in an expanding capital city like Cardiff, it's easy to see how pubs like The Vulcan perfectly represent bygone times – dusty, smoky and – without a DJ relentlessly forcing your mood – possibly too simple a prospect in the information age. But, as John Williams pointed out, it's not necessarily the bricks and mortar and added trappings that make the pub – it's the people inside that count.

In 2008, I wrote about The Vulcan in *The Rough Pub Guide*, saying it 'should be protected as a listed building. Without somewhere like this existing for future generations, people will think the only places we boozed in were Irish theme bars. At the end of the day, this really just comes down to a question of whether commerce is more important than local heritage.' Thankfully, in the time since, a group of determined people rallying under the Save the Vulcan banner delivered the pub a temporary stay of execution following concerted protest that corralled media and politicians on both a local and national level.

Coming in from the drizzle, I join campaigners Rachel Thomas and Chris Latham in the front bar to ask a simple question. In an age where we lose 40-odd pubs a week, why here?

'It's one of the last remaining pubs in Cardiff from this era,' says Rachel. 'It teems with character. I first visited the pub back in 2007 with my dad. As soon as I walked through the door, I was in love. I was in love with the pub's charm and character, as well as the friendly welcome we received from both staff and punters. That night, we got chatting to the landlady (then, Liz Smart) who told us the pub was to be demolished to make way for a multi-storey car park. It was at that moment I knew we had to act.'

Chris's experience was similarly wide-eyed. 'I was a post-graduate student at Glamorgan University's Atrium build-ing which is directly across from the pub. I loved the contrast; this little old pub that still has outside toilets nestled in among high-rise flats, modern, bland buildings and busy roads. So much of Cardiff has become uniform and boring and it seemed a real shame that this lovely old place, which appeared to be doing great business, was going to be knocked down and replaced with more of the same.'

Rachel's determination to get involved saw her utilise thor-oughly modern means to raise awareness about The Vulcan's plight. 'I searched Facebook for groups or pages about the pub. I was delighted to find that clearly there were very strong feel-ings about the pub although the groups I found didn't seem to be particularly active. I put a call out asking if anyone would like to help save it. From there, the campaign was born. We got together soon after and worked out a plan. The campaign included a peti-tion which collected over 5,000 signatures, a public meeting with over 100 attendees, celebrity endorsement and so on.'

Over the course of the campaign, the pub received supportive visits from Welsh Assembly Heritage Minister Alun Ffred Jones, Radio 2's Jeremy Vine, Velvet Underground founding member John Cale and the still fresh-faced, pre-front, bench Nick Clegg, alongside letters of allegiance from the likes of Neil and Glenys Kinnock and BBC sports commentator John Inverdale. All the while, the brewery that owned the site maintained a non-committal silence.

'Brains were relatively quiet throughout the campaign,' Rachel recalls. 'When Liz announced she was leaving Brains were very slow to reassure us that they would replace her. Liz was a well-loved character in The Vulcan and became something of an institution here. Liz worked very hard to ensure that all customers were welcome and judging by the number of people who attended her leaving do, she'll most certainly be missed. Brains eventually announced that new managers would be brought in after the real threat of direct action. We'd planned a march through Cardiff city centre and a rally at the new brewery. It was an enormous relief. I now think that Brains do truly understand the strength of feeling for the pub and I believe that they will act carefully to ensure the pub continues to thrive into the future.'

'I think it represents a triumph for all those people who are bored by the way Cardiff, and – let's face it – most towns and cities are losing their character,' adds Chris. 'Everywhere is becoming bland and soulless. The Vulcan also represents an old piece of Cardiff which is now largely forgotten and for this reason alone something should be done to protect it permanently.'

The three-year reprieve runs out in the Olympic summer of 2012. Although Brains own the pub, Derek Rapport, a local developer, owns the land that it stands on and has previously wanted to build retail units and apartments there. One stroll around the immediate vicinity where empty shops nuzzle up to glistening new constructions yet to open and it's obvious that retail units are the very thing Cardiff doesn't need any more of.

'It's likely that developer Derek Rapport will apply for planning permission to develop the site,' says Rachel cautiously. 'I sincerely hope that he'll take account of the strong feeling for the pub and think creatively about the site. There's no reason why the area around the pub can't be developed, leaving the pub alone. If this does occur in summer 2012, I have no doubt that everyone who has been involved in the campaign thus far will mobilise to object to planning applications that would see the pub demolished. Cardiff is rapidly becoming dominated by glass-fronted, laminate-floored chain pubs. There's nothing wrong with these places in principle but the pub industry must work alongside the council to ensure that our historic buildings are preserved. I personally want Cardiff to retain its character and not look like any other city in the UK. There are plenty of examples where the new and the old can work together, so The Vulcan must be protected.'

Finishing his pint while looking around the front bar, Chris sums up local feeling. 'This place is a Narnia-like gateway to a piece of Cardiff's history that's in danger of being forgotten.'

Later on that evening I'm joined by another regular visitor to the pub's snug room. James Dean Bradfield – singer and guitarist with Wales's most successful rock 'n' roll band, the critically lauded Manic Street Preachers – has been a patron of the pub for over a decade. Spending time working between London and Cardiff, it became somewhere for him to kick back anonymously in downtime; be it during post Six Nations piss-ups in the front bar or whiling away hours basking in the glow of the back room's jukebox. Having grown up in nearby Blackwood, the perfect half-light of the pub – seemingly still shot through with cigarette smoke years after 2007's smoking ban – reminded him of those intriguing closed-door venues that lined the roads of the Valleys.

'My mum always drank in a place called The Plough in Pontllanfraith, it was where her darts team met. She was the captain and secretary of the team. I'd have to run errands up there, take the accounts for the team and things like that. I'd run in and out, I'd only ever take a very quick glance. It was really simple in there, very basic, nothing spectacular at all. I was a bit disappointed to be honest. In the years since, I've come to understand that was what made it special. There was one section of the pub that only people in the team went to, that was their safe haven, their club house. I suppose when you're a kid and you don't know what something is, you want it to be like opening up the suitcase in *Pulp Fiction* – just an unearthly glow, something utterly amazing inside. And it wasn't, it was what you make it. She made it about her darts team and those social aspects. She was intensely loyal to it.'

Although Bradfield's first proper home away from Blackwood was in London, the band always used Cardiff as a base of operations. Much needed post-studio relaxation meant finding a decent boozer was an inevitable necessity.

'My first local down here was The Vulcan. I've had a really long relationship with the place over the years as – weirdly – I used to get taken here as a kid on [rugby] international days. Even though it was always a bit out of my way, I started going back here again a few years ago. I liked the fact that it was a bit off the main drag. It's worth the effort you have to make to go there. The nearest pub to where you live or work isn't always the right one, in fact most of the time it's the complete opposite. The Vulcan is isolated. It's appalling that they keep threatening to knock it down. It's a perfect example of an old-fashioned Welsh pub, beautifully tiled outside, very basic inside. These places have to be preserved for future generations, they're a reflection of the times they've survived through.'

It was Bradfield who first took me to the pub, the night before Wales's Grand Slam victory against France in 2008 after I'd interviewed his band at their rehearsal room. By five in the afternoon, the pub was packed with visiting French fans, each so hammered they'd reverted to their native tongue. Liz – the manageress back then and very much the kind to call you 'dear' irrespective of age or sex – was working up a wince-worthy bar bill by buying every other round for drinkers. The atmosphere was toasty and convivial with none of the tensions you'd imagine in a similar situation prior to a football match. Here was *liberté, égalité, fraternité* – Taff style. We sat for a couple of hours in the back room drinking and plugging coins into the jukebox, nervous as hell about the following day's match while all around us, a fantastic pissed-up chaos unfolded. James fondly recalls the spirit of that evening.

'One of the things I have always loved about The Vulcan is

that there's no division; there's no set rules for who can use the pub. I like the idea of there being no dominant tribe in a pub. A great example was the day before the Wales–France Grand Slam match. The place was full of French pissheads, all of them making a pilgrimage to the pub. It's where they'd drunk every other year, ever since they'd been coming to Wales for matches. The local boys were joining in singing with them, taking photos, playing a very pissed game of darts. There's real warmth in there. It's also really important that the person who runs the establishment will not take any kind of shit from people. Once you've crossed the threshold of the pub, you have to abide by the landlord's rules. If you don't, get out. I like the idea of there being rules in places, of a certain kind of order. It's not something you see so much now, but when I was growing up, I used to see it every single night. I think it's been drummed into me to a certain extent, the idea of living by the pub's rules.'

As someone who grew up in the seventies, Bradfield's lasting vision of the perfect pub is definitely one thick with smoke, ringing with bellowing laughter. 'People used to smoke and drink in pubs and egg each other on to tell ever more fantastical stories. People used to be able to eulogise, there was a certain kind of barroom oration about life, or at least life as they saw it. Localised, colloquial versions of Bukowski's *Barfly*. People would knit tales of the incredible deeds that they had done, or at least would profess to have done. The perfect pub for me would definitely be a little like climbing to the top of the Eiger. There would be a permanent mist like you're there at the top of the world. All made up from cigarette smoke. It's that kind of shimmer you don't see any more. It's good to think that when you walk in off the street, that you are leaving one world behind and you're making up another world inside the pub. I genuinely believe that smoking encourages people to make up so much crap in a pub. I'm not sure what the actual stimulant is that makes people talk bollocks, but I do really think it was something that made an evening in a pub more entertaining. The Vulcan has always had that ambience. The back room is somewhere with a real stillness. That would be my perfect city pub.'

Having lived between London and Cardiff for the best part of a decade, Bradfield has noticed the gradual creep of refurbishment all over the Smoke. Although it hadn't yet taken hold completely in Cardiff, places like The Yard – alongside the perpetual threat to The Vulcan – are symbolic of the 21st century's perception of how a pub should be.

'It's hard to see pubs as we know them existing for much longer because everything is so much geared towards reinvention, making things more healthy. From the food served to the smoking ban, pricing certain elements out of certain pubs. It's like the hypocrisy of banning smoking and now heavily taxing beer in pubs but not putting any kind of taxation on things like foie gras or cheeses. Most cheeses are deeply unhealthy for you, really rich foods aren't targeted like cigarettes because they are luxury goods, they are part of an aspirational lifestyle that you're sold in Sunday supplements. They give you the chance to be the perfect bon viveur. Pubs now have become the acceptable face of intellectual gourmet-ism. That's what it's becoming. You haven't got the freedom to be decadent in the working-class sense any more, you have to be decadent in the acceptable sense.'

Settling in for a final pint as the theme from *The Rockford Files* eases out of the jukebox, we muse over what would constitute the perfect pub. 'For me, firstly, it would have to have a good "team". Pub quiz, snooker, darts, whatever. It's got to be the kind of place where if someone is sitting too close to the dartboard, they have to be subservient to the players and respectful of the game. A good darts team usually means a good pub, in a social sense, in a community sense. A great jukebox can make a pub really special. Although I like a pub to be quite raucous and loud, I also think there should be somewhere where there's a certain stillness. A division between a boisterous public bar and a quiet snug. Somewhere you can just sit and read the paper.'

In fact, somewhere pretty much like the room we are sat

in. With my train due, I make my excuses and prepare to leave Bradfield and The Vulcan behind. With a firm handshake, he makes a final point.

'I think what gets lost so often is simplicity. Somewhere like The Vulcan, there really isn't that much to do here. You either drink or you play darts or you talk and that's enough. You don't need a DJ everywhere or an open kitchen where some miserable chef who thinks he's Gordon Ramsay is barking orders at people. I hate the fact that people come to places and say, "This place must change!" Why? Why does it have to conform to everywhere else? Why does everywhere have to be hauled into the modern era in the name of progress? My heart always sinks slightly when I hear about some-where that I've found solace in – a truly great pub – that's been taken over and is about to be spruced up. So many of my favourite locals over the years are now thin approximations of what they once were. And half the time, they're struggling to get customers in as they've lost all the spirit of what made them great. Progress would change everything that I love about somewhere like The Vulcan, somewhere that seems to seep history through the very walls. And that really is something that needs to be preserved.'

As the train pulls out of the station, I look out the left window to catch a final glimpse of The Vulcan in the fading light. It is a view that puts the pub and its fight for survival into sharp relief. There, totally alone, it stands ready, welcoming and still proud after a succession of potentially debilitating knocks. To all intents, it has become something of an alcoholic museum piece – a public house preserved to show future generations that it wasn't all O'Neill's this and Wetherspoon's that.

Interlude:
The Cider House Rules

Robin Turner

I'd heard talk of the Wilkins Cider Farm
for years. Friends from the West Country
would go all dewy-eyed over the place
whenever the name was mentioned. It
has obtained a properly legendary status for pretty much everyone
who managed to drag a designated driver along to ferry them in
and out. Wilkins is renowned for several very good reasons. It was
the place that sold halves of cider for pennies not pounds. It only
ever shuts on a Sunday morning (for two hours). They operate an
honour system that everyone adheres to. And it was the place that
Joe Strummer used to sit back and daydream for hours and hours
during the last few years of his life.

My first experience of Wilkins cider was at a very muddy
Glastonbury in 1997. Trudging down an country lane in pouring
rain towards the festival entrance gate I was accosted by cider sell-
ers. After buying a flagon of something local, I downed half of it
while walking onto site before a guy from the Wilkins farm stopped
me and proudly told me his cider was better than the swill I was
drinking. I lobbed the second-rate scrumpy into the hedge, bought
his murky brew and carried on towards the festival. By the time I
tried to negotiate entry, I was tripping – properly tripping, seeing
things, giggling, out of my mind. The cider effect lasted long enough
for me to watch an entire set by The Chemical Brothers facing away
from the stage. By the time I came to some hours later, I couldn't
find the cider seller again. Like an apple-cheeked Keyser Soze, he
was gone. Of course he was – it was still absolutely pelting down.

For years afterwards, I planned to head to the farm itself to stock up before the festival but time and weather always seemed to conspire against the plan. That yearly nag dissipated, eventually becoming a once in a blue moon fantasy until a chance visit to Glastonbury town hostelry The Riflemans Arms in the autumn. Prior to a bracing walk to the top of the Tor, a pint or two of fuel seemed in order (note to self – this was a terrible idea). A request for a pint of Wilkins cider was met with raised eyebrows. 'You want the rough stuff?' the landlord asked, a knowing smile creeping across his face. I can't remember a thing about the walk up but the roll back down the hill was hilarious. With that, the trip to the farm was planned for the following afternoon.

Less a pub, more a countryside working men's club and homebrew centre, the Wilkins Cider Farm is the kind of place a metropolitan drinker like myself can only fantasise about. A breeze-block outhouse in the heart of Somerset, the building is actually a converted barn that now holds a makeshift social that acts as a boozy magnet for locals and tourists alike. Somewhere between a traditional snug and a backdrop to an episode of *Countryfile*, the cider farm's whitewashed antechamber is a clutter of weathered reading material (yellowing copies of the *Daily Sport* mainly) and single shoes left by leathered visitors. The day we turn up, two Mancunians – Jimmy and Bob – have driven from the north to spend the whole weekend at the farm drinking nothing but the local laughing water. 'We came here for my stag night,' Jimmy wistfully recalls through a haze of fermented fruit juice. Bob sniggers, knowing his best friend all too well. 'He'd have come here for his honeymoon too if the Mrs didn't call all the shots!'

Proprietor Roger Wilkins has been making cider here for two-thirds of a lifetime. His grandfather started making cider in 1917. When he passed away in 1969, Roger took over the family business. One of the most genial hosts in the British Isles, it is easy to forget how much trust he puts in his punters. After all, this is his home and his livelihood; anyone whiling away sozzled time down on the farm is doing so in his back yard. Luckily for him, after so long brewing, he is still a fan of his own product. I ask how much of the punchy apple juice he drinks in a day. His answer – 14 pints – is shocking; mainly because he looks fit and full of life, partly because the stuff is utterly, utterly psychedelic when imbibed in any quantity. He recounts tales of drunkenness and revelry, each concluding with the same sweeping assimilation of the situation: 'I was pissed as arseholes I was!'

Roger's cider comes in two towering vats marked 'sweet' and 'dry'. Punters serve themselves and the amounts of each pressing are adjusted to suit individual taste. Dry is… well, dry and sweet is… you get the picture. Somewhere in the mix is paradise in a half-pint glass. Snacks for those in need of sustenance come in the form of chunks of local farmhouse cheddar and oversized pickled onions. It quickly becomes evident that these are perhaps not best designed to line the stomach after four pints. Though comical with hindsight, gnawing on a block of cheese like some gigantic pissed-up mouse is an unwise move in anyone's book.

Perhaps the Wilkins farm is sat on a tributary of the same ley lines that run through Somerset. The area plays heavily on Arthurian mythology; one look around Glastonbury town tells you that generations of people who turned up to the festival years before had stayed for the spiritual atmosphere. There are several shops specialising in crystals, a couple of New Age book-shops and the odd pub booming out roots reggae of a summer evening. A multitude of local stills offer plastic flagons of cider in the local supermarket; mainstream brands seem like an unneces-sary irrelevance. The psychedelic nature of the drink suits the cod-mysticism of the town. It is easy to be a cynical daytripper sneering at tie-dyed people sat around in pub gardens smoking weed and drinking cider all day, yet it is hard to walk away without thinking that it looks more fun than sitting in an office nervously checking emails every five minutes.

As much as the tipple seems to suit those of a hippyish bent, the music at the heart and soul of the Wilkins farm is surely punk rock.

Joe Strummer's flight from west London was well documented as being partly down to the fact that he thought 'happiness was chilling in Somerset with a flagon of Wilkins Cider'. Roger has tacked a yellowing page from an old *Q* magazine to the wall in which the late Clash frontman waxed – all misty-eyed – over the place. Nearby, there's a picture of former punk and latter-day face of British butter John Lydon mugging for the camera with his arm thrown around a bemused-looking Roger.

The place isn't supposed to be a pub – it certainly fails on most of Orwell's criteria – yet it does have one thing in veritable vat loads. That magic unknown – 'atmosphere'. Whether that's location, locals or the hallucinogenic properties of the only drink on sale… well I'd hazard a guess that Roger is running the place on equal measures of all three. Like Jimmy and Bob – and surely like Strummer and Lydon before us all – I stagger out of there rosy-cheeked and utterly elated. I feel like I've made new friends… although looking back, maybe that was me seeing double in the mirror. And maybe it was just the rapid effects of the cider on the weaker parts of my brain but I just couldn't help thinking that that crazed breeze-block outhouse was pretty much the perfect place for newlyweds to hang out.

THE STORY OF THE BOOZE

Paul Moody

Sunday lunchtime and I am drinking with a rock legend. The dapper gentleman leaning against the bar of The Grapes in Matthew Street has just introduced himself as David Byron, lead singer of seventies rock behemoths Uriah Heep. Which seems a bit odd considering he's dressed in a three-piece suit and smelling fragrantly of lavender. 'Of course, I had hair down to me arse back then,' he says, recalling Heep's appearance at Led Zeppelin's Knebworth mega-gig in 1976. 'Robert and Jimmy were great that day. I still keep in touch with them, and Eric Clapton sends me a Christmas card every year.'

He waggles a pinkie in the direction of a corner booth. 'I can still remember The Beatles sitting there like it was yesterday,' he says, clinking the ice in his whisky to suggest that, for the price of another, he might spill a few more drops from rock's holy chalice. 'John would be sitting in the corner drinking a pint of Black and Tan with Cynthia next to him. George would be dead quiet and Paul would be at the bar talking business…'

As casual Sunday afternoon exchanges go, discussing one rock star with another might seem bizarre, but then this is Liverpool, where even the glossy official brochure muses: 'Liverpool is not really the north. Not quite Midlands. Or is it just a state of mind?' and a surrealist streak comes as a birthright.

Here, bright yellow amphibious transporters nicknamed 'wacker-quackers' carry people about their daily business, a revered local landmark is called Superlambanana and the local Radio City transmits from a space age tower which, in a previous life, used to be a revolving, Buck Rogers themed restaurant. Sometimes, it's hard to tell the tangerine trees from the marmalade skies.

'It's a place where everyone and everything has to have a different name,' wrote Paul Du Noyer in his definitive musical history of the city *Liverpool: Wondrous Place*. 'It's as if vanilla reality is too hard to bear. The Mersey Tunnel is the Mousehole and you come across pubs which are called one thing but referred to as another. One is known as The Sad House. I always wondered if it had a happy hour.'

If the city's turbulent civic fortunes during the seventies and eighties were reflected by its television output (the cheery optimism of *The Liver Birds* traded for the doldrums of *Bread*; Ken Dodd's Diddymen by *The Boys from the Blackstuff*), the last 20 years have seen the city transformed from grumpy dowager to glitzy, perma-tanned princess, with 2008's European Capital of Culture celebrations (which marked the city's 800th anniversary) as a long overdue coming-out ball. Even this decision, if you believe the local barflies, was swayed by the city's pub culture.

'During their stay the judges went to see a comedian Keith Carter at the Rawhide Comedy Club who plays this boozy scally character called Nige from Toxteth,' explains Mike Chapple, author of *The Great Liverpool Pub Crawl*. 'He was encouraged to tone his act down, but instead he went at it full throttle and went down a storm. The judges later said they'd never encountered anything like it. Essentially it was the spirit they saw in the pubs and clubs which swung the decision our way.'

For Czech philosopher Carl Jung, famously, this human gumbo of hard-bitten locals, Irish refugees, Caribbean families and Chinese sailors was simply the 'Pool of Life', a 'dirty, sooty city', but also one which inspired visions of 'unearthly beauty'.

'The light comes from the water. It keeps you alive. And the pool is where we have to be. The Liver-Pool. The Mississippi, the Mersey-sippi,' The La's Lee Mavers told me in 1995, and despite the fact we were in a cramped Huyton rehearsal space with only a cup of PG Tips to enhance the mood, it made perfect sense. And the funny thing is, it still does.

'Scousers are different,' wrote Stuart Maconie in his splendid rumination on the north of England, *Pies and Prejudice*. 'They are the Basques of Lancashire, a race apart with a language and a culture that seems to bear no relation to any of the people around them.'

If this salty Scouse mentality has its roots anywhere it's in the docks, where laughter, so the joke went, was the only luxury anyone could afford.

The region's reputation as the king of cocky back-chat spread via the experiences of seamen and conscripts during the wars, fuelled by the nonsensical streams of consciousness delivered by post-war comedians Robb Wilton, Tommy Handley and Arthur Askey. This tributary flowed into the mainstream with Eddie Braben's scripts for Morecambe and Wise and its greatest living proponent is Ken Dodd, still packing out theatres with tales from Knotty Ash well into his eighties.

But then Liverpool has always lived on its wits. It's never been one for manufacturing, its seaport location enabling it to build its name and wealth on commerce, handling the produce for other towns and countries. You could even argue The Beatles themselves did the same, repackaging American rock 'n' roll, soul and R&B through a sonic Scouse filter, but it might lead to arguments. Because the city remains passionately proud of its four most famous sons and on any visit they're impossible to ignore.

It's the weekend of Liverpool Institute of Performing Art's degree ceremony and, as is customary, Paul McCartney is in the city to do the honours. Peter Grant, journalist and poet, explains that he's just come from interviewing Macca at LIPA for the *Echo* and I tell him that I'd seen him today, too, giving the thumbs-up to a coach load of disbelieving Beatles fans passing by on the Magical Mystery Tour bus. In Liverpool, Peter explains, conversation is 'like the river. At its best it comes in a relentless flow. It's about give and take. You can throw things back at people here and they'll respond. That's what makes Liverpool special. In other cities it's gone, but you can still do it here.'

At The Grapes, locals will tell you, history is literally on the doorstep. Up until its demolition in 1973 The Cavern stood opposite and the pub remains the final pit-stop for the coachloads of foreign tourists still ghost-hunting after their pilgrimages to Penny Lane and Strawberry Fields. But the pub refuses to accept its role as some kind of moptop mausoleum. Open every day from midday until 4 a.m., it has the knockabout feel of a 24-hour party which only occasionally winds down.

It's a damp Sunday lunchtime and foamy beer glasses remain uncleared on the tables, the general mood of fuzzy good humour coming with the sound of brassy hits from yesteryear: Frank Sinatra's 'Fly Me to the Moon', Dick Van Dyke's 'Chim Chim Cheree', Juanita Hall's 'Happy Talk'.

When the karaoke machine whirrs into life a couple of lads in pastel shirts immediately posit a full-blooded enquiry as to the whereabouts of Amarillo. A squad car pulls up outside to investigate the din, and the compere bellows, 'Quick lads, it's the bizzies, hide your drugs!' Anywhere else, this might have the makings of 'an incident'. Here, the police crack up laughing.

It's a devil-may-care philosophy summed up by strapping

Danish footballer Jan Molby on his arrival in the city in 1985: 'Liverpool is full of the kind of people who go out on Monday and couldn't care less about Tuesday morning.'

Mike Chapple is convinced it's a mind-set born of the city's pub culture. 'The pubs have always worked as a kind of bush telegraph,' he explains. 'You can start an evening at one end of town and you'll bump into someone who'll tell you that a friend is drinking in another pub which is only ten minutes away. So a quiet drink with your mates can soon turn into a full-on party.'

I'd had the same sense of a city communicating through its pubs and street culture when I first arrived in the city as a student in the mid-eighties. It seemed giddy with emotion, a place where every farewell came with a bear hug and every greeting like a long-lost relative, and it all seemed linked to a seaport's mentality of ships passing in the night. It all came with an urgent need to tell tall stories. People would tell you that The Vines was where the passengers on the *Titanic* spent their last night drinking before she sailed, or that Adolf Hitler spent a year in the city with his Auntie Bridgit, his art roundly rejected by everyone he showed it to. Truth or fiction? It didn't really matter. It was entertaining.

Back then, Liverpool's cultural pulse seemed to throb at three main pressure points, located around the activities of council deputy leader Derek Hatton at the Town Hall, Brookside Close and the original Probe Records on Button Street. All three have long since gone, but the hubbub and the faded grandeur of Lime Street pubs The Crown, and, most spectacularly, The Vines, remains.

Built in 1907 and known locally as 'The Big House' thanks to its location directly opposite the Adelphi, The Vines was once seen as a suitably refined destination for prosperous businessmen revelling in Liverpool's commercial role at the heart of the empire. While the pub's fortunes have varied over the years, architecturally it remains peerless; a baroque gin palace where mahogany pillars, stucco carvings and plaster friezes fight for attention and where, if you gaze upwards, you'll see crystal chandeliers dangling from an oval, stained-glass skylight, a coloured relief of a Viking ship and the signs of the zodiac engraved on the ceiling above the bar.

These days, The Vines is at its most boisterous on Sunday afternoons when local entertainer Cy Tucker takes to the stage. 'We've been playing in the pubs and clubs locally for the last thirty years and it's still going as strong as ever,' explains Tucker's guitarist and right-hand man Arthur. 'Back in the seventies we would play a lot of pubs along the Dock Road and on Scotland Road. There was a pub on every corner back then, and all of them would be packed, even during the week.' At The Vines, Arthur explains, the same spirit survives. 'People will get up and sing, strip off, anything goes. It's unique to Liverpool. We get coachloads coming in who make the trip especially to see us, from Newcastle, Derby, Crewe, Warrington, Skelmersdale, all over, and they all say the same thing: there's nowhere else like it. We've had tourists walk in off the street from Australia and Canada and they're flabbergasted, they think we're mad. But what's life without singing, dancing and having a good time?'

Liverpool's reputation as the life and soul of the pub world is hard won, however. As the embarkation point for millions of migrants headed for the 'new worlds' of America and Australia during the 19th century, the city unwittingly became home for hundreds of thousands who had made the perilous journey across the Irish Sea on vessels nicknamed 'coffin ships'. Handily for the city's bursars, these new arrivals drew a socio-economic short straw which saw them provide the cheap labour essential for the burgeoning port while living in abject poverty.

A study of the sanitary conditions of the labouring population by Edwin Chadwick in 1842 found Liverpool at the bottom of the table, with the average age of death for a working-class labourer at just 15. In the poorest areas Chadwick found 'every room of a dwelling, from stuffy attics to waterlogged cellars, crammed full of men, women and children. Their homes were damp and unventilated with no drainage system for taking away the sewage and no water supply for drinking and washing'.

However, among the arrivals at The Pier Head in 1844 was a certain James Cain and his two-year-old son Robert. Without whom, it's safe to say, Liverpool's drinkers would still be imbibing at a furious rate, but not in half as much style.

Sitting in the snug of The Lion on Tithebarne Street, Chris Routledge, author of *Cains: The Story of Liverpool in a Pint*, affords himself a smile. A university lecturer and pub enthusiast whose Phd was on American crime writer Raymond Chandler, he seems ideally suited to some booze-related detective work.

'It's doubtful how many people actually know how much of a debt they owe to Robert Cain,' he says, gesturing at the riot of dark wood panelling, intricate mosaics and etched glass. 'We certainly wouldn't be sitting here in such splendour without him.'

Robert Cain bought his first pub, on Limekiln Lane, aged 24. With Liverpool booming in the great Victorian era of industrial expansion, brewing became the perfect trade for the affluent, vibrant city and his fortunes rose with those of his adopted city. By 1858 Cain had his own brewery site on Stanhope Street, and his name rapidly became famous throughout the city for the exceptional quality of his beers, made using scientific methods and only the finest malt, hops and yeast. His pubs too, became synonymous with style and quality. Within 25 years of opening his first premises, Cain had built 200 pubs on Merseyside, including three of the most extravagant pubs in Britain: The Philharmonic, The Vines and The Central, each designed by flamboyant local architect Walter W. Thomas.

Tucked away in the Moorfields area, The Lion is one of Cain's more modest achievements, but you suspect even he would be impressed with its current state. Today a selection of guest ales are on offer, as well as specialist malt whiskys, a cheese board and award-winning pork pies.

'Cain's philosophy was that drinkers should take the time to appreciate the environment they were drinking in,' explains Chris. 'He was a remarkable man, and all the more so because he genuinely started with nothing. He was born in Ireland, but came here when he was two and grew up in the slums. His dad was invalided out of the army in 1820, after the Napoleonic War. It's difficult to find records, but his dad indentured him out to a cooper on a ship going to West Africa. So when Cain got out at eighteen or nineteen and came back to Liverpool, he started making up for lost time. He'd already seen the world.'

So what were the city's pubs like when he first got into the business?

'Pretty awful,' he continues. 'By 1850 the pubs in Liverpool were very deregulated, which meant there were hundreds of ale houses which were basically people's living rooms, and they often brewed themselves in the back yard. We're talking about random idiots with dirty fingernails. And there were thousands of those. They were absolutely lawless. And living standards at the time were atrocious, too. People would be living maybe ten to a room, with a load more in the cellars. The appeal for the population was that compared to where they were living, the pubs were quite nice. So what do you do? Sit around surrounded by kids in the filth and squalor or go to a nice warm place with a fire and have a beer?'

Routledge explains how the push towards prohibition in the 1890s forced the brewers to clean up their act. The only way to do that was to get rid of the rough houses and build big Victorian pubs.

'Cain introduced scientific brewing and built pubs which were pleasant places for the middle classes to go to. There wasn't a social stigma against drinking because at the time sanitation was so bad people were drinking beer all day because they couldn't drink the water. If you look at the newspapers from around Liverpool in that period, on the front page the brewers would advertise and the big houses in Sefton Park would get barrels of beer delivered, just because they couldn't drink the water because the sewage was so terrible.

'It was weaker than some of the beer served in pubs, but it was beer all the same. In many ways, things were still quite primitive. If you died, you were buried nearby, and there still wasn't proper regulation of cemeteries. Animal and human shit would be all over the place, and they were getting the water out of the ground, so it was unbelievably unhygienic.'

Pushing aside thoughts of decomposing bodies, I nudge the conversation back on to Cain's achievements, notably the baroque interiors of The Philharmonic and The Vines. It's clear Chris is as impressed as I am.

'These pubs were like the superclubs of the era,' he says. 'They were purposefully built in the more upmarket areas of the city, and the clientele would be the middle classes, the wealthy, and professors and students from the university. It might seem like a magnanimous act to us today, but the bottom line is that he was trying to make money. In a way Cain was a bit like Branson and jumbo jets. Once he'd started expanding, he couldn't stop.'

We discuss Cain's key role in the celebrations for the city's 700th anniversary in 1907. Will the pubs he created still be around for its 900th anniversary in 2107?

'It's a good question,' says Chris. 'I have various theories. The pub's declining place in the public's affections is a lot to do with the rise of the middle classes. Everybody aspires to be middle class now, and beer is what your granddad drank. Beer is not seen as an aspirational drink. Whereas wine makes you stylish, supposedly. And kids have been introduced to drinking things like Smirnoff Ice, which seems a bit more glamorous than drinking lager, which is what their dad drinks. The other thing is, people's lives have changed. Their homes are so much more comfortable than in Cain's day. People would rather chat and conspire online with a glass of wine than go to the pub.'

I tell him about my encounter with David Byron at The Grapes. 'Liverpool is a city where people love to talk,' he grins. 'If you hang around long enough someone will come in and say they were at the first Beatles gig at The Cavern. Here they'll start a conversation just to see where it goes.'

My last stop is Ye Cracke on Rice Street. Tucked away on a cobblestoned side street in the north end of the city between Pilgrim

Street and Hope Street, it has been a haven for a distinct breed of Liverpudlian drinker dating to the days when John Lennon and Stu Sutcliffe would drink here while bunking off lessons at the Liverpool College of Art.

In the seventies, the pub was ruled with a rod of iron by foul-mouthed landladies Marge and Daisy, swearing turned into an art form on the whitewashed walls of the outdoor gents, the 'intellectual graffiti' including a drawing of some cubist genitalia with the words 'Balls to Picasso'. Despite a disappointing scrub-up in 2009, its piratical nature continues to attract a dissolute band of students, vagabonds, anarchists, cops and robbers, as well as members of the Liverpool Philharmonic who, gagging for a drink between performances, dash over for a couple of discreet pints between the Brahms and Liszt.

Today, everyone present looks like an ex-art teacher or former member of The Scaffold. At the bar I get chatting to a craggy-faced individual who tells me he once knew the playwright Alun Owen. 'I saved his life once,' he says. 'We were on a camping trip in Wales and we were messing about in the river and he got washed away. I dived in and saved him, he was drowning.' He pauses to let this information sink in. 'He later went on to write the screenplay for *A Hard Day's Night*. That was where George met Pattie Boyd. And of course she married him and then met Eric Clapton who fell in love with her and wrote "Layla". So, in a lot of ways, I'm responsible for "Layla".'

I consider pointing out that George may well have still met Patti without Alun's involvement, but it seems to miss the point. Instead, I tell him he should claim the royalties for 'Something', too.

Which would probably be a cue for another Beatle-related anecdote were it not for the arrival of Pete Wylie. A pop star in the eighties with Wah! Heat and The Mighty Wah!, over the last 30 years he has redefined the role of musical maverick, his string of hit singles ('Come Back', 'Story of the Blues') just small splashes of colour on a much larger canvas. Having recovered from a near-fatal accident in 1991, his song 'Heart As Big As Liverpool', is now the city's unofficial anthem, played annually by Wylie at the Hillsborough memorial concert at Liverpool's Anfield stadium. He's got a reputation as Liverpool Lip and bon viveur precedes him and he doesn't disappoint.

Within five minutes he's told me about the night he asked Mike Tyson out for a fight in New York having drunk a bottle of tequila, namechecked an authentic Irish pub called The Liffey he visited with Gerry Conlon and Paddy Hill ('they loved it') and described the terrible dilemma he faced one time at the Reading Festival. 'The barman told me I could only order one more drink. I was with Hooky from New Order, so I said, "Okay, I'll have a pint of wine." Within an hour I was all over the place.'

His concern at pub closures, however, is as heartfelt as his music. In July 2011 the city's cultural mothership, The Everyman Bistro, closed down. For generations of students it had been a cheap place to eat, drink and share ideas. It was where Wah! Heat played their first gig; for Wylie it's symptomatic of the changes in the city. 'My dad died a couple of years ago and the other week I drove up to Fazakerley to visit a few of his old haunts. It's one street from Kirkby, and the number of great old pubs which have shut down is tragic, absolutely tragic. There's one every ten yards. I've said it before, but the divide between the rich and the poor in Liverpool is scandalous. It's all very well having flash new places and brilliant new shopping centres, but if you drive ten minutes out of the city centre to Anfield, Toxteth or Norris Green it's desolate. They're trying to hide the old Liverpool, pretend it doesn't exist.'

Pete sees the root of these problems in the segregation of the nation's pubs. 'I'm not nostalgic at all, but once there were scally pubs, weirdo pubs, old man pubs and there was a distinct cross-over between each. Without even realising it, they were learning from each other. The magic was in the mix. The difference is now, it's absolutely codified. It's spelt out to you: this is where you go if you're this kind of person. There's bouncers on the door of pubs now, deciding if you can come in. It's insane. There was a time when people swapped ideas whether they were conscious of it or not. That's gone.'

In 1985 Wylie had a top 20 hit with 'Come Back', a heartfelt plea to all those who had left the city in its economic hour of need to return. Now, he wishes they hadn't. 'A lot of people left the city supposedly to improve themselves, and the trouble is they've all come back as estate agents and lawyers. Thatcher's children have taken over the city. In fact, you could almost make an equation out of it. Thatcher times offspring equals disaster. It's like an episode of *Doctor Who*. First there was Davros, now there's a whole nation of Daleks running things. The trouble is, the left-wing Daleks are as bad as the right-wing Daleks. And in the middle there's the Liberal Democrats who are like the shittest Cybermen ever!'

Despite describing himself as 'a guzzler – I'll drink anything', Pete Wylie has never had a local. Instead, his passage from callow 15-year-old drinking lager and black at The Black Swan in Walton ('I thought it was exotic') to watching local bands at The Moonstone with Ian McCulloch and hanging out at O'Connor's Tavern ('the first place I was offered drugs') have come in a blur of chat, laughter and imagination.

'I'm interested in people, ideas, humour, music and art. I'll go wherever they are. The idea of staying in one place doesn't really interest me. You learn stuff about life along the way. I really like Alan Bleasdale and the way he looked at life through the lens of the pub in *The Boys from the Blackstuff* really inspired me. In fact, it made me change the way I write songs. Rather than writing songs for the people in the *NME* office, I started writing them for the people in the pub. It was a real lesson. I wasn't talking to the kid in the Rock Against Racism badge at Manchester Poly. I was talking to the guy in the corner who had seen a bit of life. Because they're the ones who genuinely need to be moved and inspired.'

This idea of, as Alan Bleasdale puts it, 'making the serious stuff funny and the funny stuff serious' is integral to the city's pub culture; waves of humour where even the *Titanic* and Hitler get washed up along the way.

'There's the Irish tradition obviously, but it's really a port thing. Every night was either a last night before setting sail or a first night back. So every night became a celebration. The port's gone, but it became a part of the city's DNA. We're celebratory, oppositional. It's about not doing what people expect of you. And going to the pub is the biggest subversion in the world.'

Walking back up to Lime Street station via the town centre I pass a mass of chain stores, chain coffee shops and chain restaurants. From The Big House, however, comes a mighty roar. The party is in full swing, Cy Tucker leading a mass singalong to Bruce Springsteen's 'Born To Run'. I can't help but think of Oceania in *Nineteen Eighty-Four*, where 'the birds sang, the proles sang, The Party did not sing.'

The locals might die younger than the average resident of Surrey, their livers pickled with booze, complexions like blotting paper, arteries narrowed to a syringe after a lifetime of Cains lager, mixed grills, vodka tonics and late night kebabs, but I know which one I'd rather share a bar with.

Outside the station I pop into an internet café, curious to find out how David Byron must have looked back in the days when Uriah Heep were propping up Led Zeppelin. A quick Google search, however, tells me that Byron died of alcohol-related poisoning in 1985. Stranger still, he was from Basildon, Essex, and was at least a foot taller than the man I'd met in The Grapes.

As I board the train back to London, even the seagulls sound like they're laughing.

Interlude:
Going Underground

Robin Turner

It's the middle of the afternoon and
I'm drunk in a converted public toilet in the
heart of Manchester. To my left, there's an Aussie bloke curled
up, asleep in a ball with his black Labrador. To my right sits the
singer in one of the city's great lost bands who – against all odds
– are about to become massive. From where the urinals used to
be, squalling guitars wail out, shaking the foundations. It sounds
as huge and frenetic as a freight train being derailed by a nuclear
missile. The Aussie guy stirs, his eyes so bloodshot they resemble
hypnosis wheels cut into fresh steak. Without so much as a grunt,
he lines up the next round of shots. After passing them round, he
returns to the warmth of the foetal position. As I tackle my fourth
Cocksucking Cowboy, it dawns on me that even when he's asleep,
Scott knock the spots off most native landlords in this country.

There's a derogatory phrase that bands and road crew use regarding Britain's more compact drinking spaces – the 'legendary toilet
circuit'. The Temple – formerly a Victorian pissoir and notorious
subterranean cottaging spot in the heart of Deansgate – redefines
that well-worn idiom. Down the stairs and into the kind of beery
fog that's so conducive to lost afternoons, The Temple is just about
big enough for a spot of impromptu cat swinging. We'd rolled in
on a Friday afternoon to find venue owner Scott spark out. Guy
Garvey, the ultra-amiable lead singer of Elbow, has just finished
mixing *The Seldom Seen Kid*. Over an initial pint, he explains about
his favourite city centre walk.

'I've perfected the shortest pub crawl in the city – three pubs within spitting distance of my flat, the whole thing takes about three minutes start to end. Kick off with beers in The Briton's Protection, a pit-stop in The Peveral of the Peak before going underground at The Temple. It's a fine bit of exercise.'

The first single from *The Seldom Seen Kid*, 'Grounds For Divorce', had just been released. Its lyrics are a paean to the wonders of Guy's favourite converted lavatory ('There's a hole in my neighbourhood/Down which of late I cannot help but fall'), making this most unlikely of watering holes something like the North West's very own *Cheers*. It isn't hard to see why he found it so easy to wax lyrical about the place. The toilets are wallpapered with sixties erotica, creating a feeling somewhere between *Carry On* titillation and peeping Tom fascination. The jukebox hurls out a thunderous selection of relentless boogie from noon to night. And Scott – sometime narcoleptic proprietor, full-time rocker – keeps the whole thing swinging.

As time wears on and the drinks change from lager to shorts to shots to anything goes, Guy wisely bails out, his pub crawl completed. Within a few months, he would be arguably the most loved man in British music. As Guy climbs the stairs, Scott stirs, sensing that it's finally time to get serious about things. As he shakes himself awake, it seems to me like the right time to address the bar with the most pressing question of the day.

'Right, who fancies coming to the Roadhouse to see an AC/DC tribute act?'

Scott nods solemnly and readies his faithful hound for the task ahead. It's going to be a long night.

ISLAND HOPPING

Robin Turner

When there is a perfectly good local just a tempting 60-second stroll from your front door, four hours each way on a boat does seem a hell of a long way to go for a pint. Lundy lies somewhere near the middle of the Bristol Channel, popping up roughly due south of Tenby and about 12 miles off the north coast of Devon. England's first marine nature reserve, home to all manner of birdlife (but only 27 people), Lundy was nominated as the country's tenth best natural wonder in the *Radio Times*. There, puffins can occasionally be seen coasting along the surface of the sea, mouths stuffed with silver-skinned fish. Grey seals wallow in the protected waters just away from the harbour. That is obviously all wonderful, but most important of all is the fact that Lundy is home to arguably the country's least accessible boozer.

If Orwell was truly searching for a pub that 'drunks and rowdies never seem to find their way' then The Marisco Tavern would have been comfortably at the top of his list. There is no short cut to get here – well, not one that wouldn't cause you to wince at the price (as with the twice weekly chopper flight from Hartland Point). Crossings can be cancelled with little warning if weather conditions turn. My first and second attempts saw the boat from Ilfracombe turn away all day passengers. Walkers, twitchers and nature enthusiasts all stepped aboard, ready to brave several days out on the rock. Us drinkers were unfortunately deemed surplus to requirements and left slack-jawed and thirsty on the pier waiting for the pubs to open. The onboard bar obeyed no landlocked licensing rules.

I vow that my third stab at getting to The Marisco Tavern will be my final one, my determination by then clouded by the thought that 'No pub is worth this must effort, surely?' I decide to change tack by trying to cross from South Wales in the temperate lull of early summer. Luckily on the day the *Waverley* – a beautifully preserved paddle steamer – glides into view. The crossing is textbook perfect. After hugging the Welsh coastline from Porthcawl to Swansea, the boat forges out towards north Devon, bobbing along purposefully packed full of daytripping Taffs. By the time the boat sets sail for the final leg of its outward journey, the majority of passengers on board have been replaced by twitchers and ramblers from the West Country.

Lundy is the original craggy island. Looming out of the sea, it sticks out like a giant boulder thrown from the shoreline by a pissed giant or the back of a terrible giant creature, felled and fossilised by time. It is truly beautiful, perfectly isolated and utterly unspoilt by the bored hands of teenagers. Most disembarking passengers stride off purposefully with the requisite uniform of slung Barbour jackets, well-worn Karrimor boots and hi-tech binoculars. There is just three hours shore leave; the sound of the ship's klaxon will sound five minutes before the *Waverley*'s anchor goes up. The challenge is to make the most of the time on the island.

I immediately make a beeline for the pub. I figure I can probably see nice birds anywhere. The only hurdle is the 45-degree incline in front of me. Alarmingly unfit and still in disbelief that I am actually here, I pretty much sprint until I'm through the door.

Sinking into my second pint in The Marisco I finally manage to relax. I take a seat next to a South Walian sea dog named Pete and ask what had brought him to the island. It turns out, weather permitting, Pete had journeyed from Porthcawl to Lundy annually for the last 45 years. Pete's original inspiration for making the trip came from the fact that Wales was once 'dry' on a Sunday. As the boat sailed on God's own day, a booze cruise up the Bristol Channel seemed like a perfect way to make up a round seven days of fully licensed bad behaviour. By the time that the law loosened in the seventies, the *Waverley* trip was part of the calendar.

In the early days, he tells me, the boat was lawless and extremely lively. 'It wasn't exactly luxury back then but people made the most of it. They'd arrive carrying flagons of beer, crates of cans, bottles as well. They'd start the real business of the day as soon as they boarded. More often than not, the bar was drunk bone dry before the boat had docked in Lundy.'

He fondly remembers regularly sailing over in the seventies with a motley crew of able-bodied piss-heads. 'We used to sail en masse – friends, family members and anyone else up for a day out. Always just men too. It was a proper day out, a bit like a sea-bound version of the Dylan Thomas story "The Outing" [which coincidentally pivots around the boat's starting point, Porthcawl]. Our extended drinking family included a chap called Chippy Hawkins. He was known as Chippy because he ran the local fish and chip shop in Bridgend. He'd lost a leg – either in the war or through some booze-based misdemeanour, I can't remember now. Anyway, when the boat arrived he'd get shoved on the back of a flat-bed tractor and driven up the hill, across fields and into the pub. He was guaranteed to be as pissed as a rat when they plonked him back on board.'

Sat here, taking in the surroundings, it is easy to see why someone like Pete would feel the urge to return time and again. The Marisco is serving the most peaceful pint in Britain. It is the perfect place to clear fog from your brain before clouding it up again with one of the island-only ales specifically brewed for The Marisco by Cornwall's St Austell. Throw in the odd lock-in, a sea shanty or two and some casual liquid-assisted twitching and one could really get used to life as a castaway. Taking a pint outside, the view is grass, sea, far-off land and bird life. There is no noise pollution here, no light pollution at night either. It feels like the most perfectly anti-social drinking experience in the world – all the details of pub life, just none of the people. No rowdies. No drunks.

KLAAAAAAAAAAAAANGGGGGGGG!

I awake from a daze to see the barman of The Marisco standing in the doorway laughing at me. I'd just dreamt my way through the klaxon and missed everyone patiently filing down the hillside. I have two and a half minutes to make the boat, otherwise I'm stuck here – homeless – for three days.

It is a very tough call.

I'd originally planned the trip to The Marisco Tavern as one half of a very short, very specific pub crawl. The second pub is also just off the coast of Devon – this time dozing out on the other side in languorous South Hams. As boozy follies go, this one is going take some beating.

Burgh Island is much closer to civilisation than Lundy. Twice daily, a sandy causeway connects it to Bigbury-on-Sea. When the tide dissipates, a contraption called the sea tractor is on hand to plough through the waters carrying visitors to the island's main attraction. The Burgh Island Hotel was built in 1929, a palatial and majestic art deco creation that had – in a previous life – played temporary home to everyone from Agatha Christie to The Beatles. Guests were required to wear full evening dress for dinner, something which gave the whole place the air of a murder mystery evening over canapés and crudités. Far more interesting to me, though, is the island's 14th-century smuggler's pub, The Pilchard Inn.

The Pilchard is as rough and tumble as the hotel is grandiose; stylistically a million miles removed from its neighbour's intricate stained glass and dinner dances, physically just a hop, skip, jump and tipsy stagger away. The pub itself is all low beams and log fires, something like a child's sketch of a pirate hideout, lacking only a couple of Johnny Depps and a few old salts sat around cackling about hauls of booty.

Sat outside the pub as evening tumbles in, it looks as if the sunset has been orchestrated solely for the viewing pleasure of the hotel's guests. The sun burns into the English Channel as advancing water somehow telescopically puts distance between the island and the mainland. Darkness and silence suits The Pilchard. There is no lock-in in the world that could substitute for that first tide-in pint, drunk in the dusk to a soundtrack that consists solely of waves lapping patiently against rocks. The fact that the place is haunted – by a ghost called Tom Crocker – only adds to the huddled-up intimacy of the bar.

Retreating inside for another pint of Beachcomber (brewed in nearby Teignmouth), I soon find myself deep in conversation with Keith, a pub regular and seasoned sea tractor passenger who introduces me to the concept of Hash House Harriers. They are, he says, 'a drinking club with a running problem'. The idea is simple. He and a group of locals get together once a week in Bigbury, run around for a bit and eventually end up for a bunch of pints in whichever pub they're nearest to. 'I was getting too fat,' Keith cheerily admits, supping foam from the top of his pint. 'But I was never going to give up boozing. Someone told me about the Harriers and I thought it sounded perfect. Burn a few calories, put a few back on.' So what distances does he cover? 'Sometimes just a couple of miles. Sometimes ten or more. Depends on how out of shape you're feeling or how thirsty you are!'

The Hash House Harriers Constitution (as recorded in 1950) states that the ethos of the club is 'To promote physical fitness among our members; to get rid of weekend hangovers; to acquire a good thirst and to satisfy it in beer; to persuade the older members that they are not as old as they feel.' The first grouping got together in 1938. A bunch of colonial officers and expats met in Kuala

Lumpur with the intention of shaking off the previous weekend's fog. Since then, the idea has snowballed to the point where a biennial Interhash takes place in different locations around the world. Having missed events everywhere from Tasmania to Cardiff, Keith signed up to run in Goa in 2002.

'I couldn't believe it when I got out there. I was used to running across a few fields over here before ending up in some cosy pub or other. There, they'd hired a train and filled it with beer. It would start rolling out slowly then we'd run alongside it during the day before diving in to get smashed. It was hilarious; I'd do it again in a second.'

I think back to The Marisco and my crazed sprint down the hillside. Out of shape and desperate, I had displayed all the tongue lolling, dribbling dignity of a three-legged dog trying to chase a tennis ball across a motorway. This search for the perfect pub is as much an excuse for drinking as it is a sociological experiment; the extra inches on my waistband really aren't that pretty. Keith's effusiveness made the Hash House Harriers sound like the solution to the problem… with a liberal dose of the problem added back in for good measure. Finally, I'd found an exercise regime I could get behind, hallelujah.

I order another pint of Beachcomber. Pretty soon, all thoughts of running and of trains rumbling across the Indian plains drift out to sea.

Interlude:
The Quest for the Holy Ale

Paul Moody

King Arthur isn't best pleased. Someone has
stolen his Round Table.

'This is the Mead Hall. This is the Roundhouse.
It's one of the only places left where we can still
gather as a tribe,' he says, sitting at a corner
table of The Red Lion in Avebury, Wiltshire.
'But people aren't coming through the doors
any more. I live in Salisbury and most pubs are empty even on
a Saturday night. It's depressing. It's as though the life is being
drained out of the country.'

Ever since a late night epiphany 25 years ago, this former merce-
nary and Hell's Angel has been redefining the term eco-warrior,
scything through red tape with his own spellbinding brand of logic,
usually clad in his trademark white tunic with Excalibur, his trusty
three-foot sword, by his side. Once, he was plain John Timothy
Rothwell, but now his passport (where he is pictured complete
with crown) reads Arthur Uther Pendragon. This Clark-Kent style
transformation to Arthurian Superman was made complete when
he purchased the Celtic broadsword used in the film *Excalibur* in a
junk shop in Aldershot.

His aim? To awaken 'the Spirit of Albion', a tribal consciousness which is 'there in all of us, and here beneath our feet in these
once green and pleasant lands, if we only realised it'. Officially
recognised as Britain's leading Arch Druid, his titles include King
Arthur, Titular Head of the Loyal Arthurian Warband and Official
Swordbearer to the Secular Order of Druids.

If we're to meet anywhere, then, The Red Lion feels like the right place. Thanks to some ingenious 17th-century stone masons, it's the only pub in the world standing within a stone circle. And not just any stone circle. Built around 2600 BC Avebury is the largest stone circle in the world, 14 times the size of Stonehenge, 18 miles down the road, predating it by 500 years. Made up of three vast stone circles, the outer one comprising 101 stones, it's positioned at the end of a pathway of a further 100 stones, also 12 feet high, called West Kennet Avenue. Trashed by the Romans and neglected for centuries, Avebury was only returned to something approaching its former glories in the 1930s by marmalade magnate Alexander Keiller, who made it his life's work to reposition the surviving stones in their original formation.

At solstice, members of the pagan community come here to celebrate the passage of the seasons and today marks the *Free and Open Gorsedd for the Festival of Imbolc*. There is a fresh layer of snow on the ground, fine as icing sugar, and a determination to celebrate the ancient start of spring. But you can tell Arthur sees these as dark days for this land, any instances of our once fabled community spirit as rare as sightings of the Lady in the Lake.

'For centuries the pub welcomed everybody,' he says gravely. 'The trouble is these days we're all segregated. There are gay pubs, biker pubs, pubs for stockbrokers. Nobody mixes any more and so the whole tribe doesn't gather together in one place any longer. Consequently they don't learn to get along.'

Back in the seventies, Arthur says, things were different. 'I travelled around the country a lot back then and it would always be the same,' he says. 'You'd find the old geezer who had been in the First World War in one corner, the young kids in the other corner, and everyone else in the middle. By the end of the evening they would all be mixing. In those days the pub had a function, because it catered for all aspects of society.'

The way Arthur sees it, the modern world has traded personality for profit. 'The pubs are being undercut by the supermarkets. Tesco is the biggest private employer in Britain, and that's a scary thought.

Because it means they have the power to put pubs out of business in the same way they've affected the rest of the high street. They're selling white goods, they're selling CDs, and nobody can compete – the bakers, the butchers, the electrical shops, the record shops, even the banks. We're being taken over by corporate interest and the ancient role that pubs and drinking had are being lost.'

While the relaxing pleasures of beer drinking are obvious, it also has the ability to enrich us on a deeper, more spiritual level. Or at least, that's a theory held by many ancient civilisations. Because far from being seen as a corrupting influence, many pre-Christian societies treated beer as a civilising, morally uplifting drink; a fact reflected in many of the world's creation myths.

In the *Kavela*, the national epic poem of Finland, beer is celebrated explicitly:

> *Let me sing an old–time legend*
> *That shall echo forth the praises*
> *Of the Beer that I have tasted*
> *Of the sparkling beer of barley*

In the 4,000-year-old Babylonian epic *Gilgamesh*, the savage Enkidu, is civilised by the humanising power of beer, while in *The Moralia*, the first-century Greek writer Plutarch wrote 'the end of drinking is to nourish and increase friendship'.

To the ancients, beer's power wasn't limited simply to being a powerful social lubricant. It was once seen as being capable of imparting wisdom, too. In the 13th-century Norse *Poetic Edda*, it's explained to the hero Sigurth by Sigrdrifa that the 'ale-runes' contain mystical powers of strength, charm and healing.

Up until the 15th century European beers contained all manner of psychoactive herbs such as gale, yarrow, rosemary, wormwood, juniper berries, ginger, nutmeg and cinnamon. Known as 'fruit ales' or simply 'gruit', these beers were highly intoxicating, acting as both narcotics and aphrodisiacs when consumed in sufficient quantity. Such was their popularity, they were even considered a threat to the power of the Catholic Church and effectively banned by the German Beer Purity Laws of 1516.

While most beers available today only provide the power to see double, they still ignite something in the soul. As William James puts it in *Varieties of Religious Experience*: 'The sway of alcohol over mankind is unquestionably due to its power to stimulate the mystical faculties of human nature, usually crushed to earth by the cold facts and dry criticisms of the sober hour. Sobriety diminishes, discriminates and says no; drunkenness expands, unites and says yes.'

So why is it so mired in rules and regulations? Barely a week goes by without a government report lecturing us on the perils of exceeding the number of 'units' we're supposed to drink, set at absurdly low levels to induce guilt in people who are simply having a few glasses of wine in the evening to unwind after a hard day at work. Arthur's convinced it's all part of a policy of divide and conquer.

'What scares me is that technology is now making social conditioning so much easier. The politicians know that. The easiest way to rule the masses is if the masses agree with what you're saying. And the easiest way to get them to agree with what you're saying is to educate them to agree with that policy. Therefore anyone voicing free expression becomes their enemy, a heretic. And if you really think about it, where is free expression? It's the pub. It's the one place where your every movement isn't being watched or where your every word isn't being recorded, like it is on the internet.'

Once, we made our own minds up about people, rubbing shoulders in the saloon bar. Now, any existing prejudices are subliminally enforced through the media. 'Pubs used to encourage tolerance,' he says. 'They were a place where everyone instinctively knew where the boundaries were.'

Arthur recalls the welcome he would get when he was roaming the country as part of infamous biker gang The Gravediggers. 'We knew our place,' he says solemnly. 'Our boundary was that we had to stay in the public bar.' He chuckles to himself. 'Equally, no one would come round to our side either. Unless, of course, they fancied a bit of rough. It worked in other ways too. If you were getting too loud in the saloon bar, you'd be asked to move into the public bar next door. Then if you behaved badly in there you'd get thrown out on your ear.'

He shrugs in a manner which suggests this was all good clean fun. 'These days you can't do anything without being caught on CCTV and the rest of it. In Salisbury they've even introduced a scheme which means if you get banned from one pub you're on a black list. It doesn't get much more Big Brother than that.'

It's only three o'clock, and The Red Lion's lunchtime trade has already petered out, leaving just me and Arthur sitting at our corner table. It seems odd to be sitting here with the Druid King of England in a deserted pub, the TV burbling away to itself in the background. He gestures at the empty tables around us, a leader without an army. 'Where have all the rebels gone? They certainly ain't here. They're probably talking online to their new best friend in Tel Aviv even though they don't even know the name of their next-door neighbour.'

He sighs. 'The other thing is, no one looks each other in the eye any more.' He means it both literally and figuratively. Wired into the grid, we've forgotten that the best thing about these islands is how different we all are. We've always been a nation of oddballs and eccentrics yet they seem to be becoming increasingly marginalised. The pubs where they once congregated are being torn down, the charts where they once wreaked musical havoc now sanitised. And anyway, isn't a lunatic, as Winston Smith suggests in *Nineteen-Eighty Four,* really only a minority of one?

When Arthur stood at the 2010 general election as an independent candidate in Salisbury, he polled a mere 287 votes, despite campaign literature which declared: 'I haven't got all the answers but I promise you this, I might not be better but I can't possibly be worse,' and included a vow to conduct surgeries in the 'streets, at markets, car boot sales, pubs, clubs and shopping centres'.

It's fun to imagine what happened in a parallel universe, Arthur storming through the Commons, raising hell in Strangers Bar and skewering slippery MPs over their expenses. He'd get my vote any day.

THE LAST DROP

What must those final drops taste like, knowing that the morning will hurtle you towards death and destruction? The elixir of life, or bitter as tears?

I'm staring up at the clock on the wall of The Sheep Heid in Duddingston, Edinburgh, and musing on what's gone before. A pub, so legend has it, since 1360, it has been a port of call for troops since the days of James VI. Frequented by Bonnie Prince Charlie's Jacobite army prior to their triumph at the Battle of Prestonpans in 1745, the pub provided a unique kind of last orders for soldiers stationed at Piershill transit camp prior to both the First and Second World Wars. As the clock ticked around to 11 o'clock, troops would fall silent, eking out their final pint, knowing that the morning would see them headed for the killing fields of France and Belgium.

'The clock dates to 1903,' says the pub's manager, D. J. Johnston-Smith. 'It's amazing how many stories you hear told about it. We had a 100th birthday party here in 2006 and it was very emotional, the memories came flooding back.'

While official records of the pub's existence only date to the 17th century (its first mention in the *Scotsman* wasn't until 1831), The Sheep Heid has a stillness in keeping with its claim to be Scotland's oldest. But then Edinburgh does 'old' better than practically everybody. A settlement dating to the Bronze Age, it was, as a friendly bloke in W.H. Smiths tells me, 'a thriving city when Glasgow was still just fields'.

Voted 'favourite UK city' for the eleventh consecutive year at the *Guardian*'s Travel Awards in 2011, its wow factor is two-fold: the sweep of The Royal Mile (even during major roadworks), and the elegance of the Georgian old town off-set by art galleries, swanky shopping malls and quirky museums.

The city's reputation as a more refined, slightly snooty elder brother to its impetuous younger sibling fifty miles to the west seems to miss something, though. A shop window off Princes Street cockily declares: 'The Kilt – have you got the balls to wear it?' and the same rakish wit is in evidence at The Sheep Heid.

A fox stares insouciantly from the front window and on a bookshelf by the bar, a stuffed squirrel clambers over bound editions of Sir Walter Scott's *Waverley* novels, while mirrors advertising Young's of Alloa reflect in cosy red lamp-light. Johnston-Smith explains he's traced the pub's history back to 1719. 'It's only a pity more people don't care about it,' he says. 'I've got a neighbour who complains relentlessly about the noise in the garden. I try to tell her there have been people drinking here since the eighteenth century, but she doesn't care. And unfortunately the law is on her side.'

Still only in his early thirties, Johnston-Smith is a new breed of pub manager. Passionate about the pub and its historical significance (he has an MA in Scottish History and Archeology), he enthuses over its past, and possible catalytic role in the Scottish

Enlightenment (former regulars including both Walter Scott and Robert Louis Stevenson). This enthusiasm even seeps into the pub's event calendar: in 2010 it hosted a Scottish history themed beer festival, featuring brews such as Claverhouse, Inkie Pinkie and Sheriffmuir, raising money for charity with the sale of Hanoverian and Jacobite cockades. He's also in line for any best dressed awards going; his dapper three-piece suit only one of a collection befitting a man with the twitter account: 'addicted to tweed'.

When Johnston-Smith arrived at The Sheep Heid in 2005, the pub had lost its lustre. The walls were bare, the ambience surly: regulars would fall silent when he entered and even get up and serve themselves. 'For me it was against the great Scottish tradition of hospitality. It's a public house, anybody should be made welcome, regardless of colour, class or creed. I took out the television and the fruit machines.' The result: 42 letters of complaint within six weeks. But he triumphed. In his first summer there were 80 complaints about noise; in the summer of 2010 there were only 20.

'It's back to how it used to be. People are talking to each other again.' To prove his point, he spins round on his chair, a blur of tweed. 'The tables are arranged so you're close enough to talk but you each have your own space. You could have a builder on one table, a taxi driver on the next, a lawyer on the next. They can talk to each other if they want, or not.'

As a Mitchells & Butlers pub, Johnston-Smith explains he doesn't have complete autonomy, but he's made conscious changes to the décor with a specific clientele in mind. Upstairs, a restaurant has been restored to its former glory, and eccentric knick-knacks catch the eye: an elephant's foot wastepaper bin (a leftover from the Raj), and a lamp made out of a goat's foot, donated by a woman from Walsall.

'I'm unashamedly catering for a middle-class clientele, but anyone can come here and enjoy a drink. We're split fifty-fifty on sales of drink and food and that's how it should be.'

The pub is progressive in other ways, too. It was the first in Scotland to implement a total no-smoking ban, two years before it became legal. 'It was the logical step,' he says matter-of-factly. 'We've become more educated, and people want to drink in a cleaner environment. The biggest change in society in the last seventy years has been the rise of the middle classes. That's unarguable. It makes up about seventy per cent of the population now. The pubs catering for the remaining working classes are filled with distractions: televisions, fruit machines. Of course what we do here isn't for everyone, but people know what they're going to get here, good beer and food in a convivial atmosphere.'

The introduction of a ban on happy hours north of the border in September 2009 was also a good idea. 'Scotland is the sick man of Europe. The government are asking people to drink responsibly. It makes perfect sense.'

Coming from Johnston-Smith, you'd imagine plans to replace beer with tap water would sound palatable. He's every inch the modern publican, adapting his premises to suit the times while keeping a curator's eye on the past. You wish all pub managers had the same enthusiasm and interest in local history and ideas. If they did, perhaps so many managed pubs wouldn't seem so lifeless and sterile, tweed or no tweed.

The Sheep Heid feels like another example of a maverick, as Paul Kingsnorth put it, 'following their star' and Johnston-Smith is already busying himself for the evening's trade. He tells me there are plans to resurrect a local culinary speciality to the menu: sheep's head broth, a nod to the days when sheep were slaughtered locally before being taken to the Fleshmarket in Edinburgh's Old Town. 'It's a novelty, of course. But it's all part of creating an atmosphere. I'm happy if people want to come in here with a newspaper and just sit quietly having a coffee. In fact, I'd take it as a compliment.'

At the pub in Fleshmarket Close there has been a grisly discovery. Underneath the freshly laid concrete in the cellar floor, the skeletons of a woman and an infant have been discovered. It's tied in with a possible racist murder in a high-rise slum estate, and the disappearance of a terrified rape victim. And it takes Inspector John Rebus precisely 90 minutes to solve it.

I'm standing outside The Halfway House sharing a fag break with a barmaid called Linda. The pub is at the mid-point of this creepy Victorian cut-through, and she tells me it is regularly visited by fans of Ian Rankin, looking to live out the cases of Edinburgh's most famous detective.

The pub itself is hobbit-sized, a short dash from Waverley station, and Linda says it has its advantages: the one-room layout means you can be on first-name terms with the regulars 'within three hours'. She explains she's worked here for 12 years on and off, returning three times having vowed to leave. She puts it down to the city's unique atmosphere, and I know what she means. The sense of the city's murky past engulfing the present is inescapable from the moment of arrival. In the *Daily Record*, I read about the latest death in Afghanistan: a 20-year-old infantry man from the Black Watch who had only been serving for four weeks since deployment from his barracks in Inverness. In some unfathomable way, death seems to stalk the city, as though it is suffused with centuries of suffered experience, an echo chamber of dreams and desires. Or maybe I've just been looking at the glossy tour brochures too long, specialising in macabre treats such as the 'Ghost Tours' (involving 'witch trials and witch burnings', 'disturbed graves' and 'Edinburgh's cannibals and vampires') and city tours, where 'murderers, witch hunters, firebrand priests and philosophers' rub along 'living on the side of a dead volcano, all fuelled by ale and whisky'.

Which certainly sounds like more fun than The World's End on the Royal Mile, the next stop on my Edinburgh tour. Here, there's no need for grisly fictions. In October 1977, two 17-year-old girls, Helen Scott and Christine Eadie, were raped and murdered after a night out here (an arrest was made for the murders 30 years later, but the case collapsed), and I sense a chill which even a thoroughly Caledonian dinner of cullen skink and haggis can't shift.

I fall into an uneasy conversation at the bar with a guy in his fifties called Ronnie. He has a deathly pallor and hair as black as licorice. When he smiles there is a hint of fang. I tell him about the book, and he reveals he's a cab driver, and has stories to make your hair stand on end. He mentions that in the wake of the World's End murders police were looking for a MK4 grey Cortina with a broken brakelight, and I feel slighty uneasy. Like David Byron at The Grapes in Liverpool, he casts a glance at his drink.

Most of the stories concern the soldiers stationed all over the city. He tells me that 84 per cent of all army personnel in Afghanistan are based at the four barracks scattered across Edinburgh: Redford, Dreghorn, Longstone and Craigiehall. This weekend the city is full of troops.

'They always use Scottish regiments when things get sticky. Wellington did it, nothing changes.' He explains that the Black Watch are in town. 'You don't realise who they are at first. They get in the cab and they look like young boys out on the lash. They're well behaved, but by the end of the night they're in bits, telling you stories about their mates getting blown to pieces.'

He tells a tale about one lad from another regiment, who had just got back from a tour of Helmand Province. 'They're basically a sniper regiment. They put them in when they need to take out someone important. This lad told me he crawled through the desert on his belly for five miles to take out a big Taliban leader. When he got there, he saw the guy was sitting there with his wife and child. He radioed back to ask what to do and they said "take them all out". So he did. That's the sort of thing you don't read about in the papers.'

Is that why I'm shivering, standing outside a grim-looking bar called Bar Salsa? To tell the truth, it's probably more to do with the fact I've spent the last few hours doing a lonely circuit of the pubs of Grassmarket. The arterially damaged heart of the city's nightlife, it's a boozy theme park where students, backpackers, hen and stag parties come to crank themselves up before plunging into local fleshpots like Sneaky Pete's, The Liquid Rooms, or, for the stag parties, pole-dancing emporium Burke and Hare's (yes, it's named after the nineteenth-century serial murderers).

There seems no option other than to give in to Edinburgh's obsession with the macabre. At Deacon Brodies' I learn the pub is named after William Brodie, whose double life was the inspiration for Robert Louis Stevenson's *Jekyll and Hyde*; at The Last Drop, named because of its grandstand view of the gallows which used to stand outside on the cobblestone square, I discover that the signature drink is 'The Executioner's Cocktail' (a kidney punishing combination of strong ale and cider). It's far less touristy, and a lot more fun, however, at Madge Kilkenny's, where Thin Lizzy's 'Dancing in the Moonlight' lifts my spirits, but, to be honest, by eleven o'clock my head feels like it's full of shaving foam. I'm smashed, and it's all in the name of research. Because I've arranged to meet a character called Craig who is part of a web group called Drunks United, whose Facebook page proclaims: 'May all drunks unite and be as one giant drunk. My goal is for everyone in this group to be drunk at the same time.' In the name of diligent research, I'd contacted 30 people before the trip in the hope of talking pubs, and I've decided to take him up on his offer of allowing me to tag along on a night out. However, the place is heaving, and I'm thinking of sliding away when I spot a character in a white tuxedo, a black shirt and a white piano key tie moving towards me. On his forehead he is wearing an airline sleep mask.

'Morning,' he says. Craig, 25, explains that he's an enthusiastic member of Drunks United, and he takes his responsibilities seriously. 'Beer is what I live for. It's the universal religion. Think about it. It links you and I to the slave workers on the pyramids. What else does that? It's the Western world's equivalent of the peace pipe. If we used it as a positive force instead of condemning it, we might actually get this planet out of the mess it's in.'

He's obviously sincere but I feel suddenly exhausted amid the bar-side crush. It's probably the combined effect of months of asking the same questions, but my dip in mood doesn't seem to phase Craig. 'Our dreams have been stolen by bureaucrats who want us to live in lives of greyness,' he says with evangelical zeal.

It's the old thing about lives of quiet desperation. You're a long time dead, man. And booze is the journey. It's like Brett Easten Ellis says in *Less Than Zero*. 'It doesn't matter where the road goes. All that matters is that you're on it.'

As the evening progresses, he becomes less interested in discussing Drunks United's manifesto and keener on hitting the dance-floor. 'I've got my hand up the skirt of the Mona Lisa!' he bellows, inexplicably, jerking rhythmically to Franz Ferdinand's 'Take Me Out'. As he spies attractive women, he voices his appreciation with quotes from his favourite film, *Austin Powers: International Man of Mystery*.

'Fembot!' he says approvingly as a girl in a gold dress shimmies by. 'Baseball, cold showers, Margaret Thatcher naked on a cold day,' he mutters, spying a girl in a micro-mini skirt.

Time to go.

'I LOVE YOU, Violet Leighton!' says a bloke in a royal blue roll-neck jumper. The object of his affections is on stage at the Scotia. 'Och, away with yer,' she says, as the soft shuffle of brushes introduces a blues-soaked spin on J.J. Cale's 'After Midnight'.

It's the next afternoon and the storm clouds have lifted, Craig and Bar Salsa already a distant memory. I've left the charm and claustrophobia of Edinburgh for the broad avenues and big heart of Glasgow, and I couldn't be happier. I'm in a pub called The Scotia and I'm struggling to think of a pub in Britain with a welcome to match it. Walking through the door on a Saturday afternoon as the city slowly cranks itself up for the alcoholic onslaught of Celtic vs Rangers, is to finally understand what the expression 'like a warm bath' means. The shoulders relax, tensions vanish. A world which seemed like a Chinese puzzle five minutes ago suddenly makes perfect sense.

A pub since 1792, its reputation as a hang out for Glasgow radicals was forged in the early sixties, when the city was buzzing with folk musicians and activists, fired up by the campaigns of the day: anti-Vietnam, CND, support for the ANC. The duffle-coats, placards and Bob Dylan albums are now gathering dust in the city's attics, but for former owner Brendan McLaughlin this idea of the pub as a hub for progressive thought laid the foundation for his own years in charge.

'I had my first pint in The Scotia in 1967, when I was sixteen. The heady days of the sixties when Billy Connolly, Gerry Rafferty, Gallagher and Lyle, Julie Felix, Donald Sutherland and Pete Seeger – who told me he once took Woody Guthrie there – were well under way. It inspired me to put the emphasis on music and literature because that's what I was interested in. Selfish, maybe, but I didn't want to be another businessman publican. I wanted to prove that the pub is a community resource instead of being a men's den of alcohol-fuelled farragos and fandangoes. Rather, it could be one of the most valuable sources of social exchange and free association. Breathing in the arts in general, but specifically music and literature was a way to the soul.'

By the mid-seventies, however, The Scotia's maverick spirit had been hijacked by the Blue Angels, Glasgow's equivalent of Hell's Angels. 'They ingratiated themselves into The Scotia Bar community in the late 1960s, giving the impression they were into the music going down at the time,' explains Brendan. 'But after an initially cool, if not rather too kindly reception, they worked their way into the core of the pub with the intention of chasing everyone else away. By around 1975 they had achieved their goal and the whole Scotia crowd moved away and left them to their lust for busting each other's brains in if no one else was around to pick on. Myself and some friends started going across the road to The Victoria Bar. Within three months everyone followed us and the "Vicky" became the in-place for singers, songwriters, poets and all sorts of long-winded literati, among them many concise thinkers with fiery passions who got everyone involved in all kinds of local issues and campaigns.'

When McLaughlin took the reins in the late eighties he barred the Angels and instigated a music, comedy and arts policy attracting everyone from John Martyn to Robbie Coltrane; Alison

Krauss to Christy Moore; George Melly to James Kelman and Sue Townsend.

A staunchly socialist agenda came with it: McLaughlin formed an action group called 'Workers City' whose monthly magazine the *Keelie* would be plotted and distributed in the pub, and all visitors had to abide by its code. 'The pub was a naturally socialist place. It got a name for the "Glasgow Banter" and belting out songs and poems of working-class struggle. It was always a place where you wouldn't get away with any form of racism, sexism or sectarianism. Nor is it still a place where cheap jokes and throwaway lines are tolerated without an explanation of why, who and what the hell.'

McLaughlin retired in 2003, but he's still a regular, seen at the bar or on stage (he recently played a gig there to launch his new album, appropriately titled *See Me I'm Always Dreamin'*).

Today the pub is run by Mary Rafferty. We're sitting in a corner booth, the soft crackle of balls fizzing across felt coming from the pool hall above our heads. Mary tells me she's continuing the tradition for live music and encouraging local writers. 'We had a poet laureate competition this year and we're starting up a battle of the bands. I'm hoping to find the next Bob Dylan.'

Mary explains that the pub is all about fostering a creative atmosphere. 'I try to get interesting people to walk through the doors, and I look for bar staff who are a bit different or a bit quirky. At the moment they're all in bands or doing art courses, one specialises in stained glass. It means that people are constantly feeding off each other, the enthusiasm comes from all sides.'

On the walls, esoteric personnel voice their silent approval: Che Guevara, Ramsay MacDonald, Ronnie Wood. A line drawing of Billy 'the Big Yin' Connolly is a nod to his days here in the early seventies, when he would play gigs with Gerry Rafferty as The Humblebums, singing songs written by local maverick Sean Tierney.

Mary explains that the flow of jobbing local musicians through the doors is constant. If a bar stool suddenly becomes empty it's probably because its usual occupant is 'in Saudia Arabia playing with Denny Laine'.

It's not, however, all about knowing your hammer-ons from your whammy bar. 'We are very careful with the music policy,' she says. 'We like to see everyone before they play. It's all about how they connect with the crowd. We had a band on the other week and their CD was incredible. But when they played live they were so introspective, it wasn't healthy. They were playing for themselves rather than the room. They won't be coming back.'

Today, the free entertainment comes from Violet Leighton. In line with the pub's socialist ideals, her set seems slanted towards songs geared to soothing a clientele bruised from all the credit-crunching. Bluesy renditions of 'Money', 'What's Goin' On', 'Inner City Blues' and 'Come Together' all conscious pleas for unity and understanding. After all the talk of big business, pub closures and the English loss of identity over the last few months, I'm blown away. Violet's in her fifties now, and explains she works in social care during the week; she gigs for fun (all entertainment at The Scotia is free).

'I'm a socialist and I don't want to bash people over the head with my opinions,' she says. 'People are drained by the end of the week and I try to address what's going on in a subtle way. Having said that, pubs are socialist places, they should be about the common good. And if I find a protest song that suits my style, it's going in the set.'

As for the pub itself, it's irreplaceable. 'I first came here thirty years ago and nothing's changed. An atmosphere builds in a place over the years, and you can feel it here.'

She tells me the bare bones of her life story, and I'm reminded of Richard Simpson's addiction to the starlight back at The Percy Arms. Mesmerised by her sister's lifestyle as an exotic dancer, she left Glasgow for the bright lights of London at 17, only to hit the bottle and give up singing, intimidated by the ads in the music papers ('I'd look in the back of *Melody Maker* and it would say "no fatties or uglies" and I'd think, oh God, I can't apply').

For various reasons Violet didn't sing again until she was 39, and only lately has she picked up where she left off, with plans to form a new band, The Bhumboogie Orchestra. I tell her she's one audition away from winning the hearts of the nation on *X Factor* but Violet shrugs; she knows the limelight comes at a price. 'I'm happy with where I am. Singing to people in a place like this is priceless.'

The next morning an odd thing happens. I'm in the quiet coach on the train back to London, when there's a sudden commotion. A group of boisterous lads clamber on at the last minute and start larking about. They're only drinking soft drinks and munching on crisps, but you can feel the carriage bristle. After 20 minutes or so, they calm down, pull copies of *Zoo* and *Nuts* from their bags and restrict themselves to snatches of conversation.

It becomes obvious they're in the army, and I ask the chattiest one, a lad called Sean, where he's headed. 'We're going back to Catterick to finish basic training,' he says, evenly. And then? 'Camp Bastion, probably.'

When the drinks trolley comes round a middle-aged woman offers to buy them all coffee, but they politely decline, and by the time the train pulls up at their station, they've fallen strangely quiet. They collect up their kit bags and troop off in silence. I can't help but think of Craig from Drunks United, barely older than these lads and with one hand up the skirt of the Mona Lisa. Maybe he was right. It doesn't matter where the road goes. All that matters is that you're on it.

At The Sheep Heid, that clock keeps ticking.

DRINKING ON THE FRONT LINE

Robin Turner

I f you squinted so hard that the HD footage blurred, August 2011 could almost pass for the early eighties. The Clash are on the cover of the *NME* and the country is at war with itself. A Conservative government is gleefully redrawing the landscape in the name of austerity. An escalating succession of lootings is taking place, first across the capital before out in the rest of the UK.

On the news, comparisons are quickly drawn with the restless summer of 1981. Back then, race riots speedballed across the country from Brixton to Birmingham, Clapham to Chapeltown. The original line-up of The Clash were still at full throttle and 'Ghost Town' by The Specials was at number one. Thirty years on, 'London Calling' has been chosen as the official soundtrack to the 2012 Olympics.

Whatever the initial root causes that sparked the disturbances, they soon faded into lawless pillaging. The civil disobedience displays all the claustrophobia and confusion of a freshly sprayed Banksy mural. At once radical and pointless, the rioters are rallying against anything and everything or – more likely – nothing.

I sit at home, watching in a dazed, impotent stupor. Living in Hackney, events are unfolding in front of my sofa. A hundred yards from the heart of the action, the sound of helicopters phase between those on the television and those some 30 feet above the house. Police vans blur past the window in a constant procession towards the heart of the problem; within seconds they are seen arriving on the grimly addictive rolling news coverage on the BBC. Cameras keep cutting between conflicts earlier on nearby Mare Street and the current police stand-off much nearer to home on Clarence Road. The news loops on, the choppers swoop on and – in search of a new angle – the camera perspective changes.

And then I see it. Caught just behind the police lines, there is my local. The Pembury.

Although not the handiest pub for anyone watching the running battle between police and Hackney's most disaffected (that honour went to The Wishing Well), on the night in question The Pembury is as close as anyone not wanting a custodial sentence will go. Cars are torched. Local branches of Tesco, Ladbrokes, Argos, JD Sports and Boots have all been ransacked. Neighbouring off-licences are still being broken into in the middle of the night after the heat had died down and the police dispatched to another postcode. The next day, it appears as if The Pembury hadn't been as much as a target. It had all but repelled the looters.

Stuck out on the corner of Dalston Lane, Amhurst Road and Pembury Road, my local is the most unassuming pub I know. One brightly lit room that fills with conversation not music. More hand pumps than keg taps. Home made pork scratchings. No recognisable brands on the bar. Board games piled high, a bar billiards table and one or two regulars who keep ferrets on leads. It is a place for daytime solace, for tie straightening, for hangovers – both making them and salving them.

The Pembury is a relic of a time before segregation in pubs. It harks back to the days before bar rooms were ruled by the invisible and inexplicable demarcations of age and class so prevalent now. Those boundaries were often based on little more than the angle of your haircut, the daftness of your trousers or the shrillness of the CDs that filled the jukebox. I had a vague recollection from when I first moved to London in 1990 of The Pembury being a kind of permanent home for the peace convoy, a lawless tie-dyed republic that never seemed to shut. Whether that was the case, no one drinking at the bar now could remember. That or they'd blanked it from memory.

Seemingly uninterested in chasing the disposable income of transient trendies, maybe The Pembury is the one throwback to the times when Hackney wasn't the most desirable address in London. And, really, that was enough for me. I'd ended up falling in love with a pub that represented everything I'd spent my youth trying to avoid.

As the clean-up operation tornadoes through the streets as fast as the looters had retreated, the news continues to portray Hackney as the archetypal broken society. Sure Start centres and youth clubs are being axed as over £32 million is shaved off the year's council budget. Elsewhere, local pubs – as in pubs used by locals – are disappearing. One of the most visible pubs in the area – The Railway Inn directly opposite the train station – is now a garish money pit, a bright green Paddy Power surrounded by the lost and desperate. Elsewhere, superfluous pub signs flap in the wind on half of Hackney's side streets – a developer's vain attempt 'to retain some of the spirit that it had back when it was a pub' as Pete Brown had said back in The Jolly Butchers.

These things surely aren't unconnected. Aspirational Hackney had been relentlessly eating up boozers for years as middle classes – I have to include my family there – elbowed our way into what had, ten years before, been a borderline bankrupt borough. Ever the savvy operator, former mayor Ken Livingstone was gearing up to fight for re-election in 2012 including a Save the Pubs campaign as one of his platforms. It would be churlish to sneer that he had been silent during the worst of the damage and that there really weren't that many more pubs to be lost in London. He clearly recognises the role of the pub as an irreplaceable cornerstone of London life. Better late than never.

A month before all the noise and confusion that followed the August lootings, I spent a couple of hours at the home of East London's most erudite biographer and critic, Iain Sinclair. A literary gumshoe, Sinclair has spent a life in books – reading, selling, writing. Increasingly his books have come to focus on Hackney; *Hackney: the Rose Red Empire* is a summation of his love-hate relationship with the borough he can't leave. Meeting such a towering intellect is a daunting prospect – I feel like I'm taking on Joe Calzaghe after spending a heavy training regime propping up the counter at KFC.

Sinclair makes no bones about his fear that the arrival of London's Olympic project will bring about a security lockdown that will turn Hackney into nothing less than a surveillance state. Three nights of riots in central London clearly wasn't going to help matters much.

I ask him about how the local landscape has changed in his fortysomething years in the area, specifically with regards to East London's pubs. He shakes his head, incredulous at the transformation Hackney has gone through.

'The pubs… they've all gone! Within this swoop there must have been seven or eight pubs and they've all disappeared within the term of the gentrification process. The Albion pub that used to sit on Albion Drive is now a very smartly privatised house but one that keeps the pub's sign as a kind of heritage street number. The Black Bull which was round the back – a really big old boozer which was squatted for a long time – that's now obliterated entirely so they can create a new canalside estate. The locality depended on these little pubs; places that bunches of people treated as a local. They had an energy and a dynamic that served the community. Now there's an economic imperative that has got rid of them because – obviously – they're worth more as housing projects, as development projects. So gradually they all disappear into history – apart from the ones that achieve gastro status and supply the new demographic in places like Broadway Market.'

I wonder aloud whether the reinvention of the local pub could almost trigger the inception point of a grand project like the Olympics. It starts off innocently enough with a chef experimenting with guinea fowl sausages and big chips, then before you know it, there is a towering Westfield shopping centre that no locals can afford to use.

'Absolutely. It's very connected. It starts off with squatting artists moving into an area. The property developers are right on their heels because they can see there's a certain mystique to the area that gives it a bit of a buzz. First off, it's all happening and then the place evolves into a lesbian quarter or something, then before very long there's the gastropub, then – boom – the next thing there's an Olympic stadium going up. I'm just interested in what happens after because there isn't any way that we can keep the whole thing running. Because the things that they couldn't keep running previously were on a much smaller scale.'

It's true, the whole landscape is changing. Train lines are being upgraded for the dignitaries of 2012, shopping malls are popping up, pubs are becoming Zagat-listed restaurants and the locals are revolting. Thankfully, as everywhere around moves with the times, my local seems content to stay the same. The day after the riots, the pub filled a gap somewhere between thriving community centre and alcohol-fuelled voluntary support group. In the middle of the afternoon, friends sat agog, unable to believe what had just happened on their doorstep, chinking glasses like fresh-faced soldiers returning from their first tours of duty.

I sit down for a pint with my friend and fellow Pembury devotee, Luke Turner. Luke lives so close to the action that he and his neighbours had hurriedly taken in their wheelie bins the night before after realising they were easy ammunition once set alight and launched towards police. That morning he wrote poetically about watching the chaos unfold out on the street where he lived on the website he runs, The Quietus. Over pints of bitter, we pick at the still bloody bones of what had happened.

'One of the things that I see as a massive problem nowadays is that everywhere you go, things look exactly the same. How can you have pride in your community if your community has three Tescos within half a mile of each other, the same bookies you see on every high street and a load of identikit pubs? But with the supermarkets the very relationship between consumer and retailer has broken down to nothing. You don't even speak to a human being at a checkout any more. The shops are full of people just orbiting each other but never interacting; that's the business model. The result is that you end up becoming annoyed with people; it promotes frustration and isolation.'

Even at a young age, it was our local's bloody-minded independence that immediately appealed to Luke when he moved to London.

'When it comes to pubs I think tastes-wise I've always been an old man,' he admits. 'I grew up in St Albans which is where CAMRA began in the early seventies and was also the home of the first ever super pub. It was originally a coaching town so it's always had a huge amount of pubs. The ones in the centre got really fucked around with, made into these big pub-cum-clubs. You'd get all these Ben Sherman-clad geezers coming into town at the weekends. Me and my mates – a bunch of Manics and Suede fans – were terrified of them. Every single time we'd try to go to one of those enormodomes, we'd either get a kicking, have to run from a kicking or – at the very best – talk ourselves out of a kicking. After a while we'd go to the pubs in the old part of town where all the CAMRA types would sit supping ale. They were all Georgian or Tudor buildings that had been really beautifully kept because they weren't trying to cater for an ever-changing youth market. I found that in that company, I started to think and drink like that. So from a very early drinking age, my criteria became "Is there a seat, is there no loud music, is there ale?" When I first moved to Hackney and came across this place, it properly ticked all of those boxes.

'This place has always reminded me of the Methodist youth clubs that I used to go to when I was a kid,' he continues. 'It's got that brightly lit church function room feel about it which weirdly makes me feel quite relaxed. I think that brings a real charm to the place, it feels like it's grown into the way it is. There's always interesting pictures on the wall, it's just a bit eccentric but not too much. When you see old photos of pubs, they actually look pretty much like The Pembury. They always appear to be pretty minimal – the kind of places where you go to drink basically! I always get annoyed when I go to supposedly rustic country pubs, those places that would have you believe they are the picture of authenticity. Most of the time, all the ephemera is just tat they've picked out of a catalogue. Horse brasses, old pictures of farm workers or sailors, a mock wood fire and stupidly puffy leather chairs. It's an affectation; a dubious post-sixties idea of what a country pub should be like.'

We finish up our pints and stand in the doorway looking outside. The predicted second night of looting is clearly not going to happen – not before kicking-out time anyway. Contemplating the local takeaway choices, Luke pauses for one more thought.

'I can remember when I first heard about Wetherspoon's opening up a pub called The Moon Under Water. I was a teenager and obsessed with Orwell. I remember thinking it was fantastic that someone had created a pub based on his ideals even if in practice it wasn't actually the way he'd have pictured things. But strangely, years after I went to the Wetherspoon's version, when I first moved to Hackney and walked in here, I genuinely remember feeling that it was as close to the written Moon Under Water as any pub I'd ever been in.'

It is weeks after leaving Iain Sinclair's house and a few days after the riots that I remember something he had written in his magnificent, occasionally exasperated love letter to E8. He tracked the flow of east London's lost river, the Hackney Brook, and how it had flowed out past my local boozer before surging onwards towards the river Lea. He contrasted imagery of the area then – the lost idyll of the 1730s – with the concrete and exhaust fumes of today.

'The point where the brook crossed Mare Street is well represented in views of Hackney as a village in the 1730s: the tower of St Augustine, The Eight Bells pub, the footbridge over the river. Then The Pembury Tavern, the riverside gardens, pictorial impressions of early balloon ascents. To reach this green table, we negotiate a set of garages tucked away under railway arches, aerosol obscenities, miracle-promising messianic franchises, guardian dogs.'

Is The Pembury's odd position – jutting out alone on a five-way junction – down to the fact that it had been near enough on the riverside in the 18th century? Did ancient liquid channels – now co-opted into Joseph Bazalgette's sewer system – once flow beside it? Is the building straddling mystical hand-pumped ley lines, acting as a spirits home for thirsty travellers from the Victorian era onwards?

The pub has a scrubby field and the beleaguered Pembury Estate to the left and a nail bar that doubles as a wet fish shop to the right. Behind it, a yawning thoroughfare leading to central Hackney. In front, railway arches filled with body repair shops for London taxis. Buses curl before it, heading out of town towards Clapton, Leyton, Whipps Cross. Police cars use the five-fingered junction like a PlayStation Formula One track. Ten thousand points for jangled pedestrian nerves. All the while, the pub stays calm – stoic and steadfast against a backdrop of inner-city insanity.

Is The Pembury truly its own island? If not physically any more then definitely still spiritually. Possibly even as much as The Marisco on craggy old Lundy or The Pilchard down south on debonair Burgh. It divined channels through the heart of Hackney and stood as one of the most visible and imposing buildings in the area yet somehow it seemed to repel so many of the grotesque trappings of the modern world. It was the kind of place Arthur Pendragon could hold a new Camelot presided over Merlin-like by the spectral presence of Orwell.

The Pembury stands alone, buffeting against heavy weather, against the lootings, against the pubcos and marketing men with unbeatable discounts on new cider launches. Against Sky Sports and DJs heavily armed with the latest chillwave and witch house WAVs on laptop. Against the properly developers and the betting shops, against a disinterested local council. Even all the drunks and the rowdies who never seem to find it.

Unless of course that drunk is me at half past closing time, valiantly attempting to proselytise about this most humble of boozers yet again.

DO ANDROIDS DREAM OF ELECTRIC PINTS?

Robin Turner

'Being in my mid-twenties, it's really difficult to appreciate what pubs meant to people twenty, thirty, forty years ago,' says Mark Charlwood, one of a new generation of beer bloggers, as we sit chatting in cyberspace. 'You've only got to be moderately interested in pubs to have heard the stats that get thrown around about how many pubs we lose each week. And that all sucks, people losing their jobs, people losing their business. Nobody thinks that's cool. But I do sometimes struggle to understand when people say that the loss of a pub is the loss of a community's heart and a community's hub. I've lived in the sticks and I've lived in the city but I've never known a community whose beating heart is the local boozer. I've known a community that has a tiny group of about fifteen people that always go to the same pub… but that's all. Is that because I'm too young to remember the times when things were different or is that because in reality pubs haven't had that role in a community for many, many years? I love pubs, but I really do struggle to believe that the Rovers Return exists outside of *Coronation Street*. I don't think enough people want a place like that any more. That's as big a reason as any for the closure of so many pubs.'

Mark seems to have hit the nail on the head. He's taken an obsession with all things ale and channelled it into the excellent Beer Birra Bier website. He is also from a generation who felt one step removed from the well-worn notions of the pub's position in society. The country's most famous pubs – The Queen Vic, The Woolpack and the Rovers – are as much fictional creations as Hogwarts or the console room of the TARDIS. In 2011, there clearly aren't real-life versions of community boozers like them on every street corner.

Mark Dredge – the award-winning writer behind Pencil and Spoon blog – is in agreement. 'The pub is what it is to the individual. I think it's only possible to speak as an individual and while it's easy to say that pubs are the most important thing in Britain and we need to save them all it's also hypocritical to say this if I only drink in the pub once a week. Taking a 1950s viewpoint of village life is just not relevant sixty years later when so much has changed. The pub's important in a different way from being the centre of the community that it used to be.'

While writing about beer might seem next to pointless to some when it is so easy just to go out and drink it yourself, there have been enough people who have tried – and a few who have managed – to capture that wondrous essence found in the bottom of a pint glass. The two Marks are perfect examples. Taking inspiration from the greats of the genre – Michael Jackson, Roger Protz and the King of Beer himself Pete Brown to name a few – they have each independently set up websites where they can espouse the virtues of foaming nut-brown ale. Unpaid, unsponsored and completely without ties to any of the old forms of media or to a structured organisation like CAMRA, they have created a forum with the freedom to write what they want when they want.

In the years since *The Rough Pub Guide*, I'd found my drinking habits in thrall to the internet. More and more often it seemed, the devil's portal was subtly changing the way I thought about drinking. Web-savvy pubs were posting updates about what was going on in the bar that day. I saw massive parallels with the way that beer was now being championed and with the way music blogs made information and music immediately accessible to all. The age of press junket and the backhander were over – bloggers with no allegiances could write what they wanted when they wanted. Why take a punt on a potential bad pint when you can easily head to a pub serving the exact beer you want, right there and then? And as in music, the bloggers acted as the vanguard, hop-fuelled missionaries preaching something akin to the gospel according to Saint Arnold of Metz (who encouraged followers with the sage advice, 'Don't drink the water, drink the beer.')

I'd chanced upon Mark Dredge's Pencil and Spoon site trying to find out more about a brewery whose beer was so good it had pretty much rendered me speechless. Mark had not only laid praise in their direction, he'd toured the brewery (with Mark Charlwood as it turned out) and had specific details about the brewing process. Though admittedly not everyone's idea of light reading, I was hooked, finding the other Mark's site soon after. From there, the web opened up – names like One More Won't Kill You, Get to the Pub, Lost in the Beer Aisle and Are You Tasting the Pith.

In the spirit of the times, I hastily convene a meeting in cyberspace. My own traditions dictate that I head to The Pembury to abuse the free wi-fi and sink a couple of pints for inspiration. The two Marks talk about beer and pubs in a loving yet pragmatic manner. There is no pretension and no one-upmanship. They are there to help, to provide a service for drinkers.

Mark Dredge explains: 'Blogging opens up avenues for people

who are interested in good beer and want to read or write about it. There aren't the opportunities to write about beer in print and the internet is without restriction. There are also lots of people who really want to talk about good beer and the nature of the internet and social media make it the perfect place to share virtual pints. Whether these people are more discerning I don't know, but there is a greater level of education and understanding about beer which is very important. There's also a chicken-egg thing going on with discerning drinkers and blogs. I do think the rise of young beer bloggers is indicative of a growing interest in beer from new drinkers. That's exciting.'

If you look hard enough, you can see that there is a sea change happening everywhere. The first decade of the 21st century has seen beer itself changing. Breweries like The Kernel and BrewDog (see next chapter) are warping concepts of what was and wasn't real ale – one of the previous benchmarks for what made a pub work. The divisions had previously been absolute – real ale came from a hand pump, anything from a keg was pretty much guaranteed to be identikit fizz brewed in an aircraft hanger on the Welsh borders. With a series of pubs springing up in London and beyond – each emphasising the quality of booze whatever the delivery method, without the selective appeal of most traditional real ale boozers – it makes sense that a new breed of writers are looking at the subject from an entirely new direction. And the internet is the perfect platform for that to happen from.

'Good beer,' ruminates Dredge, 'should be more important than beer that's "real", however it's served. The thing with most bloggers is that we just want to drink really good beer. From my point of view I couldn't care less how it gets from the brewery to my glass – cask, keg, bottle, can, bucket, whatever – as long as when I get to drink it, it tastes good.'

I am curious as to whether this new breed of beer blogger represented the 21st-century equivalent of CAMRA. In 40 years they've achieved a huge amount, campaigning for drinkers rights, but as Charlwood puts it, 'Cask ale is safe, they saved it! We need to move on and address the new challenges in the beer world; frankly there are more important issues than if my glass is full to the bloody line or not.' Perhaps this next-generation consortium of writers, brewers and pubs will all feed into a sprawling collective with a common aim of making sure what goes in a pint glass is worthy of the money paid for it, whatever the form it's delivered in?

'Talking in general terms, I think there's a new generation of brewer and drinker,' says Dredge. 'That new generation is building on our beer history and is pushing it in a new direction. I think it's also important to understand that the new generation is still tiny in comparison to the beer drinking whole in this country.'

So, will the humble pub be bypassed as the all-important venue for consuming beer? After all, what difference is there in drinking a perfectly chilled bottle at home or in a crowded boozer? Will the search for a perfect pint actually be the thing that ends up killing off the perfect pub? Charlwood sees things slightly more rationally.

'Quality transcends opinion, but opinion will always differ from one person to the next. A pub I love might be hated by someone else. And on a personal level, opinion is too dependent on things outside of our control to be consistent. On a cold winter Sunday, a pub that keeps good English bitter, has a roaring fire and serves a great roast is close to perfection. But that same pub with a no TV policy would suck when you want to go and have a pint while watching the game. A pub that only serves macro lager when you're out on a pub crawl with a load of beer lovers? Terrible. The local that I used to go to with my mates back home and go back to when I'm back visiting family? Brilliant. Does it only serve terrible macro beer? Who cares!'

It's refreshing to hear someone with an unquenchable thirst for beery knowledge say what I've been thinking for years. That it's not just about what flows from the taps and that a crappy pint in the right company is as important as a perfect pint poured in hallowed surrounds. Dredge agrees.

'It doesn't have to be a great pub and you don't need to be

drinking a great beer; it can be about the people, the food, the weather, the mood you're in. It could be that you are alone in a pub, sipping a great beer and reading a good book with locals talking around you creating a background hum of conversation, and that could be your perfect moment. Of course, it's always good to fantasise about what the perfect pub would be like – the location, the beer list, the jukebox selection, the food offering, the barmaid… I'm sure we've all got a Moon Under Water in our minds. A great pub is made what it is by the people inside it. An empty pub is very different to a busy one.'

So what then constitutes the closest thing to perfection in a boozer? While Orwell's account ran in the pages of the *Evening Standard*, what would those people using today's cutting edge information technology – people young enough to be his great-grandchildren – be looking for? Mark Dredge wastes no time in keying in his reply.

'Location first: it's not at the end of the street because if it was then I'd never leave. I need to get a train or walk at least half an hour to get to it. When I get there I'm greeted by the barman and a few gorgeous barmaids who know a lot about beer and can talk for hours. The beer choice is great but not necessarily extensive because I'm terrible at making decisions. There won't be a TV but there will be light background music. At exactly three pints into my evening, some of my favourite songs will play. There might be a piano for rare nights when I fancy live music. There will be the day's papers and an extensive bookshelf. One of the locals will have travelled the world and he will be a born storyteller filled with endless stories. There will be other locals. Mostly there for backing noise. It also needs food but it'll be snacks – Scotch eggs, sausages, chips, bread and cheese, maybe a really good burger. There will be a fireplace for the winter and a garden for the summer with a beautiful view of both mountains and the sea. Into the skip outside goes fruit machines, anything which can be described as "novelty", TVs, grumpy people, kids (I want to be able to swear and stumble around) and live animals (dead ones are fine in sausage form). They should also have nice toilets. No one ever mentions the toilets, do they?'

As I drain the last drops from my pint and shut the lid of my laptop, I find myself wondering about Mark's perfect pub. The closest match that Orwell could find in spirit to The Moon Under Water shared only eight of Orwell's criteria. I wonder whether Mark had ever been anywhere that ticked the lion's share of his; maybe there was some mythical, fantastical Pencil and Spoon boozer out there, below the mountains and next to rolling sea, serving up glorious golden pints with freshly cooked sausages on the bar and – for the good folk of the blogosphere – a broadband connection that never dipped out.

Yeah, I think, I could waste some time there. And with that, I wander off to see what kind of state the bogs are in.

THE BOTTLE OF BRITAIN

Robin Turner

Evin O'Riordan flips the top from a label-less brown bottle. We're stood in a yard out the back of a railway arch in Bermondsey. Above our heads rush-hour trains thunder along the tracks, picking up pace as they ferry commuters back home to the Garden of England, out over the hop fields where Orwell toiled while studying underclass life for *Down and Out in London and Paris*. Even out in the open air, the smell emanating from within the arch is borderline intoxicating. Deliriously woozy, it is a sublime twist of coffee and hops that seems like hangover cure and hair of the dog mashed into one. The brew is the latest in a long line of inspired concoctions that have been conjured up in this most unassuming of south London backstreets.

Evin splits the contents of the brown bottle between our two glasses. Cloudy amber in appearance with a tingling of fruit on the nose, I am curious as to what I am drinking. 'It's an India Pale Ale. Strength? About 7 per cent.' As I savour the first deeply hoppy hit of a deceptively strong beer, I roll the liquid round my tongue in an attempt to eke out the taste for as long as possible. Comparing it to standard beers is like judging *War and Peace* next to the latest Katie Price novel. It really is exquisite.

'I'd never brewed before but I was very intrigued by the culture around it,' Evin explains. 'People talking about beer, the quality of what they were drinking. When I used to work in food, I'd been obsessed with those qualities. When I used to make cheese, I could have told you what the weather was like on the day the cow was milked. But I didn't really see the same thing happening here in Britain with beer.'

Evin is the brains behind The Kernel Brewery. The brewery itself is a tiny set-up mainly producing bottled beer that is running at back-breaking full capacity. Having started out with an aim of creating 'beer that forces you to confront and consider what you are drinking', their reputation for innovation in the industry is by now a given. Gushing plaudits are commonplace and now awards are beginning to gather on Evin's mantlepiece – all the more incredible considering the brewery is just 18 months old. What The Kernel has done in that time is create a range of beers that can inspire proper followers; the kind of people who'd seek out their new beers in a hypnotic daze. People like me in fact.

Putting my own crazed fanboy tendencies aside, it is clear that there is a revolution brewing in British beer, and people like Evin are at the forefront. Beer itself is changing and pubs and punters are following suit. While the New Labour years had been synonymous with the countrywide rise of the gastropub, the prevailing trend in the early days of the coalition has been for a new type of watering hole, a different kind of drinker and a set of new, upstart breweries revolutionising what goes into a pint glass. Attention to detail is key, with presentation also playing a large part. Beer and ale have for so long seemed the preserve of a small, very male and – for want of a better description – perpetually uncool societal clique. Trainspotters ticking their way through the country's casks from coast to coast, pint by pint.

Since visiting the beer festival, I've noticed more and more often the term real ale being replaced. The buzz is all about 'craft beer' – to all intents the same thing only without all the stigma. Out were hard and fast rules about serving and presentation, arguments where 'cask means good, keg means bad'. The term is increasingly cropping up in the kinds of places where beer menus sit alongside the food listings; places like the zeitgeist-surfing Craft Beer Co or The Euston Tap, a pub located in a converted stone lodge just outside the slipstream of one of London's busiest traffic routes. The advantage of this mental rebranding is to remove the product from the image of beer festivals seemingly peopled entirely by bearded men wearing socks and open-toed sandals.

The way it looks to me is that beer culture is getting younger, less wilfully eccentric. Old delineations – socks and sandals on the left and lager louts on the right – are falling away as beer is de-ghettoised. At the time of writing, there are 840 breweries in the UK, more than at any point since the Second World War. It seems recent London start-ups like Brodies, Camden Town, Redemption, Sambrooks and Evin's Kernel and places around the rest of the country such as Harviestoun in Clackmannanshire, Thornbridge in Bakewell, Otley in Pontypridd and Brighton's Dark Star are presenting a clear message. *Drinking this stuff will not make you look like a Dungeons and Dragons fan*. All this pint-sized progress is posting a question. Will the evolution of beer help to produce the perfect pub?

The cap pops off another bottle, this time an Export Stout. To the untrained eye, the bottle would seem to be the same as the previous one – brown with a brown paper label, utilitarian simplicity at its most beautiful. Only the hand-stamped letters on the front alert the keen-eyed to the beer's recipe and strength. I am now some distance from the confines of my bar-room comfort zone (most beer I drink pours out the colour of straw – this looks like liquid coal), though that doesn't stop me eagerly knocking back the contents of my glass. My knowledge of stout doesn't stretch much further than the old bon mot that Guinness tasted better in Ireland. Here I am drinking a stout that was brewed to a recipe from 1890, a beer that has been brought back from the dead by delving deep into London's alcohol archives and is now winning brewing awards in 2011. Evin explains the interest in dusting down old recipes.

'I started out purely home brewing. I used to see this operation as a very big homebrew set-up. Pretty quickly, I got very interested in the history of British beer. I got in touch with a homebrew group called the Durden Park Beer Circle who were dedicated to keeping a lot of traditional recipes alive. These guys published pamphlets with old recipes from brewery archives, mainly from the Victorian era through to the First World War. There are lots of beers that exist on record but nobody really knows what the hell they tasted like. The Durden Park Beer Circle were dedicated to researching those old styles and pooling the recipes in order to keep them alive. You can't emulate the old styles entirely – you can't tell what the conditions of storage would have been back then or whether the ingredients you're using are the same quality. But you can try.'

The idea that London's 'drinkerati' are imbibing beers brewed to standards set over 150 years ago is both baffling and brilliant. After all, 'retromania' – as pop historian Simon Reynolds labelled it – is everywhere else. Popular culture is perpetually eating its own tail in plundering the past. Stalwarts from the world of litera-ture – from Sherlock Holmes to James Bond, even the works of Shakespeare and Austen – are constantly being reimagined and remodelled every few years for new audiences. Every discarded musical genre from the blues to synthpop has made its way up the charts and been recognised in award ceremonies. Why shouldn't food or drink do the same? What Evin and the Durden Park brewers are doing is producing something that is as fuss-free and simple as possible while doffing their caps to the past. Maybe even creating something close to what The Moon Under Water might serve.

'Well, I can't imagine 1946 was a good year for beer because of the war that had just preceded it,' says Evin. 'With that in mind, I can't really hypothesise about the quality of the beer Orwell would have been drinking but in my nostalgic view, I like to think that you could still go into a pub and expect a decent pint. That was always almost a given – some places are always going to look after beer and some places the beer is universally rancid, whatever the year. I'm trying to think whether Guinness had become ubiquitous over here by then. Porters basically died out between the wars. By the end of the Second World War there basically weren't any left, or hardly any. I think the last Worthington Porter was 1956 and they were the last brewing them. The war would have meant ingredients-wise everything was so scarce. There would have been restrictions on what people could brew with but also there were restrictions on brewing strong beers mainly to ensure that people working in munitions factories would actually get up in the morning.'

Although it is fascinating to think about brewing beer while keeping a watchful eye on the historical and sociological context, everything will always fall down if the beer isn't any good. At 35 years old, Evin's high benchmark could never have been a 1956 Worthington Porter or the ancestral version of the Export Stout he brews now. It was a regular bottled beer brewed in Chicago.

'I was working in the States and I used to drink a lot in a particular bar – d.b.a. in Manhattan's Lower East Side,' Evin recalls as the 18.40 to Tonbridge picks up speed overhead. 'They had a load of amazing beers; a load of amazing beers in bottles too. They only had good stuff and they had lots of it. It was just round the corner from where I was working so naturally I spent a lot of time in there. The beer I was drinking, I think it was something like a Goose Island IPA. It's a perfectly good beer but it's nothing that's going to change your world. I was thinking that if this is the beer at the lower end of the scale – this is the average beer they are selling – then surely everything can go up from here. I remember thinking, "If everyone in the world was drinking this beer, the world would be an excellent place."'

As I knock back the last treacle-like drops of stout, I ask Evin whether British pubs had played any inspirational role when he got back and began to brew at home.

'Not really. When I started out brewing, I had no experience of working with pubs, just drinking in them. Since starting, all of the pubs that have come on board have approached me – I've never had to hawk my wares which is really nice. Pubs weren't involved in my reckoning to start off with simply because of my own ignorance. Also I assumed that most pubs would rather sell draught beer – either keg or cask – than bottles. So pubs weren't part of any early masterplan. The one exception though was The Rake in Borough Market. It's a place where people – staff or punters – will guide you to beers you might not have tried. Pubs should offer the perfect space for that kind of engagement. A perfect pub would be the kind where a stranger might recommend you a beer, where people might sit and have a conversation about the beer they're drinking. All that interaction helps a brewery like us get going. If you've got passionate beer drinkers sat in a pub and someone walks in off the street and asks, "What shall I have?" Really, there's no better endorsement.'

A couple of days later and 581 miles north of Evin's Bermondsey railway arch, a brewer with a very different philosophy is starting work on a Saturday morning. Martin Dickie is one of the two founders of BrewDog, an Aberdeenshire set-up that is extremely good at two things: brewing and generating headlines.

Since first brewing in 2007, BrewDog has been a proper phenomenon. With a healthy disregard for any conventions or mores of the industry, two men in their mid-twenties have taken their minuscule start-up from nothing to a business valued somewhere in the region of £27 million within the space of four years.

The difference between what they and everyone else is doing is that the product is only half of the story.

'Hopefully the beers reflect us,' Martin's Scottish burr barely rising over the chaos of the brewery at full pelt. 'We were 24 when we started. When we started there was nothing that excited us in Britain. There were great beers from abroad flooding the UK but back here it was tedious. You'd get beers with names that played on some kind of nostalgic tradition. People would call their brewery The Lighthouse and beers things like Beautiful Sunset or you'd get a Scottish brewery calling beers things like Old Jock or Rob Roy. That idea had been done to death. We didn't have any interest in that, we wanted to do the exact opposite.'

And then some. The brewery's distinctive bottle designs look more akin to t-shirt logos in a skateboard shop. The beers themselves would seem no less alien to the average CAMRA member. Their regular brews – Punk IPA, Hardcore IPA, Trashy Blonde, Paradox – are complemented by the likes of the 32 per cent Tactical Nuclear Penguin and the 41 per cent Sink the Bismarck. After the Scottish Parliament made moves to ban the 18 per cent Tokyo, the brewery knocked out Nanny State, a 1.1 per cent tipple that was deemed so weak as to be below the legal classification for beer.

Beyond that, this is a brewery that created a beer that was not only the most alcoholic in the world but also the most expensive. The End of History was a 12-bottle run of a 55 per cent beer at £500 a pop. Each bottle came packaged with the body of a dead animal stitched on by a taxidermist. Although the carcasses were roadkill, animal rights campaigners were up in arms. Not that BrewDog cared. In the press release for the beer they declared it was 'to be enjoyed with a weather eye on the horizon for inflatable alcohol industry Nazis, judgemental washed-up neo-prohibitionists or any grandiloquent, ostentatious foxes… a perfect conceptual marriage between art, taxidermy and craft brewing'.

If Evin's beers are like the works of artist Richard Long (dignified, considered, minimalist and poetic) then BrewDog's are akin to those of Damien Hirst (confrontational, flashy, unhinged and unpredictable). They are brewed and bottled (or kegged or casked) to force an opinion. That said, none of the Scottish brewery's demented artifice and balls-out posturing would mean a thing at the bar if the beers weren't exceptional. Martin and his business partner James Watt are brewing challenging beers that are full-bodied, gutsy and memorable for all the right reasons. The presentation is a red herring – certainly their Punk IPA is a classic even if the name and packaging make it look like it was aimed squarely at your skate-obsessed younger brother. Or son. Amazingly, there is something even more incredible in the BrewDog story than stuffing a beer bottle inside the tyre-marked body of a grey squirrel and that is that in the height of a recession the brewery were opening up pubs as fast as they could take them on.

'When we started out, selfishly we were brewing beer that we wanted to drink because no one else was making it,' says Martin. 'Initially, we were pretty much only brewing bottles. We were brewing a very small amount of cask purely for us and our staff at the end of the month. We couldn't sell into pubs. We used to go round with the beers in the back of cars. One of us heading north and one heading south. The uptake was just horrific. We'd sell three or four cases from visits to over fifty pubs the length of Scotland. The problem wasn't the drinkers not wanting the product – they never had the chance to try it. It was that the landlords at that time were so dismissive of young guys making beers, especially beers that weren't run of the mill, average, high street stuff.'

He continues: 'Up until the point we opened the first of our own bars, we'd sold very little of our beers in Aberdeen. No landlords would ever want to take it, they didn't want to stock beers that were that strong or seemingly different. We opened a bar and filled it ninety-five percent with BrewDog beers then a handful of craft beers that we loved. Pretty quickly we had one of the busiest bars in town. The fact that we couldn't sell it wasn't down to the customers – it was down to bloody-minded, stubborn landlords, pure and simple. We'll have five bars by the end of [2011] in a market in massive decline.'

Some of Martin's observations chime with what one-time BrewDog collaborator Pete Brown had talked about – specifically that landlords attempting to read their clientele would invariably miss by a mile, usually second-guessing tastes before overcompensating with the garish and the tedious. As far as Martin is concerned the problem – that desperation to please – stems from the country's insatiable predilection for cheap supermarket plonk.

'What's the point of going into a pub and paying up to four quid for a pint of Stella. Apparently it's a specialist super-product – if you were to believe their advertising – yet you can get exactly the same thing in a supermarket for a fraction of the price. The culture of overcharging in pubs while undercharging in supermarkets is part of the inherent problem.'

I am intrigued about the brave move of opening up their own pubs in a time when most people are fretting about takings and gathering up kindling for an insurance job. The bars are a la mode – sleek concrete surfaces, sharp clean lines and more black than at an Emo wake. Martin explains the brewery's logic.

'All we've ever tried to do at BrewDog is make the best beer. Our bars are an extension of that. We try to make the most relaxed environment without pandering to any particular set of people. They're never going to become football bars or fashion bars. No one is ever excluded. Inside you'll get elderly couples next to young professionals, students, whoever… the whole spectrum of people interested in beer.

'Personally, I think the key to a good pub is to find one with passionate, keen staff. We make sure each person we employ spends a week in our brewery getting to understand how beer is made. They watch the process and see people working their bollocks off and they get to understand the ingredients and the processes and how it all comes together. By the time they start selling, they know how it all works – possibly they have even become beer snobs. Having people who will take the time to explain things is absolutely essential. If you came in and asked for Carling, they'll politely explain that we didn't sell it and try to steer you towards something else that you might like. Once you start that self-education, hopefully there's no going back. What's really cool is when you see the same person six months later in the pub drinking a third of a pint of Tokyo or waxing lyrical about Tactical Nuclear Penguin. It's fun to change people's perceptions and allow them to gain an understanding of something as simple – yet misunderstood – as beer. You'll see the guy who came in asking for lager is drinking Punk IPA or 5am Saint. And the very best thing is that when they go back into a normal pub somewhere else and walk to the bar, very soon they realise it's a pretty empty experience.'

Evin and Martin's approaches couldn't be more different yet they are both striking out in their own directions in the same industry; carving out their own utterly unique niches. The fact that they had each forged on without the help of pubs is both heartening and a little worrying. Why aren't more landlords willing to take risks, to introduce new tastes or approaches to curious customers? It baffles me. While an 1890 Porter or a bottle packed inside a stoat probably aren't to everyone's taste, surely there are enough people out there bored of the norm, bored of vertical drinking establishments or the kind of dusty, torpid last chance saloons where craggy-faced pensioners sit all day clutching half-pint glasses?

I begin to wonder. If Evin and Martin are each in their own ways trying to create their visions of the perfect beer, where are the visionaries trying to create the perfect pub to drink it in? And then, suddenly, it hits me: our search has ignored the one man who, more than any other, has attempted to bring Orwell's vision of pub perfection to life. The one whose Leicester Square pub had inspired the quest in the first place. Our journey had been into the heart of pub darkness. Now we were about to come face to face with our very own Colonel Kurtz . . .

TIM MARTIN, PUB GIANT

Paul Moody

On the walls of Tim Martin's office are a series of slogans. One features a picture of Sisyphus, condemned to roll a huge boulder up a hill as penance to the Greek gods. Another is a slogan by Wal-Mart boss Sam Walton which reads: 'We never get tired. We never get depressed.' The third, however, is less predictable. It reads, simply: 'Keep On Walking And Don't Look Back.' This dates to his teenage years when, after nights drinking with pals, Martin would listen not to captains of industry, but to Captain Beefheart.

'When I was about seventeen a pal of mine had a copy of *Safe As Milk* and when we'd been out misbehaving we used to listen to it,' says Martin. 'It was the zaniest music I'd ever heard. There's a song on it called "Yellow Brick Road" where halfway through he yells out, "Keep on walking and don't look back!" It's one of those things which has stayed with me. So whenever I get a negative thought or get down about something that's what I say to myself.'

He explains that, to lighten the mood at one of the recent weekly 'Big Meetings' at company HQ (nicknamed the 'Wethercentre'), he played the assembled reps and area managers Beefheart's 'Golden Birdies'. 'After about one minute I could see the blood draining from their faces.' He grins. 'The second half was the longest thirty seconds of my life.' He sings, '"*An acid gold bar swirled up and down!*".'

Loping into the Metropolitan Bar in London's Baker Street, Tim Martin doesn't look like your average multi-millionaire CEO. His company, J.D. Wetherspoon, by 2010, had turnover of one billion pounds. (He's worth an estimated £152 million, making him, according to the *Sunday Times* Rich List, the 428th wealthiest person in Britain.)

Jumper slung casually over one shoulder, his 6ft 6in frame comes clad in baggy trousers and a crumpled polo shirt, cascading grey locks forming the same mullet he's had since he was 15.

If his clothes appear to be from Millets, his hands are the size of buckets, his frame so broad you could ping golf balls off his chest without him batting an eyelid. He seems to be permanently surfing the edge of laughter, and when it comes, it's in tidal waves, drawing bemused looks from neighbouring tables. At 55, he could easily pass for a shambling college lecturer as he chats amiably away to bar staff, if it wasn't for the hawk-eyed attention to detail; he mentally notes a flickering light bulb on a wine box above the bar as he samples a thimbleful of one of the guest beers.

It's this obsessional desire to get things right which drives him. During the week, Martin keeps away from head office, preferring to tour Wetherspoon's 815 branches around the country, turning up unannounced like a scruffy Ulysses, making sure things are up to scratch. Last week he was in Liverpool. This week, he visited 16 pubs in the capital, and found himself on a bus in south London, travelling between Norbury and Croydon. 'I had a chat with a few of the people on the bus,' he says. 'It keeps you closer to ground level. I always try and use public transport. Occasionally I'll hire a local cab or someone to drive me from say, Southport to Blackpool. Luxury is very isolating. For a while I hired a plane and a pilot and we used to fly to somewhere like Grimsby and then get a cab, and I really didn't like it.'

Martin's intention remains the same as it has been since he launched the company in 1979: to provide good quality beers, food and wine in a convivial atmosphere. 'I'm sceptical about whether pubs are brands,' he says. 'I've always said that what people really like is individuality. There's a lot of talk in business about our portfolio, our brand. And I always think, you haven't got a brand, you've got a reputation. And your reputation is only as good as the last pint of beer you sell.'

Timothy Randall Martin grew up between New Zealand and Northern Ireland, the son of an Irish mother and a Kiwi former fighter pilot turned Guinness rep, both of whom, as he puts it, enjoyed 'a tincture'. He went to 11 schools as he pinballed between the two countries, and learned how to drink in the student pubs of Belfast, notably The Botanic. He drank his first pint at 13 in the beer garden of a pub called The Mondesir in New Zealand. 'I was already six foot three by then, and the old man figured if I was big enough, I was old enough.'

Struggling with a law degree at Nottingham University, he acquired a taste for real ale. It would be the making of him. Martin dropped out, and got a job working in a pork pie factory ('I was putting the jelly into pork pies; I really enjoyed the work'). Aware that he should knuckle down to a career, after six months he moved to London with a vague aim of becoming a barrister. Every night at 9 p.m., after a day studying for bar exams, he would travel five miles from his flat in Wood Green to a bar called Marler's in Muswell Hill. 'The pubs around where I lived were terrible, the beer was rubbish. And this guy called Marler served a decent pint of Abbot Ale.'

Opening a pub was the last thing on his mind.

'I used to play a lot of squash and my initial idea was to try and start a squash club. But I didn't really know how to go about it.

And then one night this guy Marler said to me: "I've got an eight-year lease running this pub, I hate it, do you want it?" So I said: "Yeah, okay." And it went from there.'

Three weeks after Martin took over, a brick came flying through the front window. The glass was still emblazoned with the word 'Marler's' and his original thought was simply to change the pub's name to 'Martin's'. But then he wondered what Captain Beefheart would do. On a whim, he decided to call it Wetherspoon's, after an ineffectual primary school teacher he remembered from New Zealand (the J.D., inspired by J.D. Hogg from the *Dukes of Hazzard*, would come later). 'At the time everyone was giving their companies these over-serious names. The full name eventually became the J.D. Wetherspoon's Organisation Limited. When we were floated on the stock market they tried to get me to change it to JDW or something, but I said no. Although I did cut out the "Organisation" bit.'

He explains that he always had the idea that his pubs should be, as Orwell put it, 'quiet enough to talk'. 'It was trial and error really. I had an idea the music shouldn't be so loud as it is in most pubs. At the first one I found that if the staff liked a track, they'd turn it up. It was impossible to control the atmosphere. So I took the music out, which was slightly controversial. The pub started attracting less trade, so we did a beer festival where you got two and a half pints for a quid, and it was packed again. So we started having keen pricing, and no music. I suppose it was slightly revolutionary at the time but I've always preferred pubs with no music. It brings out the sociable side of people. I've never been a fan of television, anyway. It's really disorientating, it's almost as if you're not really there.'

In 1985, six years after Tim opened his first pub, a reporter from the *Daily Telegraph* visited The White Lion and Mortimer in Stroud Green, north London, eager to quiz the young entrepreneur (Martin was still only 29) on his drink-and-think philosophy. 'The pub was in a converted car showroom and this journalist came down and said to me: "This is like The Moon Under Water."

I'd never heard of it until that point and we'd been going for a while by then. So I read it and it made perfect sense. The irony is that we completely modernised that pub a few years ago. It was a total disaster. After that I said never again. Now, if we take over an old pub, we'll restore it back to how it was before.'

Martin didn't let the matter rest there. Instead, he set about opening up a chain of Moon Under Waters across the country, based, to the best of his abilities, on the Orwell blueprint. Acutely aware that attempting to make a chain out of the perfect pub was counter-intuitive, he tried to instil the values he'd learned from his business heroes, Wal-Mart boss Sam Walton and General Electric's Jack Welch.

'What I learned from them is that the company has to have an identity that's positive. It has to have some values. People might think, "Oh, this isn't perfect" when they walk into a Moon Under Water or a Wetherspoon's but they can identify with what you're trying to do. We still try as best we can to provide all the things he [Orwell] suggests. Preferably the pub itself has to have a landlord, like Orwell's landlady and the staff, who know your name. And if it's an old pub we restore it to its former glories. Instead of china mugs we put the emphasis on sparkling clean glasses, because there's nothing worse than a pint in a dirty glass. You'll never get a hundred per cent of the way there, of course, but you might be able to get seventy-five.'

As for the pub closures, Martin lays the blame squarely on the usual suspects: greedy pubcos, government ambivalence, voracious supermarkets. 'I think you can relate it to what happened with the banking sector. There's a syndrome where the private equity type of business over-borrows, and when the debt finally registers, things collapse. This hit the pub world in a big way, with large swathes of it being run by financial engineers. But the real blame lies with tax and regulation. Because the tax we pay now is forty-two per cent of our sales. It's ten pounds of tax for one pound of profit and that's with an efficient company. It's overkill. If you drill down further, eating out is what people like to do these days, and yet supermarkets pay no VAT on food. Pubs pay twenty per cent. Which makes it so much more attractive to eat at home than go out for a meal.'

The way Tim sees it the solution is simple: cutting tax. 'What I'd like to see is VAT on pubs set at a reduced rate, as it is in France, of five per cent. Then you'd find there would be a massive increase in village pubs and community pubs. Pubs will thrive again because they'll be much more competitive.'

As for government guidelines on drinking, he thinks they're ridiculous. 'People talk a tremendous load of bollocks about everything. The politicians got it wrong about the euro, that was never going to work. Twenty years ago they said you shouldn't eat more than two eggs a week. These rules are equally daft. Twenty-one units for men and fourteen for women? I think in New Zealand it's fifty-six for each, or some huge number. There's no medical basis for these figures. There's a lot of rubbish talked about alcohol consumption, and it's often by highly educated people because they have the confidence to talk rubbish.'

The recession has only spurred him on to make greater efforts. Sisyphus would be proud. He's in the gym by 7 a.m., has read the papers by eight and is constantly working on ideas to keep the company in profit. A recent initiative saw all branches of Wetherspoon's open at 7 a.m. to cater for the breakfast trade.

'We're having to run very, very hard to stay up with the pace. We break even on that early trade. It's mostly coffees and breakfast, so it hasn't been rocket-fuelled. Given how hard we work and how much capital we've invested, we've only just been able to keep our end up, as James Bond put it once. It certainly hasn't sent us into the stratosphere.'

Tim worries that over-regulation and the endless price increases have already succeeded in putting a younger generation off the pub. He was horrified the other week when, on coming home unexpectedly to his home in Exeter, he found his 20-year-old son and his mates sitting at home with a 'heap of bottles and spirits from Tesco'. 'I found it really sad in a way. They'd rather sit at home drinking and playing computer games. I found myself saying, "Why the hell don't you go to the pub?" That's the real worry. The pub is becoming marginalised without a doubt, because the melting-pot aspect of pubs has been drastically reduced.'

He explains that presenting a united front to government to push changes through is difficult when the sector is so riven with conflicting interests. 'You'll be surprised at the great difficulty we've had in galvanising the chief executives of the pub companies themselves to understand the problem,' he says. 'The family brewers are good. Michael Fuller, the guys from Youngs, the guys from Robinsons. Those sort of guys tend to be a bit remote because the company has been in the family for a couple of hundred years, but they do understand we've got a real problem with pub closures. But the chief exec of your typical PLC who's on a five-year term is only looking at the short-term outlook. It's too much of a long-term commitment for him to try and change the system.'

Occasionally, ministerial apathy about the pub's plight seems to border on outright hostility. He's had problems with his pubs at Heathrow and Gatwick because there's a perception from government that they're somehow not the right image we should give to travellers from abroad. Which is ironic when you consider, as Brigid Simmonds pointed out, that most tourists list a visit to the pub as one of the nation's top three attractions.

'They have to be careful they don't look down too much on pubs,' he says with a touch of irritation. 'We've got regular travellers who happily enjoy a pint or two in the Red Lion in Gatwick prior to a trip. But they (the government) want it to be more upmarket. They think that by having a Gordon Ramsay restaurant there it will somehow put Britain in a better light.'

So, does it annoy him that the chattering classes, too, still see Wetherspoon's as hang-outs solely for penny-pinching students and pensioners? 'No, it doesn't annoy me,' he shrugs, genuinely unphased. 'The fact is that people may have been in our pub in, say, Turnpike Lane, and thought "it's a bit tasty in here", which it sort of is, and thought, "this isn't quite for me". That becomes their impression of every Wetherspoon's. And perhaps there's an element of snobbery to it. Wetherspoon's appeals to a very broad spectrum of people and some people don't like to be a part of a broad spectrum. They would rather stick with their own kind.'

He likens the pub's role to that of the church, bringing together disparate elements of the population. And like the churches, thousands are now lying empty. We're learning to live away from each other, in our tiny mini-cliques, and I can tell it frustrates Tim no end.

'A few years ago, when we moved out of London to Exeter, me and my wife started to get involved on the dinner party circuit. Most of them were doctors and lawyers, and to use my own cockney rhyming slang, it drove me chicken jalfrezi. Their views were so narrow. They were all very nice, but when I go out I like to see young, old, rough diamonds, people who work in offices, the whole spectrum. The other advantage, of course, is that you can also get up and leave if you don't like it. Whereas at a dinner party, you're stranded!'

We start talking about the state of our town centres and the hundreds of empty pubs around the country. 'We never used to be able to get our hands on them before, but there are quite a lot in market towns we're looking at. In fact about fifteen per cent of the openings in the last four years have been old pub premises. Some of them are doing surprisingly well, too.'

As much as the cut and thrust of business appeals, part of the pleasure for him comes in renovating local landmarks. 'Seeing a really nice old building get a new life is always good. The Opera House in Tunbridge Wells, The Ralph Fitz Randall in Richmond, which is a converted post office. The Hamilton Hall in Liverpool Street station is a hell of a pub.'

The pub we're sitting in, The Metropolitan, squeezed between Baker Street Tube station and Madame Tussauds, is the former offices of British Rail. They've retained many of the original fittings, county shields lining the vaulted ceilings.

'What we're desperately trying to avoid is cloned bars,' he says, reading my mind. 'It's all about getting the design and the feel right.'

He explains that he was recently chatting to a market researcher who stressed the importance of 'pub values'. 'I think that's what you're really talking about with this search for The Moon Under Water, isn't it? The idea that there should be a real mix of characters. I'm pretty certain you'll find that in any Wetherspoon's.'

Emboldened by a second pint of Buxton Blonde, I feel compelled to ask him whether his wealth has led him to a greater enjoyment of life. He famously eschews the trappings of success paraded by some of the self-made millionaires of, say, *Dragons' Den*. His one major indulgence over the years was a brand-new BMW he bought when the company was first floated on the stock market. It got broken into nine times in two years, and he went back to driving a Volvo.

'You certainly ain't going to be any happier if you've got a yacht, if that's what you're asking,' he says. 'I wouldn't like to preach to people but what makes me happy is working. You can't do fuck all. People think, "If I wasn't working I'd be so happy," and retired people know that isn't true. Secondly, you need to avoid what I call SOYA. Sitting On Your Arse. If you've got those two things then you're on the way. And avoid too much bloody TV as well!'

In his spare time, Martin listens to music ('I downloaded a hundred tracks by Yehudi Menuhin for £4.99!') or heads to his house in Cornwall, and out on to the waves. 'I've taken up surfing again after a break of thirty-eight years. A very late midlife crisis I suppose. I've persisted with it, and I can get up on my feet now.'

Does it represent a release from the brutally competitive world of business? 'Well, it takes you away from the world, and there's a sense of fear, too, because you'll never be able to dominate the ocean. But human nature will always be the same. There will be competition and ego, kindness and cruelty, all these different things. It's a question of trying to channel them towards a positive outcome. It's difficult to be more precise, because where would we be without competition and ego? Nothing would ever get done.'

When he says this, it's easy to picture him as a cross between Richard Branson and Patrick Swayze in *Point Break*; a zen surfer who also happens to be a master of the universe.

Martin's complete lack of self-importance isn't so much disarming as unnerving. At one stage, as we're edged off a table by a large group of foreign tourists, he happily gives up the terrain and moves us onto another table, totally unphased. And all without the vaguest hint of a press officer, an entourage, or a buzzing phone to remind you of his status. It's clear that the picture on his office wall has a deeper meaning too: Sisyphus was punished for the crime of hubris, believing himself to be smarter than Zeus, and it's this humility which works as Wetherspoon's secret weapon.

He meets as many staff members as he can on his travels as 'undercover boss' and proudly explains that the average manager stays with the firm for nine years, and many a lot longer than that. The manager of The Metropolitan, he tells me, has been here 20 years, and that's why, in his opinion, 'It's one of the best pubs in London.' Tonight, it's hard to argue. Conversation is buzzing on all three sides of us, spilling over so you can't help but hear. There's a bloke in a suit talking about his first deep-sea dive with a mate, a gay couple talking about the latest blockbuster, a foreign exchange student being guided through the drinks options by a tutor ('It's called Wetherspoon's – it'll be dirt cheap!'), a guy in his twenties chatting up his date.

What would Tim say is the definition of success? 'Knowing that the part-time barmaid in Windsor became the pub manager in Swindon.'

His phone rings. It's his wife, reminding him they're going out this evening. He says he'll meet her in a pub down the road. He usually has a couple of pints at the end of each day, and it looks like this won't be an exception. 'I wouldn't like anyone to think I'm a Spartan,' he says, still mulling over our earlier discussion. 'I'm gonna have a pint in someone else's pub now and it's going to cost me £3.70.'

And with that, he shakes my hand, gets up from the table, and keeps on walking. He doesn't look back.

THE REVOLUTION STARTS AT OPENING TIME

Paul Moody

'**M**e, start an effing normal pub? Never, not in a million years,' says Martyn Hillier, leaning against what could pass for a pulpit at The Butchers Arms, in Herne, Kent.

'All those smokers and lager drinkers? No thanks.' It's 9 p.m. and that rumbling sound I can hear isn't breakers hitting the shore at nearby Whitstable beach, but the sound of a revolution frothing and bubbling to the surface.

As landlord of what is surely Britain's smallest business empire (assets: one 14ft x 12ft room; staff numbers: one; expansion plans: zero) Martyn is one of a new wave of British publicans. One for whom despair is replaced by optimism and resignation is washed away on the tide. And if you'd told me about it two years ago, I would have taken it with a pinch of salt.

As the weeks and months have gone by since we set out travelling the country and hearing tales of pub-related woe, Paul Kingsnorth's words about how soul-destroying such research would be have rung increasingly true. All too often a lead about a quirky neighbourhood pub which has gone strangely quiet resulted in us turning up outside only to find the phone cut off, the doors bolted and a 'For Sale' sign on the upstairs window. But along with the casualties there have been whispers of strange and remarkable recoveries. Of pubs which had previously been displaying only the faintest pulse suddenly bursting back to life and displaying strange new character traits.

Inspired by a scheme initiated by Prince Charles encouraging pubs to diversify, hundreds have taken up the challenge, incorporating shops, post offices, play areas, developing allotments and, in the case of The Nightjar in Weston-super-Mare, even a Sunday morning church service.

A central player in this rebirth has been John Longden, a 65-year-old father of three from Harrogate, and founder of The Pub is the Hub. Set up as an advisory body to help rural pubs diversify, working directly with licensees, private and public sector partners and rural regeneration schemes, its volunteers have been helping keep pubs stay at the heart of communities by pooling the resources of everyone involved. There's even a Hollywood-style twist: participants include everyone from concerned locals to CAMRA, the British Beer and Pub Association and all the major pub companies. Is it a case of all parties healing rifts for the greater good?

Running through the scheme's success stories is heartwarming.

At the Black Swan in Ravenstonedale, Cumbria, the scheme supplied landlords Alan and Louise Dinnes with half the cash needed for a £12,000 conversion of an unused bedroom into a shop. This is now so successful it has created four part-time jobs, and means villagers can buy fresh bread, sausages and bacon, locally made soap and homemade greetings cards (the milkman's profits have soared by £600 a month, too). And all without making the 12-mile round trip to the nearest supermarket.

At The Queens Head in Hawkedon, near Bury St Edmunds, landlord Scott Chapman, 42, opened a butcher's shop within his pub, frustrated at local prices. The pub now sells beef, pork, lamb and even muntjac deer, with 40 sheep grazing in a nearby field.

Over at The Queens Head in Monmouth, landlord Neill Bell has found a cure for deathly Monday nights by installing a lending library in one bar. A pub with books? Why didn't anyone think of it before? Better still, nothing is accepted without a short critique explaining why it should be included.

It's the example of Martyn Hillier, however, which really reads like something out of fiction. Leaving school at 16 to do a catering course at Thanet Tech (alongside a certain Gary Rhodes), he packed it in for a job on a building site, leaving his weekends free to indulge his first love, motorbikes. A regular at Brands Hatch on his 900cc Honda, his reckless enthusiasm soon won him a place on the front row of the grid, but would almost prove his downfall. Messing around on the roads one night, a major crash resulted in six months in hospital and his left arm paralysed. Martyn's never-say-die spirit prevailed, however; he went on a ski-ing trip soon afterwards to prove there was nothing he still couldn't do, and landed an unlikely job as probably the world's first one-armed chauffeur. Driving the likes of Michael Caine ('lovely') and Bonnie Langford ('a very pleasant lady') only confirmed what he'd always suspected: that self-made stars best appreciate privilege.

At 30, bored of the backseat egos of the famous or, as he puts it, those 'who thought they were famous', he took his mother's advice and took over the running of The Canterbury Bottle Shop.

As passionate about real ale as he was about bikes, the business boomed. That is, until what he calls 'the big boys' took an interest.

We're in The Butchers Arms as he runs me through this brief personal history, and it's hard to concentrate because the pub is overwhelming in itself. A former butcher's in the genteel village of Herne, ten miles outside Canterbury, it's crammed to the rafters with oddball clutter. Plastic lamb chops, joints of ham, pheasants and geese dangle from the ceiling (a nod to the pub's previous incarnation), meat hooks, antique scales and brightly coloured beer towels line the walls. The sight of a shrivelled waxwork of Michael Jackson in one corner – complete with spangled glove – only confirms the notion that as pubs go, it's pretty off the wall.

Martyn goes into the back room and returns with a pint of Hop Head (there's no bar or till, and you pay at the end). A youthful 51, his acquired wisdom is delivered in terse, staccato sentences laced with an acid wit. There's no room for interruptions ('Shut up, I'm talking now,' he says at one stage) and as he tells his story it feels a bit like being filled in on a briefing about a nasty bank blag over Hammersmith way by Jack Regan.

'Let's start at the beginning. In '85 I was up in Highbury, London. I was a lager drinker but I tried a pint of Whale Ale. Loved it. No gas, loads of flavour. Converted. I used to live in Putney, and in some pubs the beer would be good, in others not so good. But they were all Fuller's pubs. The same brewery. I realised it wasn't the brewery at fault, it's the publican. So I decided to open a real ale off-licence [The Canterbury Bottle Shop]. Only sell decent beer.'

His troubles started when the chain off-licences (or 'the big boys') found out how well he was doing. 'They came along and opened one up two hundred yards down the road. Bigger and better than me, they said it would be. It only lasted eighteen months. But in the meantime it put me out of business because you can't fight the big boys. You can only fight them with money. If they've got more money than you, they win. It doesn't matter how good you are. You can't keep affording to lose money. They can.'

It strikes me his passion for speed and restless energy have somehow seeped into what neurologists call the Broca region – the brain's motor centre for speech. The words come out in bursts, like someone revving a motorbike, with deliberate comic timing. You can't help laughing.

Martyn took on the current premises with his ex-wife, running it initially as a florist's, with an off-licence at the back. 'Men like flowers. Women like beer. Or something like that. Anyway, ex-wife left so I sacked her. Got another florist. Good, but no money in the till. Third one, pregnant straight away. Not by me. Maternity pay. Fucking nightmare.'

And then came the epiphany. During a visit in 2003 by the local licensing officer, he casually mentioned that, due to the change in the licensing laws, Martyn could convert the florist's to a pub without negotiating a mountain of red tape.

'No brainer,' he says. 'Realised I could run the pub exactly how I wanted. No lager drinkers or smokers. No jukebox or quizzes. Just good chat and decent beer.'

In the past, any new independent pub would immediately have come under pressure form the big pubcos. Now, they couldn't do anything to stop him. 'There's only four reasons why people can object to you getting a licence,' he says with a hint of glee. 'Health and safety, law and order, protection of children and you have to have been a good boy. Previous to that Mr Shepherd Neame, Mr Enterprise Inns and Mr Punch Taverns and the rest of them would have been banging the door down with their barristers and solicitors, raising objections. Now, they can't.'

This isn't pubco paranoia, either. He explains that a friend who applied for a licence before the act spent 18 months and £12,000 fighting off repeated applications to magistrates from the pubcos, claiming that another pub in the area would present a threat to law and order.

The freedom also extends to what he sells, and his opening hours. With only one member of staff (himself), these are limited by his moods. 'I only open when I know my customers want a drink,' he says. 'I'm closed Monday and Sunday evening. The other times are on the door. It's an hour and a half at lunchtime, and in the evening it's six until nine, or later. If it's pissing down with rain and I haven't seen any of my regulars, I'm not going to sit here until half past ten or eleven o'clock just for the odd person who wants a pint of beer. Bottom line. If you want a decent pint of beer, get your arse in here between six and nine. If you leave it until later, I might not be here. Your risk. If you haven't drunk enough by eleven, have a takeaway. I'm not going to sit in here until half past one listening to people talking shit. I'm not interested.'

Is Martyn Hillier the embodiment of the grumpy landlord following his star? Unquestionably. And beneath the grouchy exterior, he's not even all that grumpy, although it's certainly enough to put off the faint-hearted.

The attraction of The Butchers Arms, apart from the non-stop repartee, is, Martyn explains, good beer, sold at sensible prices. There are always six real ales on offer, and the choice revolves according to demand. 'I listen to what my customers tell me. If they come in and say such and such beer is good, I get it in. The most expensive beer I've got is £2.95. You go to any other pub and it's £3.10.'

How so? 'Because I buy direct. There's no middle managers taking their cut and my overheads are low. Turnover's not bad. If I've got five pound more in my wallet at the end of the week than at the beginning of the week that'll do for me. It's as simple as that.'

There are other benefits to drinking at The Butchers Arms too: no hangovers. 'Beer goes off. You've got three days to sell a cask once it's opened. The beer won't get any better after the third day because the air's got into it and started oxidisation.' He tells a possibly libellous story about standard practice at certain chain pubs, where, thanks to a process called 'blanket pressure', beer from the barrel is still served after two weeks using CO_2, causing killer hangovers. Fresh beer, however, he assures me, leaves you 'clear as a bell'.

The way Martyn sees it, the high street pub has become its own worst enemy. 'The trouble is they try to please everybody, and they end up pleasing nobody. They're trying to do too many things. They're trying to entertain you, feed you, offer wines, spirits, the rest of it, when all you want is a decent pint of beer. You can't please all the people all the time, so why bother?'

He explains that the wine list at The Butchers Arms isn't exactly extensive. 'People come in here and say, "What wine have you got?" and I say, "White." That's it. It's white wine. I'm not sure what it is. Maybe Pinot Grigio. Narrowing the choice down makes things easier. If you're driving there's cloudy or real lemonade, which is free.'

Is it any wonder The Butchers Arms has been a triumph from the off? Having already been voted CAMRA's East Kent Pub of the Year it also signifies something far more intriguing, the idea that the 'micropub' represents a way out of the slump for the nation's publicans, or even enthusiastic amateurs. Even to my own novice eyes, the logic is brilliantly simple: like the pub version of punk's independent labels, micropubs cater for street level demand, bypassing corporate strategies in the process. I'm reminded of Paul Kingsnorth's idea about the modern-day Moon Under Water needing only four things: authenticity, integrity, character and independence. They're all right here and it feels like a case of the revolution starting at opening time. Which is any time you want.

Martyn, not surprisingly, sees it in similar terms. 'Totally. You can start your own micropub with five grand. The point is that you can't franchise it. You can't tell them what beer to have or slap their wrists. Everyone doing it has got to put their own spin on it.'

He explains how back in 1830 the Duke of Wellington's Beer Orders saw the creation of 25,000 new pubs almost overnight, and I'm sent spinning back to my discussion with Jack Adams at the Pub History Society. If history is on a permanent repeat cycle, is the pub about to experience an unlikely boom?

'I'm surprised that more people haven't picked up on it already,' he says, explaining that CAMRA asked him to their AGM to deliver a 15-minute presentation on how micropubs work. 'I went down there and explained how simple it was. I don't think they could believe it. There was a bloke there from Hartlepool called Peter Morgan who said I'd changed his life. He'd been made redundant, he didn't know what to do, and now he's opened a micropub called The Rat Race in an office at Hartlepool railway station. Another guy from Newark, he had a few problems I helped him with, and he ended up opening one called Just Beer. The ball's rolling.'

Just Beer's website exudes an almost evangelical zeal for the project, and includes the lines: 'Let's not rest until we have a micropub in every city, town and village.'

I can almost hear Orwell cheering.

I ask Martyn what other publicans who have lost their pubs make of it? 'The interesting thing is that publicans will hear about it and start wondering why they're paying over the odds for their beer and why they're not allowed to get different beers in, even when their customers want them. Now, if there's an empty shop just down the road, and they can get it licensed and put a sign above it, you've got your own free house.'

The root of the problem, as Martyn sees it, is that cost-cutting measures introduced by major pub companies have backfired. Traditional pubs which once had three separate bars catering for three types of customers were knocked through en masse because it would be cheaper to have one big bar served by one bartender. 'What that means is, three different sets of people, the lads playing pool, the girls having a chat and the blokes listening to the juke-box, have to mix. They don't like it, so they stay away. That's how I see this place. It's the real ale bar in a pub. Except there just isn't anything attached to it.'

Apart, that is, from the regulars. By 7 p.m., the place is filling up with an oddball clientele which almost gives Straw Bear a run for its money. A pinstripe-suited banker rubs shoulders with a craggy Catweazle lookalike, muscle-bound rugger types crack jokes with softly spoken student types. And all of them part of one big, never-ending conversational flow which seems to involve every-body present. It's unnerving at first, especially when the attention of 15 people is suddenly drawn to the one stranger in the room. But the drink flows and it reminds me that this must have been what all pubs were like once. When there was nothing to do but talk to each other, find out about how other people see the world and then trundle off home.

I remark to one local that Martyn may just be the landlord of the county's best pub. 'I know, it's good, isn't it?' he grins. 'But please don't tell him that, his head is big enough already.'

'Only serve beer,' says Martyn on his return from pouring more pints. 'Because hops are soporific. They're related to the cannabis plant. So if you have too much you fall asleep. When people drink too much lager they want to fight each other. No thanks. There's never any trouble here. People might start talking shit when they're drunk. Piss ripped out of them. When they come back, tail between their legs.'

Martyn shows me how he 'taps' a new barrel and serves custom-ers, all one-handed, and some new friends insist I try some local cheese with one of the pickled eggs nestling in a jar on the side-board. They're both delicious; taste explosions to match the rich hops of the beer.

As I say my goodbyes, I realise it's the best night I've had in the pub on the whole trip. Martyn sees me to the door. Firm hand-shake. Steady eye contact. 'Remember,' he says. 'No hangover!'

JOURNEY'S END

Paul Moody

As soon as my eyes blink open it feels like a dazzling black flash-bulb is being stamped straight onto my retinas. I screw my eyes tight shut again, but it only triggers a meteorite shower exploding backwards into my skull, an interplanetary pile-up where galaxies collide at split-second intervals. Diamond mines are crushed by steamrollers. Nuclear power plants combust in chain reactions. A million castaways beg for water.

'Remember, no hangover?'

Maybe it was the cheese. Still battling the effects of the world's worst hangover courtesy of the world's smallest pub, I begin the daily trawl of the internet. Inevitably, this is the day something lands in the net which is so jaw-dropping I almost throw it back in sheer disbelief.

According to an article in the *Letchworth Comet*, a lady called Irene Stacey had been in contact with the paper about their plans to launch an Orwell Festival to commemorate the author's time living in Wallington, Hertfordshire. Mrs Stacey, now 94, explained that as landlady of The Plough pub, she knew Orwell as her next-door neighbour, and that he would regularly pop in for a pint. It seems so implausible it must be true, and sure enough, when I ring her, thanks to a friendly scribe at the *Comet*, my spirits rise further: Irene's voice is crystal clear down the wires, and she happily agrees to a visit, explaining with a laugh that she's in heavy demand these days: someone from BBC radio came to see her last week.

She then rattles off directions on how to get there which leave me scrambling for a pen ('Turn right out of the station, go past the bus garage, then over the bridge, left past a dramatic building, take a right, then a left and you're there') and leave me wondering not whether she'll be able to keep up with me, but the other way round.

On the train to Letchworth, I can't help thinking about Orwell's own state of mind in the winter of 1946. As he typed the words to 'The Moon Under Water' in Canonbury Square was he planning an escape to his own perfect hideaway from the world?

Seriously ill with lung disease, his worst fears about his own deteriorating health were confirmed the same month when he began to cough up blood: a certain sign of TB. Desperate to escape the hubbub of London life and telling friends he felt 'smothered by journalism', the chance of escaping to the Scottish island of Jura to formulate ideas for a new novel, tentatively titled *The Last Man in Europe*, seemed too good to turn down. Prior to departure though, there were loose ends to be tied up in London and at the cottage at Wallington, which he'd leased since 1936.

Tucked away in a small village deep in the Hertfordshire countryside, the cottage had acted as the perfect rural idyll for him and wife Eileen. The couple kept chicken, geese and goats and converted the front room into a general shop, called The Stores, selling mostly sweets to schoolchildren. The peace and quiet had been productive, too: *Road to Wigan Pier* and *Homage to Catalonia* were both written there, and *Animal Farm* was even modelled on the Manor Farm up the road (he changed the village from Wallington to Wallingdon), even basing the characteristics of the pigs on the locals.

The obvious question, then. Was The Plough a partial (or even the whole) inspiration for The Moon Under Water? And could Irene Stacey be the barmaid who always addressed him as 'dear'?

Sweet suburbia. Letchworth in the June sunshine looks just how the town planners must have imagined it. Street-level fountains add sparkle to the pedestrianised precinct, and a hairdresser's with an outsize sign seems to capture the sense of civic pride: Dead Swanky.

Founded in 1903 by the social reformer Ebeneezer Howard and designated the world's first 'garden city', Letchworth's design was intended to incorporate elements of both town and coun-try, putting the emphasis on trees and open space. Mocked by the press, it chimed with the ideas put forward by H. G. Wells that a modern utopia would be alcohol-free, because the town only lacked one thing: a pub. Or at least, one which served alco-hol. Instead, the town had The Skittles Inn, opened in 1907 and serving only Cydrax (a non-alcoholic apple wine), Bournville's Drinking Chocolate and tea.

It seems like a delicious irony our search should end up in a town famous for not having a pub, and stranger still that it wasn't until a referendum in 1958 that the town finally overturned the decision, with The Broadway Hotel opening in the town centre. Even now, Letchworth boasts less than half a dozen, meaning that the town after dark is usually a haven of peace and quiet. Was H.G. Wells's vision of utopia as being alcohol-free right all along? The place certainly seems mellow enough today, and everyone seems to glow with a contentment which makes me think Howard and Wells might even have colluded to slip a little soma into the water supply.

I turn a corner into a quiet, well-tended cul-de-sac, full of pretty herbaceous borders and identical maisonettes. The numbering system doesn't conform to any logical pattern and I'm wondering how I'll ever find the flat when an upstairs window opens and a crystal-clear voice shouts: 'Are you looking for me?'

This afternoon, Irene is watching the Tour de France on a flat screen TV in the sort of neatly ordered front room which puts younger generations to shame. She's bright-eyed, sparky and full of life, and she puts her enthusiasm and general fitness down to life behind the wheel.

She's always been a keen cyclist and has prepared a pile of pictures and documents for my visit. The first is a black and white photograph of a leggy, dark-haired teenager in a cream blouse and shorts. It's Irene, just after she joined local cycling club The Hitchin Nomads in 1935. She used to ride a tandem in those days, and says she is looking forward to the club's 80th anniversary later this year. 'I think I'm the only one who can remember the day they started it,' she adds.

As the conversation turns to Orwell, Irene explains that, homeless when her husband was demobbed in October 1945, the young couple applied to Simpson's brewery at Baldock to see if they had any pubs which needed running. To their surprise, Simpson's said there was one they could have: The Plough in Wallington. 'I know why, because no one else would have it,' she says tartly. 'It was falling down. The foundations were rotten. The walls were crumbling plaster. I don't think anything had been done to it for three hundred years.'

She takes me through her daily routine at The Plough. With the pub barely profitable, her husband would take any work he was offered, leaving her to run it largely on her own. She would open 'every day of the year apart from Christmas Day' at ten in the morning and then close at two, reopening at six until ten every evening. With no running water other than a single tap, she would regularly need to fetch water from the local well using a yoke, a large wooden beam strapped across her shoulders, balanced by two large pails of water. The pub had no gas or electricity either and she would light 13 small paraffin lamps each evening. 'By the end of the night the ceiling would be completely black.' She grins, and I'm instantly reminded of Orwell's words: 'the florid ceiling stained dark yellow by tobacco-smoke'.

As she talks about her daily routine it feels like we're surfing a subject which has never really gone away, the generational rift which says we've got it easy these days. 'People haven't lived,' she says, but there's no malice in her words, only laughter. 'You know, everything is so easy today; you just flick a switch and it's there. You don't know you're born.'

With no bar, every order for drinks (a straight choice: Mild or Bitter) would mean descending the 13 steps to the cellar and pulling pints straight from the barrel. It was damp down there, newts and frogs hopping about in the darkness, and Irene often had to vent the barrels herself, hammering in the beer tap with a wooden mallet which would regularly leave her showered in beer. She would then carry a maximum of six pints back upstairs on a tin tray, dodging frogs as she went. Little wonder that by the time the pub closed at ten o'clock each night, Irene would be so tired she would blow out the lamps and leave the empty glasses where they stood. It sounds back-breaking, but when I suggest as much she shrugs it off: that was just the way things were. And besides, there was still fun to be had.

A thriving black market ensured fresh rabbit pie was always on the menu, while the local beekeeper provided hundreds of pots of honey and gallons of highly potent mead.

She explains that the locals, mostly farm labourers, were always happy to buy her a drink and play games of darts and dominoes, and larger than life characters abounded. A local stockman called Gerald would regularly park his dray outside and bring his thirsty pony into the bar for a pint. Paralytic by the end of the night, they would carry Gerald out and place him in the back of his dray, a cue for his pony, slightly sozzled himself, to trot slowly back down the country lane to Gerald's farm.

I tell her it sounds like something out of G.K. Chesterton's poem 'The Rolling English Road' ('The rolling English drunkard made the rolling English road/A reeling road, a rolling road, that rambles round the shire') and she pulls out a copy of *Illustrated* magazine from June 1939 and starts leafing through it like it's this week's *Heat*. She stops at a page showing a group of five men enjoying a pint in a rural country pub. It's the sort of image we've all seen hundreds of times, a group of flat-capped locals crowded around an open fireplace, light streaming in through leaded windows. Except, Irene explains, the picture is of The Plough, and she's talking about the men in the picture ('That's Ted Ridley, the Youngs, Harry Keep, Fred Hatchett…') like they're old friends because, well, that's what they are.

It's a weird, almost unnerving feeling, almost as if I'm back in the booth at Colindale, except this time with an audio commentary which will answer any given question. I gently enquire if everyone in the village knew who George Orwell was.

'Oh no. That's the funniest thing,' she says with a laugh. 'No one had any idea who he was. He was only known to us as Mr Blair. I remember someone came to the village for some magazine article or other, asking: "Do you know George Orwell?" No one had a clue. But we all knew Mr Blair.'

Irene explains that the author kept very much to himself, never mentioning the war or 'his wound'. I also find myself faintly disappointed to hear he looked 'exactly like he does in the photographs', 'always very neatly turned out', and was never anything less than 'the perfect gentleman'.

'He would usually only come into the pub if he wanted some cigarettes,' she says. 'Oh, he was a dreadful smoker. He would buy his pack of Player's, say good morning and something like, "I've got to get back and milk the goat," because he kept one next door. If I'm not mistaken he had a beehive, too.'

Apparently, because his cottage was so small, Orwell's literary friends who came to visit would always stay at The Plough. 'I rented the upstairs rooms out as a B&B for half a crown for a little

extra money,' Irene says. 'There was a Baroness Orczy and I definitely remember a Mr Crisp…'

I almost have to pinch myself when she says this. George
Orwell and Quentin Crisp, close friends? It makes me think back
to my meeting with Alan Avenall at The Fitzroy Tavern, and muse
on how many of those decadent denizens of Soho might secretly
have craved fresh air and early nights.

'Of course I was so ignorant I had no idea these were people
known all over the world,' she continues. 'If I did I would have
asked for their autographs! I cooked their breakfast for them and
they were perfectly pleasant. They weren't snobs. They just pigged
it same as we did. I remember Mr Crisp as always being what I'd
call very tidy, he carried himself in a certain way, but very polite
with it.'

Irene explains that Orwell and his guests would regularly
come in for their evening meal, cooked on the pub's coal-fuelled
Rayburn stove, and I can't resist asking if jam roly poly and liver-
sausage sandwiches were ever on the menu?

'Oh no, he'd have made those himself if he wanted,' she says
breezily. 'He might have had black pudding from me. On a
Saturday I'd make a big steak or rabbit pie with vegetables, and I
could always do a trifle. And in the evening, there would be cheese
and pickles.'

And large biscuits with caraway seeds? To tell the truth, I can't
bring myself to ask. Never in my wildest dreams did I think that
the search for The Moon Under Water might lead us to his old pub
landlady, but here she is, living flesh and bright as a button, and I
idiotically ask what Orwell would be drinking. Which seems a bit
pointless when the pub only served two drinks: mild or bitter (or
mild and bitter for the adventurous). But the answer comes as a
curveball.

'Oh, he didn't drink in The Plough,' she says. 'He always took
the drink back to his cottage. I had a china mug which he would
borrow and then he would bring it back the next day. In fact, I've
still got it.' She goes over to a glass-fronted cabinet and takes out a

small white mochaware jug. It's an extraordinary thing; cold to the touch, and with a tortoiseshell motif and a thin pale blue band at the lip.

'He borrowed it many times and he really liked it. In fact, he offered me half a crown for it but I said no. I thought if it's worth that much to him, it's probably worth a lot more to me.'

If it's not the strawberry-pink china mugs that are mentioned in 'The Moon Under Water', it's pretty near. It feels like I'm close to the journey's end, in this neat sitting room in Hertfordshire, and I thank Irene for sharing her memories, and helping solve at least part of the riddle.

Then, splendidly, she says: 'Pubs are closing down all over the place now and it saddens me. I even saw a programme on television saying old people are drinking too much at home these days. Well, they haven't got a choice if the local pub has closed down. Personally, I think the supermarkets have got a lot to answer for.'

Somewhere in heaven I can hear Orwell raising a glass (or even a china mug) to this display of the crystal spirit, and it seems like a good time to go.

As I'm packing away my tape recorder she says I should send her a signed copy of the book when it's finished. It might be worth something one day. I assure her that won't be the case but Irene's not going to take a chance. She's clearly going to live for ever, and, with this in mind, I voice the concerns which have been bothering me ever since Blackpool. It's a sprawling, mostly incoherent, speech about how we seem to have lost sight of the values she's been talking about, of quiet decency, honour and local communities muddling along together. I end up blurting it out: but aren't things better now than they were then?

She pauses for a moment. 'There's a lot to be said for today. People say, "Oh, it's not like how it used to be," but I think there's a lot to be said for both.' Her voice lowers slightly, and she says, 'There wasn't so much expectation back then. You just lived your life and enjoyed it in the best way you could. The wider world didn't seem to matter so much. You just did what you did. So in a way, we were freer.'

We say our goodbyes, and the paradox of ending our search in a town famous for not having a pub feels like the punchline to some elaborate cosmic joke.

'Before writing off our own age as irrevocably damned is it not worth remembering that Matthew Arnold and Swift and Shakespeare – to carry the stock back only three centuries – were all equally certain that they lived in a period of decline,' wrote George Orwell in 1948. And in Letchworth on a glorious mid-summers afternoon, it seems easy to view the future of pubs in a positive light.

But will all our cities, as Ebenezer Howard envisaged, one day be pub-free? They will be if we let it happen. We can shrug our shoulders at pub closures, lose ourselves in identikit bars and listen as the doom-mongers tell us the pub's golden age is over. But if we cherish and support pubs with authenticity, independence, character and integrity, we may yet break free from the chains. And besides, by my last calculation, there are still over 47,000 pubs left to visit.

There's half an hour until my train, and my euphoric state leads me to the pub across the road, where I offer to buy the barman a drink. 'No thanks' he says, 'Rules are rules'. He pours me a pint, and a quizzical look spreads across his face as I run through the highs 'n' lows of the last two years. A mini-tsunami of foam engulfs his fingers and drips onto the bar. 'All due respect, mate,' he says, sliding the glass towards me. 'But you've hardly even started.'

EPILOGUE

Robin Turner

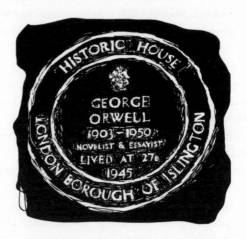

As I step out of The Compton Arms, I wave goodbye to my newest friends – Andrew, Emily and Fabian. It is funny to think that just a few hours before I'd never even met them. They turn back to the bar as I walk away, picking up the open-ended conversation that I am certain I could join again sometime in the future. Their cheery banter was the only sound in the pub that afternoon; music and sport mercifully banished.

With my bearings knocked after three lunchtime pints, I stop and take in the pub's surroundings. Just off from the main drag, The Compton Arms is the kind of place that quietly minds its own business – the crowded shops and bars of nearby Upper Street, Islington, are a world and a half away.

My bus stop is a two-minute walk away, and I start an ungainly jog-cum-lurch. With Highbury Corner looming into view, the world becomes a little less sepia, focus pulling back to normal. The streets ring with London's incessant summer soundtrack of wailing police sirens. Serenity shattered, the few hours I'd just spent are already beginning to feel like a strange fiction.

I pass The White Swan – an anonymous-looking Wetherspoon's pub – and The Famous Cock, a pub I'd always avoided thanks to wall-to-wall sports coverage. Outside The White Swan, a whip-thin, sallow-faced smoker sucks the last dregs from the butt. Through the window of The Cock, a dozen or so drinkers sit hypnotised in front of telescreens, watching silently as England's cricket team thwack willow on leather in Edgbaston.

On the top deck of the Number 30 I flick through my notebook, pausing on pages scrawled out in my erratic shorthand. Scanning quickly, the black scribbles prove what I hoped. Orwell's pub – the Moon Under Water – was real. This I knew because I'd spent the afternoon drinking there.

I'd arranged to meet Andrew Gardner outside Highbury and Islington station. Just a lifetime or so ago, cigarette smoke had billowed from its depths. That hellish fug had inspired the title of the 1939 novel *Coming Up for Air* by regular commuter George Orwell.

Andrew is the chairman of the Islington Archaeology and History Society and has been leading walks around the north London borough since 2008. I am interested in trying to get Andrew to lead a very specific walk indeed. I charge him with the job of turning a piece of 20th-century journalistic fiction into 21st-century fact by asking him to take me to the very source, the inspiration for The Moon itself. Luckily, when following the right guide, it is possible to trace Orwell's thirsty ghost throughout the area. He'd been generous enough to leave clues everywhere.

Warming to the idea of a historical reconstruction-cum-pub-crawl, Andrew quickly reroutes our tour. 'The Moon Under Water was very much an amalgamation of each of the three pubs that Orwell drank in during the time he lived around here,' he explains. 'At the time he wrote the piece, those pubs represented – for him – creator, redeemer and sustainer. The Hen and Chickens, the creator and inspiration for one of the most memorable scenes in one of his greatest works [*Nineteen Eighty-Four*]. The Canonbury Tavern was very much his redeemer, where he could relax with his son. And The Compton Arms… well, that was sustainer – the provider of liquid bread!'

The Hen and Chickens is a theatre pub just the other side of Highbury Corner from the station. The last time I'd ventured there was to see an Edinburgh warm-up by Russell Brand, recently released from a sex addiction clinic and about to embark on a stratospheric ascension that would eventually see him wave good-bye to north London and leave for altogether sunnier climes. A cursory look at the ceiling shows earlier structural divisions long since removed. The pub had once been separated into three distinct sections – snug, lounge and public bar. Andrew points out of the window in the direction of the station.

'If you look around the pub and imagine back to the original structure, a very close reading of *Nineteen Eighty-Four* will tell you that this was the basis for the interior of the Chestnut Tree Café. When Winston and Julia are rehabilitated they meet in Highbury Fields and stroll across to the station. Back then there was no traffic island – a terrace of houses stretched across. They were eventually brought down by a rocket bomb. This was one of the pubs he'd frequent, popping in for a Scotch egg and a pint. You can still see the Bass sign outside. That was a particular favourite ale of his.'

Leaving the pub, we walk towards 27b Canonbury Square, the flat Orwell kept from 1944 until the end of his life. These days, Islington may have been more famous for another Mr Blair and the deal supposedly struck with Gordon Brown just a few hundred yards down the road in the long-gone restaurant Granita. Back then though, the area was thoroughly working class, all but shattered after nightly visits from the Luftwaffe.

'This was where the proles lived,' says Andrew. 'After the war, everyone who had the means had moved out of the city. New towns were being built and there were railways to bring them in and out of the capital. The only people left in London were those who couldn't afford to move out.'

A few hundred yards east of 27b stands The Canonbury. These days a pretty nondescript gastropub conversion, back then Orwell would sit and write in the garden while his adopted son Richard played in the open air. Andrew points to the towering tree that dominates the garden.

'"Under the spreading chestnut tree / I sold you and you sold me..." We're stood in the exact spot under the exact tree that inspired those words from *Nineteen Eighty-Four*. In this garden, Orwell can see that the boy is safe because there's a brick wall surrounding the garden. American visitors go absolutely bananas when they see that tree. It's like there's a greater physicality to the tree than the flat he lived in. This tree will probably be here long after anyone drinking here today has shuffled off.'

The inspirational chestnut tree is indeed a glorious thing, well over a hundred years old and utterly majestic. The only downsides are the B&Q spot lamp chained to the trunk and the depressingly modern concession to health and safety – a laminated sign demanding no customers risk life and limb by climbing it.

'It's enormously important when you're looking at how pubs used to be, the roles they filled, exactly why they were so important back then,' continues Andrew. 'With more and more closing every week, you look back to what the pub represented. Truly it was the community hub, a communal living room that was infinitely warmer and more populated than what awaited at home. You look back at pictures of Islington in Orwell's day and you can see the utterly squalid conditions people were living in. For so many, the pub was something of a salvation.'

We walk on towards the last pub on the trip, The Compton Arms. I ask Andrew what he thinks Orwell would make of today's drinking culture. 'Personally, I think if Orwell had lived long enough, I imagine he would have been a founder member of CAMRA. The thing that Orwell would have appreciated about them – besides the attention to detail with beer – was their determination to preserve old interiors. Having won the battle if not the war about real ale, they now take a massive interest in buildings. And as every generation despises the architecture of the one before, there's always a case to be made to preserve buildings. If you think of the description of The Moon Under Water, it still features the "solid, comfortable ugliness of the 19th century".

'You have to remember that all through his life, Orwell was irrepressibly middle class. He was the kind of person who thought marmalade should not be served in a jar, it should be served from a bowl with a spoon. The pub Winston Smith goes to in *Nineteen Eighty-Four* where the proles demand pints of wallop was a mishmash of London pubs where the great unwashed would get so drunk they could hardly string a sentence together. Pubs like that are the equivalent to today's vertical drinking establishments.'

Entering The Compton Arms, Andrew is greeted by both customers and staff like a war-weary battle veteran returning to his village of birth. On stools at the bar, Emily and Fabian sit discussing the art of chivalry. Emily waves a £20 note in our direction. 'Andy, may I buy you and your friend a drink?'

The pub is situated on a side street far enough from the hustle so as to seem like a best-kept secret only locals knew about. Customers occupying the same chair as much for the conversation as the beer – my beer benefactor is proof positive of that. Quiet enough to talk? Pretty soon we are all debating the virtues of gentlemanly conduct. After half an hour, Andrew and I break away. He points at the bar and begins to hypothesise about a mythical meeting of minds.

'I'm speaking absolutely speculatively now and obviously you need to take the timeline into account and the lifetimes of the people,' says Andrew, warming to a personal theory. 'But had Orwell lived longer – say to his mid-seventies – you could theoretically have seen at stools along this bar all the people known to have drunk in The Compton Arms. That could have included Malcolm Muggeridge, Arthur Koestler, George Orwell, John Betjeman and Joe Orton. As opposed to today when you get me and Emily and Fabian! You see, pubs really do go up and down over the years…'

Staring out of the window of the eastbound Number 30, I lose myself in a daydream. I am picturing the public bar of The Moon Under Water, all grained woodwork and cast-iron fireplaces, pewter pots and history-lined faces at the bar. I imagine Orwell sat in this imaginary public bar with a legendary line-up of thinkers and drinkers. Irene pours pints from the jug. In the corner, Pete Brown and Evin are sampling 21st-century takes on a Victorian recipe. Nearer the door, Paul Kingsnorth is deep in conspiratorial conversation with King Arthur and Pete Wylie, exasperated about where things were going wrong nowadays. At the bar, Tim Martin talks shop with Martin Hillier; Pat from The Falcon is on hand and ready for action come kicking-out time.

A disembodied voice from somewhere shakes me awake. I've been travelling in the wrong direction. The Moon Under Water – a second ago so vivid in my mind – is all but gone. I desperately try to remember the conversations, the expressions – anything. But, like any dream, it blurs to nonsense within minutes. As the bus pulls to a halt, all I am left with is a holistic glow, the warmth of knowing that that very afternoon, I'd been staring at The Moon Under Water – mentally and physically. Now all that is left is my own reflection in the bus window.

As I alight, just there on the other side of the road are frosted windows, an open door, and a group of people lost in the afternoon. I had ten minutes. If I am honest, I always had ten minutes. Might as well pop in for one.

POSTSCRIPT TO THE PAPERBACK EDITION

'Do you know The White Horse in Parsons Green?'

'The Golden Fleece in York?

'You must know The Cobweb in Boscastle?!'

During the fifteen months since *The Search for the Perfect Pub* was published, it has been my pleasure to field such enquiries – usually delivered with the intensity of a doctor to an ailing patient – on a daily basis.

Each time my response is the same. I reply in the affirmative, nodding sagely, while making frantic mental notes to check out the pubs in question, secretly convinced that I have finally discovered the coordinates for pub Xanadu.

Which is a bit daft, when you think about it. Because, fun as it is to pretend, we all know that stumbling upon the perfect pub is about as likely as waking up on a chilly morning in Hades on the day England have won a major football tournament and *The X Factor* has produced a genuine talent.

It was George Orwell himself who said that 'the essence of being human is that one does not seek perfection'* – and when you come to think about it, even *defining* perfection is a tough nut to crack, especially after that fourth pint of Bishop's Finger.

According to the eighteenth-century philosopher Immanuel Kant, perfection depends on whether you're a relativist or an idealist. So, at risk of sounding a little Kant-ish, if after a long walk on a cold winter's day a relativist stumbled upon a cosy country local with a log fire, they could argue that they'd achieved pub perfection. For an idealist, however, the experience might be ruined completely by the fact that they only served Carlsberg and the menu stretched as far as Bacon Bites.

Some people, eh? But you get the drift.

And so while we always secretly hoped we might stumble across a living, breathing version of The Moon Under Water on our travels, it was never our sole aim.

The truth is, we wanted to write a book which examined the state of Britain's pubs in the twenty-first century and discover what, exactly, was going on out there in our cities, towns and villages. A book – if we might be so bold – which might just serve as a valuable resource for future, erm, pubologians, just as John Byng's *Vision of Britain* (1789) and John Hissey's *A Tour in a Phaeton through the English Counties* from exactly a century later helped shed light on contemporary fears about everything from the coffee house to the advent of the railways.

Of course, we didn't know when we set out that we'd find ourselves coming face to face with pissed-up Power Rangers, grumpy Archdruids or tooled up Hell's Angels, but, then, that was

---

*Admittedly, in an essay called 'Reflections on Gandhi' as opposed to musing on his local pub.

half the challenge. Or, as our friends at *The London Drinker* put it, 'The authors put themselves in the firing line without any worries for their own health or, at times, sanity.' Move over Bear Grylls, is all I can say.

Thankfully, the warm reception the book received from everyone from the *Financial Times* to the *Big Issue* suggests we did a reasonable job. During the last year, we've talked about pubs everywhere from 6 Music to ABC News in New York (which was a story in itself), but before this starts to take the tone of an Oscars speech, I'd like to let off a little steam.

Because while spreading the pub gospel via press and radio had its benefits – as our publishers regularly reminded us – it did throw up a few unwelcome home truths, which, at the risk of sounding ungrateful, I'd like to share. Most notable was that coverage of pubs in the media is often treated as a temporary relief from the non-stop diet of bad news we endure daily, rather than as a serious topic in itself.

During one radio interview, I found myself sandwiched between news pieces on the increase in cases of depression brought on by the double-dip recession and the dangers of older mothers having Caesarean births. Not exactly a gag-fest. Yet our role as a chink of light in the gloom often meant that the bigger story – about how the pub's traditional role in our lives is being eroded – was, it seemed to me, too often ignored.

A few more facts, then, before we go. In the peak beer drinking months from July to September 2012, Britons drank 117 million fewer pints than they did the previous year. And this in a summer which included the Olympics, the Diamond Jubilee and Euro 2012. Sales of home-brewing kits in the same period, however, increased by 46 per cent. You don't have to be Roger Protz to figure out what's going on there. We are changing our drinking habits as a nation and will continue to drift away from pubs until something is done to stem the tide.

In the week of writing, another pub-related news item caught my eye. Tucked away on an inside column in the *Evening Standard* was a small news piece about the closure of a pub called The North Pole in North Kensington. The local neighbourhood pub for 173 years, it had been earmarked to become a branch of Tesco Metro, despite the fact there were already seven other branches of Tesco within a two-mile radius. This had so infuriated local residents that they'd organised a 1,000-name petition and erected a large 'Bog Off Tesco' sign across the front of the pub.

None of which is particularly remarkable until you discover that The North Pole also happens to be David Cameron's local. Now, if the prime minister is unwilling to save his own local from the military-like advance of the supermarkets, what chance do other communities stand?

This lack of interest in the pub's future by both politicians and the media (touched upon by Paul Kingsnorth in the 'Clocking On at the Fun Factory' chapter if you're an academic from 2115) brings me to another of my pub-related bugbears. Nowadays, it seems anyone with a Twitter account can add to the chorus of agreement about anything from Bruno Tonioli's haircut to Iran's nuclear-weapon capability on programmes ranging from *Strictly Come Dancing* to *Question Time*. Which is fine. Some might even argue that it is proof of a healthy democracy in action.

Personally, I'd rather hear views being beamed live and direct from the nearest pub. Because if there's one thing I learned from my travels, it is that the best conversations are often with those with whom you have the least in common. Sounds perverse, doesn't it? And yet while it was fun and informative talking to the likes of Guy Garvey, Pete Wylie and Paul Heaton, I'll remember the conversations with a retired policeman called Steve and a former Hells' Angel called Arthur a lot longer.

Why? Because at the risk of sounding like a cracked record, they taught me something new about the world, rather than simply shoring up my own viewpoint. What I'm getting at is this: whereas social media encourages us to agree with like-minded people, the pub challenges our preconceptions and makes us think about ourselves and the world in a different way.

Now, I hate the boorish, sometimes bigoted views of the local pub bore as much as anyone. But I love the unexpected wit, intelligence and sheer *joie de vivre* that you can find there twice as much. I'm as uncomfortable in a pub close to Millwall's ground on match day as the next man, but the experience means that I'll enjoy the calm of a country local in mid-afternoon all the more.

The pub is the nation's traditional debating chamber, and as technology takes over as our primary medium of communication, it feels as though something very human is getting lost (I'm sure someone called George touched upon some of these themes in a novel which came out a few years ago).

If this all sounds a little high-minded, blame Lucy Norton. She's my local representative of a group called Philosophy In Pubs who encourage complete strangers – of all political persuasions – to discuss matters ranging from David Cameron's Big Society to the nature of solipsism. And all without a crossed word or a Twitter 'troll' in sight.

Does that sound awfully pompous? It's not meant to. I'd be just as happy talking about Barnet's chances away to Doncaster next week, if I'm really honest. I'm just trying to make the point that pub discussions encourage us to expand our experience of life, not reinforce what we already know.

One day, I'd like to think that an enlightened government will come down hard on voracious supermarkets (maybe using the slogan 'Bog Off Tesco'). Soulless property developers will be forced to live in cramped 'studio' apartments, and the pub will be restored at the heart of the nation's life. Taxes on locally made beer will be slashed, and every pub in the land will be encouraged to work with their nearest microbrewery. Smokers will have their own snug bar if they desire it, and vintage jukeboxes, dart boards and skittle alleys will be dusted off, restored and made available for those who want them. Prospective landlords, meanwhile, will be actively sought from the ranks of former professional footballers, actors and musicians.

Until then, let's make the most of the pubs we've still got.

Let's roll out the barrel, admire the landlord's daughter and keep ordering two pints of lager and a packet of crisps, please. Because, as we mentioned 100,000 words or so ago, great pubs are like songs, and the best ones stay with you for ever.

Now, if you'll excuse me, I must dash. There's a little place in Parsons Green I need to check out . . .

Paul Moody
April 2013

If there's one positive that can be taken from the closure of The Vulcan, it's that when the end came it was mercifully quick. There was no protracted, last-minute fight to save the Cardiff landmark, no picket line with hand-drawn placards and no drawn-out week of closing parties during which regulars whispered their final goodbyes to the pub whilst sobbing gently into their pint pots. No, when The Vulcan stopped tap for the last time, it was a surprise to nearly everyone.

The Vulcan's lease was due to expire on 31 May 2012. Many of those who had campaigned since 2008 to save the pub from closure still hoped for a reprieve. At the very least, those thirsty supplicants thought they'd get to say a decent farewell to their beloved bricks and mortar should – *God forbid* – things not work out.

On 3 May the Vulcan was administered its lethal injection. That night as the pub shut up shop few were aware that it wouldn't open for service the next morning. Or ever again. Brains – the brewery behind the pub – had long since given up their part in the fight. The site developer clearly felt that those petitioning to save the pub – from Jeremy Vine to James Dean Bradfield to Rachel and Chris (the campaigners I talked to) and each and every regular who propped up the bar over the years – had been humoured for quite long enough. Progress couldn't be put on pause for ever.

After the closure, the site was quickly prepared for a very controlled demolition. Each brick, each beam, each font and optic was photographed and documented as part of the preparation for The Vulcan's relocation to St Fagans National History Museum. That rebuild will take anything up to half a decade. Future generations will indeed get to experience The Vulcan – only as a museum piece, painstakingly reconstructed five miles away from its original home in an open-air heritage park, where historic buildings are granted architectural afterlife.

In place of The Vulcan, there's now an overspill car park. There's space for a handful of Fords, a couple of Peugeots, the odd Skoda and the occasional BMW. Soon, a new shopping centre will rise there. In the meantime, John Lewis is a hop and a skip away. The Saturday-afternoon crowds queuing for a lunch table at Jamie's Italian could be waiting in line on any high street anywhere in the UK. Back on Adam Street, there is no trace of The Vulcan. It's as if it never existed.

Untouched since 8 May, the final post on the *Save the Vulcan* blog questions the motives of the developers whilst trying to make sense of the events that had just unfolded. Administrator Jez signs off with this eulogy:

'Terms like "end of an era" get thrown around far too readily, but for those who ever got a chance to experience the unique energy and charisma that The Vulcan had, it rings with absolute truth.'

The Vulcan was that rarest of pubs. Just a stroll away from a frenetic city centre, where a hundred happy hours blur together and Jägerbombs go off in the queues for cabs home, it was a proper local. It was stoically impervious to modernisation, and all the better for it. Personally, I loved the atmosphere in the front bar on evenings before internationals, and I loved the sobering trip to the outdoor gents toilets in the middle of winter. I loved the resolutely untrendy jukebox and the 'that'll do' Brains economy-range beer selection. I loved the bar staff and the regulars and the chapel-like mid-afternoon light that always made a pint – any pint – seem truly heavenly.

The Vulcan's tale isn't unique – it just happens to be one I took a particular interest in. Back in London, New Cross institution The Montague (another favourite of the authors of this book) quietly called a final 'Time!' at the end of 2011. In doing so, south-east London's community of art students and non-conformists was robbed of the kind of eccentric boozer that no one would dare open nowadays. How could anyone even begin to piece together such a magic kingdom as The Montague? Could anyone begin to accumulate the decades' worth of much-loved clutter, detritus and dusty objects-of-unknown-origin that filled the pub's every available space? Would a true individual with an unconventional vision – Alan at The Yew Tree, for example – even enter the pub trade now?

Despite a slowdown in closure numbers, local boozers are still disappearing at an alarming rate. Since the coalition took power in May 2010, more than 2,300 British pubs have closed. As ever, the same factors are to blame – the beer duty escalator, cheap plonk in supermarkets and the smoking ban. Recent additions to that list are maybe the most significant of all – a seemingly permanent VAT hike and the real-time effects of a prolonged recession.

Everyone knows the problems yet nobody seems empowered to help. More than 100,000 people signed an online petition asking the government to scrap the beer duty escalator (a New Labour initiative which effectively increases the price of a pint by 2 per cent above inflation); the point was raised in a debate in parliament on 1 November 2012. At the time of writing, there's been a lot of furrowed brows in Westminster, a lot of cross-party talk that 'something has to be done' and not a lot else. It's unlikely the austerity chancellor will peel back any easy sources of tax revenue anytime soon.

Elsewhere in pub world, the craft-beer revolution rolls on apace. Even as a card-carrying craft convert myself, it's hard not to view many aspects of that particular trend as blatantly opportunistic. Craft beer has seen the humble pint elevated to artisan status. It's perfectly acceptable to charge upwards of £3.50 for a half pint in many London pubs. Invariably, the beer has taken a journey from brewery to bar top of no more than a couple of miles.

The Craft tag has made beer an aspirational product. It's cherished by the kind of people who regularly patronise farmer's markets and organic chain stores. Bottles sit there in the fridge next to the sourdough starter and the knobbly organic carrots. It is a product half designed to be consumed at home; the pub loses out again. Although the chance of being sold a bad pint has dropped dramatically, the average price of beer has risen astronomically.

Honestly, it's enough to make you turn to drink.

A couple of weeks after deconstruction work began on The Vulcan, I'm sat in the back bar of a pub at the other end of Wales. Less than a year old and housed in a beautifully preserved art deco building, The Albion in Conwy certainly looks the part. Press coverage of The Albion talked of the pub's unique business model and – more importantly – the exemplary nature of the place itself.

Soundtracked by little more than gently inebriated chatter, The Albion is immediately warmly welcoming. Most of the beers on the bar – seasonal specials from small local breweries – are unfamiliar; mainly they are short-run casks that haven't travelled far from their source. Pints are reasonably priced, as real ale should be. Food is purely line-the-stomach minimal – a pie here, a bag of crisps there. After four pints, I'm of the distinct impression that this is a very, very good pub. Dare I say, it's pretty close to perfection.

Back in London a few days later, I find myself musing over what made The Albion so special. Over the years, I've been to countless pubs with flawless interiors, ditto praiseworthy, unique beer. I phone the pub's manager Stuart Chapman-Edwards in an attempt to put my finger on what makes the pub so special.

'Two years ago, The Albion pub was put on the market by

Punch Taverns. They didn't see a future in it. A North Walian living in London working in the city saw the pub was up for sale and thought it represented a good investment. He bought it off the internet, just like you'd buy a book off Amazon. Before starting work on it, he approached a few local breweries and said, "If I spend money on refurbishing the place, would you like to rent it off me?" Jonathan from Great Orme Brewery said that their set-up wasn't really big enough to stretch to owning a pub, but having worked with three other local microbreweries on various beer festivals he thought that maybe it would be a good idea to approach each of them to try to run it as a collective. Those breweries were his (Llandudno's Great Orme) as well as the Conwy Brewery, Bragdy'r Nant from Llanrwst and Purple Moose from Porthmadog. Without fail, we always have at least one of each of their beers on.

'It works like this. The four brewers allocate each other a role which changes year on year. Lawrence from Purple Moose is this year's chairman, Dewi from Bragdy'r Nant the treasurer, Gwyn from Conwy deals with house issues and Jonathan from Great Orme deals with marketing. They'll change roles on the anniversary of opening each year. A few people told me it's bound to implode, but it works perfectly at the moment.

'The Albion has been brought back to its incredible 1920s glory. The art deco interior was lovingly and painstakingly restored. The original concept for everyone was to take the pub back to its roots. We don't have fruit machines or a jukebox. A pub is about socialising – or at least it should be. Everyone involved wanted the pub to be filled with conversation. We picked massive tables so that people would be forced to sit together and hopefully encouraged to talk. I stand behind the bar sometimes, and I see disparate groups of people come in and before long they're chatting away like friends. On paper you worry that it might not work, but then you see it in action and it's absolutely heart-warming.'

I say goodbye and think about what he's just said.

Collaboration. Conversation. Good beer. Socialising.

If it all seems so simple, that's probably because it is. The tenets that Stuart and the four local breweries behind The Albion adhere to aren't that different from George Orwell's criteria when he wrote about The Moon Under Water in 1946. The key aims that Stuart pinpoints for The Albion are collectively what Orwell called 'atmosphere' – the great intangible that makes a pub . . . well, a pub.

Punch Taverns and the pubcos may move on when the figures don't add up, and developers will always place a higher value on twenty more parking spaces than a living, breathing piece of pub history. The government – whoever it is – will probably always see the drinker, grumbling about the price of a pint yet still paying up without fail, as an easy target. And the opportunists will always follow trends in order to make a buck or two. Last year's gastropub becomes this year's craft-beer bar becomes next year's . . . port and zydeco bar? Who knows?

That said, there will always – *hopefully* – be those who see the pub trade as something more than a money-spinner – publicans and brewers who see pubs and the pursuit of simple pleasures as a calling and have a natural affinity with the people they serve. There will always be those who recognise that a good pub's place in the community represents everything from matchmaker to lifeline for the lonely. Those who understand the recuperative effects of the warming hug of a busy snug bar and appreciate the restorative power of a full pint served by someone who knows your name.

And maybe even calls you dear.

Robin Turner
April 2013

Acknowledgements

This is a book written by enthusiasts, and in our enthusiasm we may well have made errors that an expert in the field of pub history, brewing and pub folklore may not have. Equally, there is probably someone, somewhere, who knows more about every sentence in this book than we do. The difficulty is that they're never likely to be the same person twice. With that in mind, we can only apologise and pledge our undying thanks to the following sources, whose writing on pubs and culture continues to shine through the years: Michael Jackson – *The English Pub*; Paul Jennings – *The Local: A History of the English Pub*; Steven D. Hales – *Beer & Philosophy*; Geoff Brandwood, Andrew Davison, Michael Slaughter – *Licenced To Sell: The History and Heritage of the Public House*; Paul Kingsnorth – *Real England*; Stuart Maconie – *Pies and Prejudice*; DJ Taylor – *Orwell: the Life*; Peter Stansky, William Abrahams – *The Unknown Orwell*; Paul Du Noyer – *Liverpool: Wondrous Place; Music From the Cavern the Coral*; Mike Chapple - *The Great Liverpool Pub Crawl*; Barry Miles – *London Calling: A Countercultural History of London Since 1945*; John O'Farrell – *An Utterly Impartial History of Britain*; Paul Chatterton and Robert G. Hollands – *Changing Our Toon: Youth, Nightlife & Urban Change in Newcastle*; Jason Wilson – *Boozehound*, Ian Marchant – *The Longest Crawl*; Thomas Burke – *Travel In England* and *English Night Life*, A.A Gill – *The Angry Island*; Richard Boston – *Beer and Skittles*; Nigel Barley – *Native Land*; Tom Hodgkinson – *How To Be Idle*; Dan Kieran – *I Fought the Law*; Jonathan Raban – *Soft City*; Iain Sinclair – *Hackney, That Rose-Red Empire*; Pete Brown – *Man Walks Into A Pub*; Jeremy Paxman – *The English* and, of course, George Orwell – 'The Moon Under Water'.

To all the following, without whose time and thoughts the search might have happened, but it wouldn't have been half as interesting: Simon Fowler, Jack Adams (humanrightstv.com), Alan Avenall, Stan Pownall, and all at The Montague Arms, Freda Searle, Dot Gasson, Gerry Foster, Frog Morris, Kate Burt (savetheboozer.blogspot.com), Patrick Chaplin (aka 'Dr Darts'), Paul Heaton, Polly Birkbeck, Gerry Sutcliffe, Kirsty McCaskill, Greg Mulholland, Neil Williams, Brigid Simmonds, Bill Hamilton and Vickie Dillon at A.M. Heath, Paul Kingsnorth, Josie Appleton, Joe Jackson, Arthur Pendragon, Terry Dobney, The Bard Of Avebury, Brendan McLaughlin and Mary at The Scotia, Violet Leighton, Linda at The Halfway House, D.J. Johnston-Smith, Ian Ward, Richard Dollimore, Keith Armstrong, Richard Simpson, Rachel Thomas, James Le Fanu, Chris Latham, John Williams, Steve Williams, Steve Brown, Terry Dix, Tony Foster, Chris Corcoran, David Jackson, Pete Brown, Mark Charlwood (beerbirrabier.com), Mark Dredge (pencilandspoon.com), Jeff Barrett, James Dean Bradfield, Alan East, Roger Protz, Luke Turner, Iain Sinclair, Evin O'Riordain from The Kernel, Martin Dickie from Brewdog, Emma and all at the Jolly Butchers, The Good Beer Guide, Andrew Gardner from the Islington Archeology and History Society, Guy Garvey, Scott from the Temple, Peter Grant, Pete Wylie, Lisa Southern, Ian Prowse, Ian McNabb, Tim Martin, Tina Coppitters, Martyn Hillyer, Simon Armitage, Ewan Foskett, Irene Stacey, Rich Cochrane, Neil Thomson, Steve and all at the Pembury, Roger Wilkins, Nick Dewey, Leanor and Pip for saint-like patience and much needed company on half the journeys, Jane Pickup for putting up with the mood swings, Simon 'Six Bottles' Benham, and the countless others who gave their time and energy for free. We owe you all a drink. Some interview dates and locations have been altered in the interest of trying to tell a good story – apologies to anyone who unexpectedly found themselves down the pub.

Special thanks to Peter Turner, whose sketches brought so many events in the book back to life, and to our editor Ian Preece, without whom this book would have been one of those pub conversations which remain just that.